LOVERS' GUIDE TO AMERICA

IAN KEOWN

Illustrations by Claude Martinot

Macmillan Publishing Co., Inc.
NEW YORK
Collier Macmillan Publishers
LONDON

Thank you, in alphabetical order, Betty, Lynda, Margrit, Mary Ann, Susan, and the others who've since run off and got married.

Library of Congress Cataloging in Publication Data

Keown, Ian.
  Lovers' guide to America.

    1. Hotels, taverns, etc.—United States. I. Title.
TX909.K46 647'.9473 73-21692
ISBN 0-02-562300-1

Copyright © 1974 by Ian M. Keown

All rights reserved. No part of this book may be reproduced or transmitted in any form or by any means, electronic or mechanical, including photocopying, recording or by any information storage and retrieval system, without permission in writing from the Publisher.

Macmillan Publishing Co., Inc.
866 Third Avenue, New York, N.Y. 10022
Collier-Macmillan Canada Ltd.

Library of Congress Catalog Card Number: 73-21692

First Printing 1974

Printed in the United States of America

CONTENTS

INTRODUCTION   *xiii*

The New England Coast
and Long Island:

  1. Gurney's Inn   3
  2. Earl of Stirling Bar   5
  3. Three Village Inn   7
  4. Griswold Inn   8
  5. Gray Gables Ocean House   12
  6. Clauson's Inn & Golf Resort   13
  7. Wychmere Harbor Club   14
  8. Ship's Knees Inn   16
  9. The White Elephant   17
10. Jared Coffin House   19
11. Ships Inn   20
12. Wentworth-by-the-Sea   22
13. Seacrest Inn   24
14. Shawmut Inn   26

Green Mountains,
White Mountains:

15. The Inn at Sawmill Farm 31
16. The Old Tavern at Grafton 34
17. Bromley House 38
18. The Four Columns Inn 40
19. Chester Inn 43
20. Woodstock Inn 44
21. Hawk Mountain 47
22. The John Hancock Inn 49
23. The General Wolfe Inn 52
24. Wolfeboro Inn 54
25. The Inn at Steele Hill 56
26. Stafford's-in-the-Field 57
27. Farrell Lodge 60
28. Tecumseh Inn 60

In and Around the
Bosky Berkshires:

29. Red Lion Inn 65
30. Blantyre Castle 67
31. Orpheus Ascending 69
32. The Flying Cloud Inn 71
33. Stagecoach Hill Inn 74

34. Old Deerfield Inn 75
35. Lord Jeffery Inn 78
36. The Publick House 79
37. Longfellow's Wayside Inn 82
38. The Mayflower Inn 86
39. Kilravock Inn 89
40. Harrison Inn 91
41. Swiss Hutte 93

From the Shawangunks
to the Alleghenies:

42. Mohonk Mountain House 97
43. Auberge des Quatre Saisons 100
44. 1740 House 101
45. Tulpehocken Manor Farm 103
46. Century Inn 106

In and Around the
Chesapeake Bay:

47. Robert Morris Inn 111
48. Maryland Inn 114
49. The Tides Inn 116
50. The Tides Golf Lodge 118

The Shenandoah Valley—
Up Hill and Down Dale:

51. Wayside Inn 123
52. Narrow Passage Inn 125
53. Skyland Lodge 126
54. Big Meadows Lodge 127
55. Sky Chalet 128
56. The Homestead 129
57. Valley View Inn 132
58. Peaks of Otter Lodge 134
59. Boar's Head Inn 135
60. The Greenbrier 137
61. Pipestem Resort 140

From the Carolinas
to the Keys:

62. Holly Inn 145
63. The Carolina Hotel 146
64. Mills Hyatt House 147
65. Hilton Head Inn 151
66. The Cloister 153
67. King & Prince Hotel 157
68. Greyfield 158
69. The Breakers 161
70. Boca Raton Hotel and Club 165
71. Pier House 167

The Heartlands and the Deep South:

72. The Golden Lamb   173
73. Wells Inn   174
74. The Inn at Pleasant Hill   175
75. Lodge of the Four Seasons   178
76. Hotel Maison De Ville   180
77. The Saint Louis Hotel   182
78. Grand Hotel   184

The Rockies and the Mesas:

79. Far View Lodge   189
80. Strater Hotel   191
81. C Lazy U Ranch   192
82. The Timbers   194
83. Sundance   195
84. The Lodge at Snowbird   199
85. Alta Lodge   202

The Deserts and Resorts of the Great Southwest:

86. The Bishop's Lodge   207
87. Rancho Encantado   210
88. Tom Young's Tres Lagunas Guest Ranch   213

x

89. Sagebrush Inn   214

90. Thunderbird Lodge & Chalets   216

91. Saint Bernard Hotel & Chalets   216

92. Hotel Edelweiss   216

93. Hacienda de San Roberto   217

94. Arizona Inn   218

95. Hacienda del Sol   221

96. Tanque Verde Ranch   223

97. Wild Horse Racquet and Riding Club   227

98. Saddle and Surrey Ranch   229

99. John Gardiner's Tennis Ranch   230

100. Marriott's Camelback Inn   232

101. Casa Blanca Inn   233

102. Hermosa Inn   235

103. Arizona Biltmore Hotel   236

104. Carefree Inn   239

105. The Wigwam Resort   241

The Sunny Coast of Southern California:

106. Inn at Rancho Bernardo   247

107. Rancho La Costa Resort Hotel & Spa   249

108. La Valencia Hotel   251

109. The Inn at Rancho Santa Fe   254

110. Beverly Hills Hotel   257

111. Bel-Air Hotel   261

112. Santa Barbara Biltmore Hotel   264

113. The Alisal   267

San Francisco and Its Neighbors:

114. Del Monte Lodge 271
115. Highlands Inn 274
116. Pine Inn 277
117. Cypress West Inn 278
118. The Sandpiper Inn 280
119. Normandy Inn 281
120. Big Sur Inn 282
121. John Gardiner's Tennis Ranch 283
122. Quail Lodge 285
123. Miyako Hotel 286
124. Alta Mira 288
125. Sausalito Inn 289
126. Sutter Creek Inn 290
127. Hotel Leger 293
128. The Mine House 294

Northern California and All the Way to Oregon:

129. Timber Cove Inn 299
130. Sea Ranch Lodge 301
131. Heritage House 303
132. Little River Inn 306
133. Ireland's Rustic Lodges 307

xii

134. The Inn at Otter Crest   308
135. Salishan Lodge   310
136. The Inn of the 7th Mountain   314
137. Sunriver Lodge   315

INDEX   321

INTRODUCTION

"O for a seat in some poetic nook,
Just hid with trees and sparkling with a brook."

This is a book of nice places.

Old inns. Hideaways. Resorts. Trysting places. Shangri-las. Places to nip off to for a few days to be together and alone. They're for people who enjoy the finer things in life. Not necessarily the expensive things, but *good* things—watching sandpipers at sunset, munching freshly picked apples, scrambling over rocks, sipping mulled cider, listening to a log fire, biking through lanes of moss-covered oaks, trudging through the snow, listening to Mozart under the stars, riding desert trails.

It's primarily for lovers—boy/girl, boy/boy, girl/girl, mature woman/young boy, old lech/young girl—but it can also come in handy for anyone planning a first, second or third honeymoon, or for someone who's fed up to the teeth with the kitchen and wants to get away, *away* for a few days.

It's *not* for swingers. It's *not* for people who'd rather see a floorshow than the moonlight, who'd rather listen to a crap table than the surf. It's *not* for people who want heart-shaped bathtubs in bathrooms that look like grottoes, or mirrors on the ceiling and walls, or tiger-skin bedspreads and tiger-skin rugs in rooms with fountains dribbling down purple walls (don't snicker, these places exist). These people will be bored out of their skulls by the places in this guide.

Setting the ground rules

All the inns and hotels in this guidebook have something special going for them. The something special could be antiquity (the Old Tavern in Grafton, Vermont, the Publick House in Sturbridge, Massachusetts, or the Wayside Inn in Middletown, Virginia), location (Far View Lodge in Mesa Verde National Park, Colorado or Skyland Lodge in Shenandoah National Park, Virginia), charm (the Inn at Sawmill Farm in West Dorset, Vermont or Greyfield Inn on Cumberland Island), nostalgia (The Wentworth in Portsmouth, New Hampshire or La Valencia in La Jolla, California), luxury (the Bel-Air in Los Angeles, the Breakers in Palm Beach, Florida), remoteness (Sundance, Utah or Mohonk Mountain House, Mohonk Lake, New York), sports (The Cloister, Sea Island, Georgia or the Arizona Biltmore, Phoenix, Arizona)—or a combination of several of these features.

They're places where you won't be embarrassed if you forget to write Mr. and Mrs. when you sign in, where bellhops won't snicker if the initials on your luggage don't match, where chambermaids won't come barging in on you in the morning, where you won't have to sit down to breakfast with nosy old ladies who'd just love to know what you were really doing up there.

They're places where you can escape neon, piped music, plastic, television, juke boxes, coach-loads of tourists, conventions and swarms of children. Well, more or less. The advantage to writing a book is that you can make your own rules—and then break them.

Breaking the ground rules

Some of the places listed in these pages *do* have piped music, television and conventions, but they're included because they have other qualities that compensate—or, as in the case of conventions, because it would mean eliminating virtually every entry in this guide. First, conventions. There are conventions and there are groups, seminars, annual meetings, workshops and a score of other assemblies. Any excuse to get away from the office is reason enough to hold a meeting in a hotel these days. Meetings can be anywhere from half a dozen people up, and nowadays even the smallest hotels rely on groups of some kind to keep themselves alive during the off-season months. However, none of the hotels in this guide are able or willing to handle the mob conventions of beer salesmen or politicians; when they do have meetings, the groups usually consist of high-level executives, professors, governors, company directors and others who can usually be relied upon to conduct themselves in an unobtrusive manner. Most of the inns and hotels in this guide can be enjoyed by a loving twosome, even with a seminar or group in the house; however, to be on the safe side, when you make your reservation, ask if there's a large group scheduled for that period. Most hotels will understand your concern; in fact, several of them will tell you automatically without having to be asked. And you can do some preliminary research yourself by reading the "Seasons" category in the individual hotel listings, where you'll find a rough guide to the convention/group situation in each hotel.

Now, about children. Very few hotels actually exclude children, but many of the larger resorts have separate play areas, dining rooms and dining hours for children. They won't be much of a problem in the places listed in this guide, even during the school holidays.

Pet peeves

You'll notice several references throughout this guide to things like television and piped music. They're among my pet peeves, and even if I end up sounding like a curmudgeon, here's why. You go away for a quiet weekend together, and you deliberately pick out a spot where you think you'll be allowed to enjoy the quiet and the atmosphere so you don't want to sit down in the bar or dining room and have to listen to what someone else has decided you ought to listen to. It just doesn't make sense to search out an old Colonial tavern in New England, order lobster or pumpkin pie, and have to listen to "Down Argentine Way" or some hack's orchestral arrangement of the love duet from *La Bohème*. What's the point of creating a Colonial atmosphere, and instantly destroying it by adding a cha-cha-cha?

Ditto TV. Take one example: The John Hancock Inn, in Hancock, New Hampshire. You drive around this "Currier & Ives" countryside, lapping up the fall foliage and the solitude, and you arrive full of the joys and glories of nature at this lovely old inn, go into the tap room to savor the local brew and *zap*—there's an ugly TV set perched on the bar with the same puerile commercials and gunfire you're trying to get away from. (This is not to say that inns and hotels *shouldn't* have television sets if their guests want them; I just feel that they should be in places where people can watch them without having them interfering with guests who don't want to watch.) The innkeepers usually justify TV and piped music on the grounds that their clients like them, but the truth is more likely that the *staff* enjoys them. If you feel the same way about TV and piped music, ask the innkeepers to turn the bloody things off. Tell them you came out to the country to listen to the birds and the crickets rather than Guy Lumbago or Lawrence Belch.

Live entertainment is another matter. You can't very well ask the innkeeper to tell his musicians to go home, and the best you can do here is to ask them to restrain the amplification. Most of the places with live entertainment in this guide are big enough to give you an opportunity to slip off to some place where even amplification can't penetrate.

How to understand rates

All the room rates quoted in this guidebook are for *two* people.

Hotels have different ways of establishing their rates, and what you're going to pay depends on variables like twin beds, double beds, with bath, without bath, facing the front, facing the rear, lower floors, upper floors. I haven't spelled out all the variations because I assume that you like each other so much that tiresome details and a few dollars won't come between you.

The basic types of rates are:

EP   European
         Plan: This means you pay for the room
                            only, no meals, not even breakfast,
                            except where mentioned

MAP   Modified
         American
         Plan: Room with breakfast plus *one*
                            meal—usually dinner

AP   American
         Plan: Everything—breakfast, lunch,
                            afternoon tea (when served)
                            and dinner

AP and MAP mean that you order meals from a fixed menu, usually with a choice of dishes, and often with extra dishes available for a small surcharge (unfortunately, usually the dishes that you really want—like lobster in Maine). Some hotels don't give you any choice, and you have to go along with AP or MAP rates, especially during their peak season. Where you can, however, try to arrange an EP rate, so that you have the option to eat where you choose.

Off-season pleasures and prices

Avoid peak seasons and weekends if you can. Obviously, this is not always possible, and there are times when you'll want to go on weekends in peak season to catch, for example, the music festival at Tanglewood or a candlelight tour of the mansions in Charleston.

However, there are so many advantages of the off-season that it's worthwhile making the effort to go somewhere when most other people have left. If you're looking for peace and quiet, the advantages are immediately apparent. If you're counting pennies, the rewards are greater still (see the listings for resorts like The Breakers in Palm Beach, Florida or the Camelback Inn in Scottsdale, Arizona for just two examples of the off-season savings). Think twice about the weather: the idea of Cape Cod in summer is very appealing, but for many people, May, June, October and November are the best months for beachcombing —and it's not unknown to get a sunburn on the Cape in June. Other benefits: in the off-season you get a better choice of rooms, and you probably don't have to stand in line for a table or wait for service at mealtimes (in fact, you can sometimes be *swamped* by service in the quiet months).

The peak and non-peak seasons, of course, vary from region to region, but sometimes they also differ for different hotels in the same region. In Vermont, for example, the Inn at Sawmill Farm in West Dorset is usually busy during winter weekends because it's a five-minute drive from the ski slopes, whereas the Old Tavern at Grafton, only an hour's drive away, is less crowded because it doesn't have a ski slope on its doorstep.

The basic seasons for each hotel are listed in the following pages. Note them carefully: they can make a big difference when you're trying to get reservations—and in determining how much value you get for your money.

Checking in, checking out

Nobody bothers to check credentials nowadays, so just sign in as Mr. and Mrs., or Mr. and Ms. Even nice little old ladies at reception desks in Maine don't care, unless one of the partners looks very, very young. *If* anyone should make a fuss and ask for identification, show them something and explain the different names by saying that you both have your own professional lives and therefore prefer to use your own names.

Don't do as one sprightly old fellow did. He called ahead discreetly to ask the manager if it was okay to bring a young lady who was, well, *you* know . . . and the manager told him he couldn't care less; but when the couple arrived they checked into one room, then signed the register *and* their checks separately with separate names. Don't embarrass the staff by doing anything that gauche.

Signing bar and restaurant checks

This is often a giveaway, and/or a bookkeeping bother, because a young lady may instinctively start to sign her own name. You should remind her occasionally. Also, if you have a strange name, like Keown, better make sure she knows how to spell it. And pronounce it. If you're *both* signing in under assumed names, make sure you have plenty of cash, because there are few innkeepers willing to let John Smith pay his bill with a credit card that has someone else's name on it.

Reservations

It's always a delightful and carefree feeling to drive around casually and stop where and when you like. But that's not always possible, and there's nothing more frustrating than being all ready to tumble into bed only to discover that the place you wanted to tumble in is full, and so is the other one down the road, and you waste hours driving around looking for something only to end up in a dispiriting motel. Don't take chances: make your reservations in advance, even if only a few hours in advance. This is almost essential if you want to specify a particular room, or a double bed, or a room with private bath, and so on.

Most hotels will hold your room until 6 p.m. If you plan to arrive later than that, tell them to hold your room; otherwise, they may rent it to someone else. This is particularly true in small inns where they can't run the risk of an empty room; *conversely, if you make a reservation and then decide you don't want it, call the inn and let them know so that they can rent the room to someone else.*

The inn thing

You'll find many old-time inns listed in these pages. They are not everyone's cup of tea, and several innkeepers tell me they're concerned that people sometimes arrive on their doorsteps and are disappointed with what they find.

Here are some of the *non-features* that may disappoint: You usually won't find a porter to carry your luggage; occasionally the innkeeper himself will help, but you should try to keep your luggage manageable because one of you may have to carry it up two or three flights of stairs.

You usually won't get room service in an inn. No breakfast in bed—unless one of you goes and fetches it. Also, don't expect the sort of service you'd get at the Beverly Hills Hotel or the Greenbrier; these places just don't have the staff to cope. They can offer you friendly personal service—but not night and day, and not in matters beyond the call of duty.

You may not find phones, radios, TV or wall-to-wall carpet in your room. Or even a bathroom.

The plumbing may be rebellious; the floors may creak, and if you get back late you have to remember that other guests have come for peace and quiet. Tip-toe. Also don't *arrive* late at night, because the innkeeper is in bed since he has to be up early the next morning; if you must arrive late, call ahead and say so.

Most of these inns are operated on precarious budgets, and survive on love rather than cash flow. We should all be grateful to all those innkeepers who get up at the crack of dawn to prepare breakfast, do the marketing, organize the staff, greet the guests, stick around the bar until after dinner, and probably get only a couple of weeks vacation themselves in a year. Play the game. If you make a reservation, keep it; if you can't don't just shrug it off, but call the innkeeper or drop a line and cancel it, as far in advance as possible. One empty room in a twelve-room inn can be the difference between an inn's profit and its plot of land being bought up by a motel chain.

Who wants to stay in an inn, in that case? A lot of people—because inns offer other attractions that more than compensate for occasional drawbacks, as you'll see in the following pages.

The prices

Many of the prices quoted in this guide may seem steep; but remember that what you're looking for in these places is peace, quiet, something out of the ordinary. These commodities don't come cheaply these days. It costs a fortune to convert and furnish an inn like Sawmill Farm in Vermont, and to maintain a palace as impeccable as the Greenbrier in West Virginia. Economy comes from standardization, and that means the type of accommodations you get in motels. But have you checked motel prices recently? Even a good motel in a moderately desirable location will cost you $20 to $30 a night. Of course, you *can* find less expensive motels alongside highways far out in the country among the telephone poles and power cables and truck stops, but that's not what you're looking for.

Remember: when you look at the prices, check if they're for room only, or room with dinner and breakfast, or room with all meals (see page xvii). A quick glance at The Homestead, Virginia, for example, may look prohibitive, but remember that this includes a whopping great breakfast, gargantuan buffet lunches, afternoon tea and a five- or six-course dinner. Calculate what all that would cost you in motels and restaurants.

Remember: when you read about a hotel that takes your fancy but seems to be too extravagant, check the off-season prices—they may be in your range.

Remember: in these days of Women's Lib and Gay Lib there's no reason why both parties shouldn't pay their own way. Go Dutch and you can afford places you thought were over your head.

Remember: all rates are for DOUBLE rooms.

A Cautionary Note

Hotel prices are highly susceptible to inflation, and in these ultra-inflationary times it's almost impossible for innkeepers to calculate rates more than a season in advance. A lot of care has been taken to get all the rates in this guide as accurate as possible, but the depressing thing is that by the time you read this many of the prices will be out of date. This is nobody's fault, certainly not mine, nor Macmillan's. Don't blame us if you turn up at an inn or hotel or resort and have to pay more than the price indicated in this guide: you should always check the hotel for up-to-date rates before you leave home. If, on the other hand, any hotel or inn quotes a rate *significantly* higher than the one quoted in this guide, we'd like to hear about it.

Double or single beds?

Hotels nowadays have more twin beds than double beds. The reasons are that a surprising number of American couples prefer solitary slumbers; also, with so much convention and business traffic, hotels have to be able to accommodate a couple of executives in one room, but apparently American corporate team spirit hasn't yet reached the point where executives want to bunk down in the same bed, even when they're with the same company. However, most of the hotels, inns and resorts in this guide have both twin and double beds. Always specify which you prefer when you make your reservation; if all the doubles have gone and you really must have one, most hotels will bully their maids or handymen into pushing the twins together and making a double. (This may not be true in smaller inns where the manpower situation is more critical.)

The ratings

All the inns, hotels and resorts in this guide are well above average, in one way or another; but some are obviously better than others and to make life easy for you, and possibly suspenseful for the innkeepers, I've rated the individual establishments with cupids, champagne bottles and crossed tennis rackets. Unlike other guides, such as Mobil, which seem to rate hotels by a formula relying heavily on the number of elevators and coin laundries, this guide's ratings are highly personal and subjective.

Cupids represent the *romantic* qualities—the hotel's personality or charm, the attitude of its staff, the decor and ambience, the location and what the hotel does with it (the ecology bit), the flowers and the birds and the bees.

Champagne bottles evaluate the wining and dining aspect of your stay, and this includes the overall *attitude* to food and wine, the competence of the staff, as well as the quality of the wine cellar and the food that's actually placed before you. In other words, a hotel that gets only two bottles might deserve three for the food but loses out because the waiters are sloppy and noisy, or because the wine cellar is skimpy; on the other hand, a hotel that doesn't pretend to serve haute cuisine but does serve good food, and where the waiters don't pretend they're graduates of the Tour d'Argent in Paris, may get a high rating.

Tennis rackets give you a rough guide to the availability of diversions other than the one you really came for. The facilities can be either on the premises or easily accessible in the neighborhood.

Here are the ratings:

 For a one-night stand or stopover

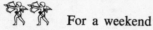 For a weekend

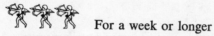 For a week or longer

 Happily ever after

 Sustenance

 Good food

 Cuisine

 A few diversions

 Lots of things to keep your mind off sex

 More diversions than you'll ever have time or energy for unless you have a spat

The ¢ symbol identifies inns, hotels and resorts which cost
less than most—say, $20 or less for a double room *without
meals* (which means that one or two inns with ¢ symbols will
have prices higher than $20 because they include one or more
meals).

Getting there

Most couples will immediately think of hopping into a car and
driving off, and undoubtedly that's the coziest, most convenient,
least expensive way to go off together for a few days; but when
you read through this guide you'll probably discover some places
you'd like to try which are just beyond your customary driving
distance. Question is, should you skip the place, or drive like
crazy to get there and then drive like crazy to get back? Few
things in this world are less conducive to love than long taxing
drives on highways with lots of traffic. For those special places,
consider the other possibilities of getting there.

Flying is the obvious one. Now that most of the domestic air
carriers have developed the habit of introducing special low
fares for off-peak periods, think of flying somewhere for a few
days—say, with after-dinner or nightcoach flights between New
York or Chicago and New Orleans, or with special eight-day
tickets between New York and Los Angeles or San Francisco.
Unfortunately, the airlines never seem to be able to resolve
their fares far enough in advance to be able to supply information for a guide such as this, so you'll have to check out the
possibilities with your local travel agent when the time comes.

Also, don't overlook the possibilities of commuter airlines like
Air New England which can speed your travel time between
New York or Boston and places like Nantucket, Vermont and
Maine; or from Atlanta, Air South, which will get you sooner
to bed in Hilton Head.

Air travel is something of a hassle these days, however, with
security checks, so you may want to consider another way of
getting around the country—train. By *train?* Who's he kidding?

The best way to get through Iowa and Ohio is in bed, tangled together in your sleeping compartment, watching the scenery, such as it is, roll by (but remember to lower the shades before the train pulls into a station—Ohio and Iowa are not ready for that sort of thing yet). Just think of it—you can love your way clear across the continent; and you can even arrange for your conductor or waiter to bring your meals to your berth.

Amtrak is trying to perk up America's trains; it's a struggle, because they have to make do with existing equipment for a few years, and some of the cars are a mite grubby, depending on which route you're on. If it's any consolation, your berth may once have been pressed into service by movie stars and moguls shuttling to and from Hollywood in what the Amtrak crews refer to, rather unloyally, as the good old days. Give the train a try; at least wander round to your local Amtrak office and pick up a schedule.

When you get to your destination, by train or plane, you can usually have your hotel send over a limousine to pick you up; alternatively you can rent a car and drive off in style. Here again there are some surprising bargains going around these days. For example, the Avis Discover America rate that gives you a full-size sedan for $110 a week with *unlimited* mileage (with a few qualifications, of course, none of them serious). Other rental companies have roughly similar plans.

THE NEW ENGLAND COAST AND LONG ISLAND

One day I wrote her name upon the strand,
But came the waves and washed it away . . .
SPENSER

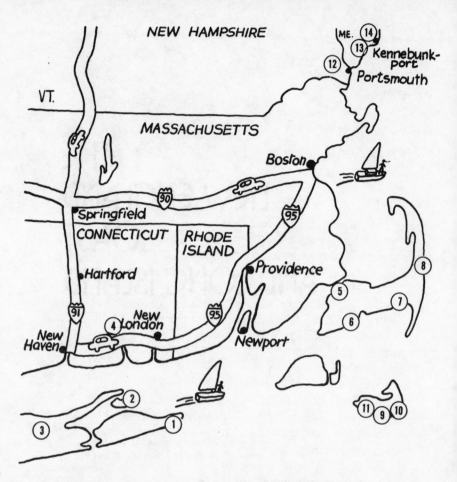

1. Gurney's Inn
2. Earl of Stirling Bar
3. Three Village Inn
4. Griswold Inn
5. Gray Gables Ocean House
6. Clauson's Inn & Golf Resort
7. Wychmere Harbor Club
8. Ship's Knees Inn
9. The White Elephant
10. Jared Coffin House
11. Ships Inn
12. Wentworth-by-the-Sea
13. Seacrest Inn
14. Shawmut Inn

GURNEY'S INN
Montauk, Long Island, New York

You can't get much closer to the beach than this without living in a sand castle. And what a beach! Mile after mile of Johnson's Baby Powder. You can jog on it from here to forever. It's almost the end of the world. The Atlantic comes rolling in on one side, hundred-foot-high hills shut out the world on the other, and 120 miles of Long Island separate you from New Yukk.

The inn is actually a collection of cottages and motel-like units, by the edge of the beach or up on the hill, spread comfortably over eleven acres, brightened with bubbly-trimmed bushes, trees and nooks of flowers.

It's an everything-or-nothing place. You can lie on the sand in front of the inn all day, or you can jog off together to a secluded corner of the dunes. You can go surfbathing, sailing, water skiing, riding, fishing or golfing, or play a set or two of tennis. You can drive over to Montauk and sniff around the fish market, or continue to Montauk Lighthouse and scramble among the rocks at the very, very tip of Long Island. In the evening you can get involved with combos and dancing in the inn, or you can go to the John Drew Theater in East Hampton. Best of all you can kick off your shoes and chase the moon along the beach.

This is a great place to be in summer, but it's sensational in the fall and winter when you have the beach to yourselves, and you have to huddle up in sweaters and scarves, and the spray comes whipping across the sand.

Then after your walk you come back to a lovely warm room, a warm shower, a warm bed. You can even have your dinner shipped over from the dining room—lobsters or roast beef or a thick steak.

You have quite a choice of accommodations at Gurney's. Make your days together a special event and have the inn's best love nest—the Crows Nest (a self-contained cottage right by the edge of the beach, with a living room, fireplace, hostess pantry, patio and bedroom), or a room in the Foredeck (a three-story lodge unit with pine-paneled walls, armchairs, individually controlled heat and air conditioning, telephone, television, tile bathrooms, his and her vanities, and a patio).

But just about any room is worth the drive out to Montauk, and the inn has plenty of quiet corners where you can be alone. You can even turn your back on the world when you're sitting on the Riviera Patio sipping a cocktail and watching the gulls.

NAME: Gurney's Inn

INNKEEPERS: Joyce and Nick Monte

ADDRESS: Montauk, Long Island, N.Y. 11954

TELEPHONE: 516-668-2345

DIRECTIONS: Just keep driving; when you hear a splash you've gone too far.

RATES: Very complicated, rather expensive, but basically MAP only, from May through October—from $52 a room to $76 for the Crows Nest in spring and fall; from $60 to $88 in summer.

MEALS: Breakfast (to 10 a m.), lunch, dinner; room service; although it's MAP you have a wide choice of dishes, and the food's good.

SEASONS: Open all year; crowded in summer, glorious in winter if you have strong lungs.

THE EARL OF STIRLING BAR
at Shelter Island House, Shelter Island, New York

What do hot-shot photographers do with their fees? In the case of David McCabe, one of the English stars who arrived in America in the Sixties, he went looking for a pub—not the East Side Manhattan imitation, but someplace where he could create "you know, a true pub feeling, a gathering place for friends, with darts, a piano, sometimes an accordion player to get people dancing . . ." He found what he was looking for on Shelter Island in the form of a nondescript hotel built back in 1891, brought his parents over from their restaurant in Cornwall to manage the place, and together they went to work transforming it into the Earl of Stirling Bar at Shelter Island House. They fancied up the dining room with greens and whites, planted roses alongside the veranda, prettified the guest rooms with frilly curtains, jolly wallpapers and bright bedspreads, and opened for business in the winter of 1972.

Darts, chats, pints of ale

They ended up with what they set out to create—as authentic a pub as you'll find west of Cornwall, a place where you can drop in for a game of darts, chat with the locals, take your pint of ale out into the garden to sit on a bench and admire the roses —Golden Prince, Bewitched, Mister Lincoln. Landlady Phyllis keeps an eye on your welfare with an authentic "Everything all right, dears?"; and John Hacking, surely the most immaculate chef in the Northeast, occasionally arrives from the kitchen where he's preparing unamericanized Yorkshire pudding, roast beef, sherry trifle, and flounder and lobster fresh from the waters off Long Island. The Earl of Stirling does what a good pub should do —it makes you feel relaxed, convivial, at peace with the world, and in the mood to enjoy life's simpler pleasures. Take a walk up past the golf course and around the clifftop. Stroll down the hill, no more than a quarter of a mile, to the local beach, a quiet half moon on Peconic Bay. Go for a stroll after dinner, along leafy moonlit lanes whirring with the night sounds of crickets and frogs. It says a lot for the disarming mood of the inn that you don't notice until later that the rooms are a shade expensive for what they are—charming for sure, but small; and some of the private showers share air space with the semi-private shower next door. If you want luxury and convenience try the motel down the road; if you want a place with personality, visit the Hackings and McCabes.

NAME: The Earl of Stirling Bar at Shelter Island House

INNKEEPERS: David & Christine McCabe, John & Phyllis Hacking

ADDRESS: Stearns Point Road, Shelter Island Heights, N.Y. 11965

TELEPHONE: 516-749-0122

DIRECTIONS: By car from New York, take the Long Island Expressway or Southern State Parkway, and a few local roads to the ferries at Greenport or Sag Harbor. From New England, take the ferry from New London to Orient Point; then the ferry from Greenport. You can also go by rail to Greenport; the hotel limousine will meet the ferries on request.

RATES: EP—$25 (with washbasin and toilet) and $30 (with private bath) from June 1 through September 30; $20 and $25 remainder of the year.

MEALS: Breakfast (to 10 a.m.), lunch, dinner (to 10 p.m.); no room service; "acceptable dress" required in the dining room, which doesn't mean you have to wear jacket and tie, but doesn't mean that you can turn up in bare feet and T-shirt either.

SEASONS: Open all year.

THREE VILLAGE INN
Stony Brook, Long Island, New York

The inn is best known as a restaurant, an hour-and-a-half drive from Manhattan, but you can stretch the evening into a night because there are a few guest rooms upstairs. Storybook Stony Brook is one of the oldest settlements on Long Island (it was founded sometime in the 1660s), a seafaring town where men built ships and then put to sea in them. The inn was built in 1785 by one of these versatile seafarers, Jonas Smith, who also happened to be Long Island's first millionaire; it stands at the end of the village green, down by the harbor, a white clapboard building sheltered by locust trees and surrounded by shrubbery.

Drive out here and stuff yourself on Stony Brook Harbor clams on the half shell, New England codfish cakes, sautéed Long Island bay scallops or roast turkey with chestnut dressing; but it's the inn's dessert list that will make you thankful you had the foresight to book a room for the night—Colonial nut layer cake, steamed fruit pudding with rum hard sauce, ginger sundae, fresh persimmon with cream, Concord grape fluff with soft custard sauce, New England mince pie. Etcetera.

The alternatives to the Long Island Expressway turn out to be seven pretty little Colonial-style rooms above the Tap Room, all with private bath, air conditioning, wall-to-wall carpeting and television.

There are also a few rooms in cottages and a motel unit around the corner, overlooking the yacht marina and a few yards from a stretch of sandy beach where you can rest up before dinner.

NAME: Three Village Inn
INNKEEPERS: Monda and Nelson Roberts
ADDRESS: Stony Brook, Long Island, N.Y. 11790
TELEPHONE: 516-751-0555
DIRECTIONS: Sixty miles from New York City, by Long Island
    Expressway to N.Y. 111 (Exit 62), then north to N.Y. 25a

and northeast to Stony Brook Road. From New England take the ferry to Port Jefferson, a few miles east.

RATES: EP—$22 to $25 in the inn, $26 to $28 in the motel cottages, year round.

MEALS: Breakfast (to 10 a.m.), lunch, dinner (to 9 p.m. weekdays, to 10 Friday and Saturday), supper (to midnight); no room service; jacket and tie for dinner.

SEASONS: Open all year.

GRISWOLD INN
Essex, Connecticut

After dinner, stroll down to the boat jetty, perch on a bollard and look across the still estuary. Sniff the night air. Listen to the clink of rigging on masts. Watch the moon shimmying across the water. It's the perfect public ending to a day at a sea-loving spot like the Griswold Inn.

The Griswold is the same age as the United States; in the 18th century they used to build ships across the street, and during the War of 1812, the British sneaked ashore one night and burned the town. But not, praise be, the inn, and drinks and dinner at the Griswold are still a tradition with yachtsmen on this part of Long Island Sound. There's no reason why land-lubbers shouldn't have some of the fun, too.

Essex is a lovely old Colonial seaport, its main street lined with houses that have weathered many a gale. The inn is three stories of white clapboard (with, oh dear, green plastic shutters) anchored to a two-story annex, the Hayden House. It has a small lobby-lounge with a large goblet full of jelly beans, and delightful new innkeepers. Until 1972, the Griswold had been in the same family for 140 years; now it's been taken over by a young couple, Bill and Vicky Winterer. Bill Winterer was once a Coast Guard officer, and then an investment banker, who also happens to be a gourmet cook and natural host. But he wanted to be near his thirty-six-foot yawl, so now he has a 200-year-old inn, with his yawl moored at the bottom of the street.

Steamship prints, antique pistols

The dark-hued Tap Room (originally the first school house in Essex) is dominated by a girthy Franklin stove that once warmed the audience at the Goodspeed Opera House in East Haddam. Here you get your first introduction to the inn's unique collection of steamship prints and handbills, including a turn-of-the-century advertisement announcing sailings of the "*State of New York* (new and elegant steamer) leaving Hart-ford Wednesdays and Fridays and arriving in New York in time for early trains to the South and West . . ."

The main collection is in the adjoining dining room, called the Covered Bridge Room, where the walls are awash in prints —some by Jacobson, others by Currier and Ives—and here and there a helpful if unheeded temperance poster (my favorite: "Large Streams from LITTLE Fountains Flow, GREAT SOTS from MODERATE Drinkers Grow"). The six-foot-wide log

fire crackles away during the winter months to cheer the land-bound sailors waiting for the first glimmer of spring and a chance to unwrap their boats.

The newly-restyled Library Room is a second restaurant, decorated in this case with antique pistols, revolvers, flintlocks, carbines and muskets; and off the main lobby there's a third dining room, the Steamboat Room. This one resembles a cabin of a posh yacht, looking aft; an illuminated painting of Old Essex, recessed into the wall, rocks gently to and fro to give you the idea you're at sea. (There's some speculation that this "motion" may be cutting down the bar sales.) That's a lot of eating and drinking space for one small inn, but in fact on summer weekends it takes all three rooms, with three sittings in each, to accommodate all the yachtsmen who come here. It's not because there's no other spot on the Sound, but because the menu is excellent—fried Cotuit oysters ($4.75), fried Cape bay scallops ($6.85), broiled bluefish ($5.75) from the list of local specialties; pumpkin soup, sweetbreads Virginia ($6.25)

and broiled quail Virginia ($7.95) are among the menu's sur-
prises. The wine list is short—enough to launch a meal, if not a
ship.

Upgrading the upstairs

The inn's eighteen guest rooms don't have quite the style of the
public rooms—at least not yet. The Winterers are working on
it, and already they've upgraded a few of them. At the moment
six of the rooms have private baths, with one bath to two rooms
for the remainder. (Note: The "private" bathroom may be a
pullman-type affair, installed in a room that was never intended
to hold a private john, and may offer less privacy than some
couples might prefer; if you're on a first outing together you
might feel more comfortable without the not-so-private private
facilities. Check out the situation when you get there.) Otherwise, the Griswold's rooms are as fresh as a ten-knot wind,
with print wallpaper, homey furniture, scatter rugs, and here
and there a few apt antiques. Most of the rooms are air condi-
tioned, but the towels are skimpy.

What do you do in Essex if you're not a sailor? Plenty. Take
a trip up the river on the "River Queen." Take in a play at the
Goodspeed Opera House or the Ivortown Theater. Drive over
to the charming town of Old Saybrook at the mouth of the
river. Or just sit on a bollard and dream.

NAME: Griswold Inn
INNKEEPERS: Bill and Vicky Winterer
ADDRESS: Essex, Conn.
TELEPHONE: 203-767-1812
DIRECTIONS: Take Exit 64 on Connecticut Turnpike, then go
    north 5 miles on U.S. 9.
RATES: From $10 to $22 year round, EP.
MEALS: Lunch and dinner; breakfast in spring and summer only;
    no room service.
SEASONS: Open all year, busiest during the sailing season.

GRAY GABLES OCEAN HOUSE
Bourne, Massachusetts

This was Grover Cleveland's summer house. He built it in 1880, on a tiny peninsula at the western tip of the Cape Cod Canal, after experts assured him that this was the spot least likely, within the entire continental United States, to be struck by lightning.

The President summered here from the time he married his wife Frances (twenty-seven years younger than Cleveland) until 1902, when his son was killed (not by lightning). He never again visited the house, which became an inn in 1905 and went through several owners; the most recent owner, Arthur de Saulniers, arrived in 1972, and things look promising.

At least, through all its tribulations and remodelings, Gray Gables hasn't lost its sense of history. The posts of the staircase leading to the gallery still have the marks where Cleveland recorded the heights of his children and grandchildren.

Room 106 was the former President's library, a studious place with wood-paneled walls, a fireplace and built-in closets, but no books; the other guest rooms off the second-floor gallery are small but charming, and they all make up for their skimpy space with lively views of boats jostling for position at the entrance to what is reputed to be the busiest canal in the world. (If you arrive by boat you can even pull up at the inn's private jetty, originally built so that the President could step directly from his gunboat to his garden.) The ground floor is almost entirely given over to drinking and dining, and the big dining room has a view of Buzzard's Bay that competes with the flickering flames in the fieldstone hearth.

The virtue of Gray Gables is that it's far from the beaten path, at least from the landlubber's point of view. It's surrounded on three sides by water (and parking lot), and on the fourth by private summer homes; it has its own pool, and there are beaches nearby (but you have to drive some distance to the nearest tennis court or golf course).

NAME: Gray Gables Ocean House
INNKEEPER: Arthur de Saulniers
ADDRESS: President's Road, Bourne, Mass. 02532
TELEPHONE: 617-759-5722
DIRECTIONS: Just off Mass. 28, 2½ miles southwest of Bourne Bridge.
RATES: EP—$30, July and August; lower in April, May, June, September and October.
MEALS: Dinner only (to 10:30), but "you can always have a cup of coffee for breakfast"; room service (to 11:30); informal.

(Since this book was written, Gray Gables was destroyed by fire. A new hotel—built in authentic Cape Cod style but not a reconstruction of the original—will be built sometime in 1974 or 1975.)

CLAUSON'S INN & GOLF RESORT
North Falmouth, Massachusetts

A hundred and fifty years ago when it opened, Clauson's was just a small Cape Cod inn; now the small Cape Cod inn is surrounded by a 400-acre estate with its own eighteen-hole golf course, mile-long lake, sailboats, private beach, riding trails and tennis courts, plus cottages and a motor lodge. It can get crowded in summer—especially during the jazz jam sessions on Sunday afternoons; but the rest of the year you can have acres to yourself for walking in the woods, skiing on the lake or playing a game or two or three of tennis. The most charming rooms are the ten in the inn itself—wood-paneled nests with white ruffled curtains, twin beds and private bathrooms with shower stalls; and the pride of the inn is a two-room suite with a gabled, beamed ceiling (ask for rooms #1 and #1a). The inn is a rambling affair, in typical New England fashion, with built-in settees under stairways, hearthstone fireplaces, antiques and wing chairs everywhere; the main lounge, with a baby grand piano, Governor Winthrop desk and bookshelves stacked with first editions, leads into several small dining rooms, so that even when the inn is busy with hungry golfers and sailors you can still find a quiet corner for your meal. Except during the jam session.

NAME: Clauson's Inn & Golf Resort
INNKEEPER: Paul Simpson
ADDRESS: Route 151, North Falmouth, Mass. 02551
TELEPHONE: 617-563-2255
DIRECTIONS: Just across the Cape Cod canal, on Mass. 151, a few miles west of the intersection with U.S. 28; by air to Hyannis.
RATES: EP—$14 in fall, $16 in summer for rooms in the inn; motor lodge and cottages from $16 to $20 in fall, from $18 to $24 in summer.
MEALS: Breakfast, lunch and dinner; informal.
SEASONS: Open all year, busiest July and August, delightful in the fall.

WYCHMERE HARBOR CLUB
Harwichport, Cape Cod, Massachusetts

From your room in one of the hotel's five villas you can almost reach out and grab the tiller of one of the sailboats sidling in to Wychmere Harbor—a tiny cove ringed by saltbox houses, jetties ajumble with nets and lobster pots, seagulls perched expectantly on bollards, sloops and schooners casting off for

Nantucket. The sights, sounds and smells tell you you're in a typical Cape Cod harbor—and you have to walk only a dozen paces to be in your hotel room.

The Wychmere Harbor Club was built eighty-five years ago by the family that runs it today, and the main lodge hasn't changed much since then—parlor after parlor of overstuffed Victoriana; upstairs, narrow corridors like the passageways of an ocean liner lead to thirty-one friendly rooms in period style, with private bathrooms and room phones, but without modern frills like television and air conditioning (you don't need it, since the sea breezes never stop breezing). If your bedroom tastes run to something more modern, the Wychmere also has the five villas along the channel breakwater, each with a communal lounge and elegant, spacious bedrooms with big windows, patios overlooking the channel, and modern frills like cable TV.

The remainder of the inn's eight acres is taken over by an obtrusive parking lot, putting green, lawns; a Cabana Club with heated, glass-screened pool, dining room, sundeck, terrace bar and gazebo bar (guests of the hotel can become members for $1 a day); and a small private beach by the edge of Nantucket Sound.

If you're looking for real Cape Coddy atmosphere, you'll find it here.

NAME: Wychmere Harbor Club
INNKEEPER: Eleanor Thompson
ADDRESS: Snow Inn Road, Harwichport, Mass. 02645
TELEPHONE: 617-432-1000
DIRECTIONS: Just off Mass. 28 in the center of Harwichport; by air to Hyannis
RATES: AP, sometimes EP, and rather complex, so check with the hotel before you make your reservation—$52 to $88 AP in July and August; $52 to $60 AP (including tips) from Labor Day to January 1; EP rates available if you ask for them (which you should do since there are fine restaurants in these parts).
MEALS: Breakfast (regular to 9:30, Continental to 11 a.m.), lunch, dinner (to 9 p.m.) in season—AP guests can also eat

at the dockside Clam Bar; room service; jacket and tie required in Cabana Club dining room.

SEASONS: Currently closed between January and March, but may be open year round by the time you read this; small groups throughout the year, except July and August, the Social Season.

SHIP'S KNEES INN
E. Orleans, Cape Cod, Massachusetts

¢

It's not a cutesy-pie title; a ship's knee is a block of wood that connects deck beams to the frames of sailboats, and when this shingle house was built 150 years ago it was held together by ship's knees. "Now I'm having a fantastic love affair with Ship's Knees," says Jerrie Butcher, who took over the house a couple of years ago and charmed it into the most decorative hostelry on the Cape. She scoured local antique stores for ship's trunks, old whaling prints, antique maps, Windsor chairs, decoy ducks and braided rugs; then she sorted out her finds in rooms designed in one of three basic colors and fitted them out with carpets, towels, bedspreads and sheets in coordinated colors, making simple but delightful nooks for love affairs, fantastic or otherwise. The ships' knees hold together just ten rooms, four of them with private bathrooms and color television, and one (#3) with beamed ceilings and a fireplace. There's a small lounge where you help yourself to fresh-baked popovers and doughnuts and coffee for breakfast, and out in the garden you can toss a frisbee, play volleyball or lounge in patio furniture till the stars come home. And that's it—quiet, unassuming, impeccable, escapist. The Ship's Knees sits at the junction of a couple of residential streets, under streams of telephone company spaghetti, and across the street from an unusual little restaurant called The Quacker, where you can have simple snacks on a rustic terrace or buy the ingredients for a tasty picnic to take to the beach. Just wait till you see the beach! Nauset Beach is part of the Cape Cod National Seashore, mile after unspoiled mile of sand and dunes, just a three-minute walk from and five-minute walk to the inn. This is paradise for off-season beachlovers, a place to walk when the winds are churning the ocean and the seagulls are flying backwards, when the twilight comes early and eerily and turns the surfcasters into balloon-legged silhouettes; then, when your faces are all tingly, you can hurry up the hill to the color-coordinated warmth of the Ship's Knees' bedspreads and sheets.

NAME: Ship's Knees Inn

INNKEEPER: Ms. Jerrie Butcher

ADDRESS: Beach Road, East Orleans, Mass. 02643

TELEPHONE: 617-255-1312

DIRECTIONS: Follow U.S. 6 to Orleans exit, then go east on Mass. 28 to E. Orleans and follow the signs for Nauset Beach; by air to Hyannis.

RATES: EP—$24 and $26 with private bath and TV, $13 and $16 without private bath from late June to Labor Day; from $9 to $14 remainder of year. Prices include Continental breakfast.

MEALS: Continental breakfast only (to 10:30 a.m.); Ms. Butcher will give you a list of quayside and countryside restaurants for lunch or dinner.

SEASONS: Open all year, busiest in July and August, at its best in spring and fall.

THE WHITE ELEPHANT
Nantucket, Massachusetts

You wake up in the morning in a flower-covered cottage to see seagulls preening themselves on the bollards and schooners riding at anchor in the harbor. If it's sunny and warm you can slip into the pool or wander over to the beach; if it's cool and misty, the way Nantucket should be, you can hop on bicycles and ride across the moors of Sargent juniper and Warminster broom. In the evening, wander down to the wharf for a moon-light view of the harbor before you return to your flower-covered, saltbox cottage.

Nantucket is a nautical town, and the White Elephant is a nautical hotel, right down on the waterfront, with its lawns ending up in the harbor. It was built in 1963 by Walter Beinecke, Jr., of S&H Green Stamps, who took over most of the Nan-tucket waterfront and revitalized it (he's had his critics, but most people seem to feel he's done a tasteful job, remodeling the place with a feel for its shingle-saltbox heritage).

This elephant comes in three parts: the main two-story lodge with spacious, modern rooms; the Spindrift Cottages, on the lawn by the water, with roses growing up the walls, neatly furnished living rooms and bedrooms, and windows facing the harbor (which makes them the most popular rooms in the hotel); and the Captain's Court, a bunch of typical Nantucket homes the size of doll houses, grouped around a lawn with loungers spread out beneath the locust trees. The suites in the Captain's Court cottages give you a chance to live in the style of a Nantucket seafarer—pine walls, beamed ceilings, sturdy furniture, fireplaces, and old prints and maps on the walls. (The hotel is also building a new extension a few doors down the street, also on the edge of the harbor, with twenty-six deluxe rooms; when they're ready, the hotel may remain open year round.)

NAME: The White Elephant Inn and Cottages
INNKEEPER: Richard W. Davenport
ADDRESS: Nantucket Island, Mass. 02554
TELEPHONE: 617-228-2500
DIRECTIONS: By ferry from Woods Hole or Hyannis; by air from New York, Boston or Hyannis, by Air New England.

RATES: AP from $43 to $57 for rooms, $36 to $137 for cottages, from mid-June to Labor Day; slightly less in spring and fall.
MEALS: Breakfast (to 10 a.m.), lunch, dinner (to 10 p.m.); room service in summer; jacket and tie required in evening.
SEASONS: Closed October through May (but may be open year round by the time you read this), busiest in July and August.

JARED COFFIN HOUSE
Nantucket, Massachusetts

Step inside the lobby and you're back in the days of the great whaling fleets of Nantucket. The public rooms are filled with Chippendale, Sheraton, Directoire and American Federal furniture, antique oriental rugs, Chinese coffee tables and Japanese lacquered cabinets; a sweeping stairway with a white balustrade leads you up to your guest room, which will be decorated with period furniture, authentic Colonial wallpapers, and traditional Nantucket curtains and bedspreads hand-woven by local ladies. Jared Coffin, one of the wealthiest shipowners in Nantucket, built this red brick mansion on a street of mansions in 1845, and furnished it with treasures brought back from around the world by his ships. It still looks like a private home, although Coffin lived here for only one year before it was bought up by the Nantucket Steamboat Company and turned into a hotel in 1846; the Nantucket Historical Society took it over in 1961 and restored it to its original state.

The Jared Coffin House is the most famous and most popular inn on the island, which means that in summer its garden patio, Tap Room and dining room are swarming with overnight visitors and day trippers; but it remains open throughout the year, which means you can visit Nantucket at its most Nantucketty. The islanders themselves rave about November in

Nantucket, when the moors are a carpet of fall colors; but October is also a lovely month for hopping on a bike and riding along the clifftop roads, and May and June are great for tennis, golf and playing leapfrog on the beach.

Just bring lots of sweaters to keep you warm on the moors and beach; the Nantucket embroidery will keep you warm in bed.

NAME: Jared Coffin House
INNKEEPER: Philip Whitney Read
ADDRESS: Nantucket Island, Mass. 02554
TELEPHONE: 617-228-2400
DIRECTIONS: On the corner of Broad and Centre Streets, near the top end of Main Street; to get to Nantucket Island you take the ferry from Woods Hole or Hyannis, or fly Air New England from New York, Boston, Hyannis and other points.
RATES: EP—from May 1 through October 31, $36 to $40 in the original Jared Coffin House, $26 to $30 in the newer wings; from November 1 through April 30, the rates are $26 and $30, $18 and $22.
MEALS: Breakfast (to 10 a.m.), lunch, dinner (to 9 p.m.); room service breakfast only; formal and informal.
SEASONS: Open all year, busiest July, August and over Christmas and New Year's; small groups at other times.

SHIPS INN

Nantucket, Massachusetts

The Ships Inn is to the Jared Coffin House what a ship captain is to a ship owner. This clapboard house is a modest version of the Coffin house, built in 1831 by Captain Obed Starbuck as a cozy place to come home to after long voyages. It's now a cozy place where John Krebs came to after a spell as a stockbroker in Baltimore in the heavy seas of the Sixties. The furniture is sturdy rather than stylish, the walls are lined with prints of whaling ships and flowers, the door jambs are askew, the rooms are named for the ships Starbuck commanded, and all in all it has a salty Nantucket air about it. It's on a quiet street at the top of Main Street, away from the rabble, but still close enough to the wharf and bars and goings-on.

Downstairs, the Krebses have installed their own cocktail lounge—an unusual place where you can sit at a bar shaped like a whaling dory and have a drink while you're waiting for your place at the Captain's Table. Their restaurant has an interesting menu—beef, cheese and seafood fondues, and baked stuffed Nantucket quahaugs. The menu is inexpensive, but the inn is a shade overpriced in the peak season; however, that's only three months of the year, and the remainder of the time it's a comfy little harbor to return to after days of exploring the island.

NAME: Ships Inn
INNKEEPERS: John and Bar Krebs
ADDRESS: Nantucket Island, Mass. 02554
TELEPHONE: 617-228-0040
DIRECTIONS: On Fair Street, which runs off to the left at the top of Main Street.
RATES: EP—$26 with private bath, $24 with semi-private bath from June 15 through September 15 (including Continental breakfast); $18 with and $16 without the remainder of the year (without breakfast).
MEALS: Breakfast (Continental, to 10 a.m.), dinner (to 9:30 p.m.), closed Tuesdays; no room service; informal.
SEASONS: Open all year, busiest in summer.

WENTWORTH-BY-THE-SEA
near Portsmouth, New Hampshire

This is a veritable "Queen Mary" of resort hotels, a leviathan with elegant salons and hallways and dining rooms, with balls and parties, dance bands, cabarets—even its own Symphonietta. It rides the crest of one of the small islands at the mouth of Portsmouth Harbor, its gleaming white superstructure rising above an ocean of trees.

The Wentworth is an immense place (200 rooms), rather posh, but it sails into these pages because of location—and nostalgia. It's ironic that hotels of the Colonial era seem to be thriving more successfully than hotels of the Victorian era, that hotels built to cater to the stagecoach trade are doing better than hotels built for the carriage trade. The Wentworth is an exception.

The first carriages started driving up to the Wentworth in the 1870s, and the hotel reached its pinnacle of fame in 1905, when it hosted the diplomats who signed the Russian-Japanese treaty. Ever since, it's been hosting the families of the well-heeled as well as a sprinkling of celebs—Gloria Swanson, Richard Nixon, Sir John Gielgud, Ted Kennedy, Duke Ellington, Goodman Ace, Anthony Burgess and the late Ogden Nash. A motley crew.

The hotel's rooms are big, plushly carpeted, with the gracious air of a country mansion. Each room is different. They all, of course, have private baths, and the lanai suites also have enclosed porches with luxurious terrace furniture. But you don't have to stay with the crowd. The hotel has a few New England-style cottages scattered around the grounds, most of them across the street in the gardens above the sea. Ask for the Boat House cottage; it has its own garden, living room, double bedroom, kitchenette and bath, and a sun deck facing the water, about two blocks from the hotel. The other cottages are larger, with several apartments in each; but if you want luxury and privacy there's nothing to prevent your renting an entire cottage.

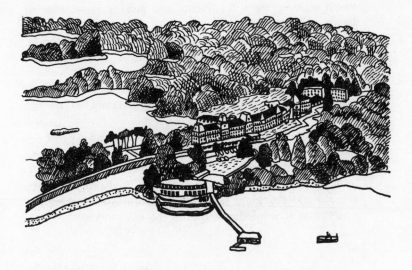

Park-like grounds

Although the hotel is immense, you don't feel crowded because the grounds and the surroundings are so spacious. Walk across the street, through the gardens, around the pitch-and-putt course, and you come to a heated swimming pool of Olympic stature, or the sandy beach. The hotel's private golf course, eighteen holes, skims alongside the shore half an island away, and there are first-class tennis courts out back. The amiable president-owner and his resident manager occasionally throw out a challenge to guests to a set of tennis or a round of golf; if they lose, the guest gets a free night's lodging. Don't dream—they gave away only two rooms last summer, even though the president is a shade older than, say, Bobby Riggs.

NAME: Wentworth-by-the-Sea
INNKEEPER: James Barker Smith (owner/president)
ADDRESS: Portsmouth, N.H. 03801
TELEPHONE: 603-436-3100 (summer), 436-4410 (winter)
DIRECTIONS: From Interstate 95 northbound, take exit 3 about an hour after Boston, then follow the signs to U.S. 1a, where

you'll pick up signs for Wentworth and/or Newcastle; or by air, to Portsmouth.

RATES: AP preferred—$54 a room, $54 for a room in a cottage, $62 a suite (you may be able to arrange EP rates in the off-season).

MEALS: Breakfast, lunch, afternoon tea, dinner, coffee shop; room service (even for the cottages); clambakes on the beach.

SEASONS: Open May through October only; July and August are the Social Season; May, June, September and October tend to be convention months (but not the beer-salesmen type—more likely a group of heart surgeons discussing the aorta valve), and the hotel will always inform you if there's a convention scheduled at the time you plan to visit.

SEACREST INN
Kennebunkport, Maine

This is a place to be in a gale, by the window, a roaring fire at your back, a roaring sea outside, hands clasped around mugs of mulled cider. Rocking chairs on the big veranda and picture windows in the dining room make sure you never miss a single wave.

This old seafarer's home, a green-timbered house with a steep red roof, overlooks a rocky garden, the rocky shore and the rocky sea; a skinny road runs between the garden and the shore, and there's nothing else around but private summer houses.

The inn proper has three rooms with private baths, and two bathrooms for the remaining half-dozen rooms. Try to get one of the two big rooms facing the sea, painted in soft pastel shades with turn-of-the-century Maine furniture. Most of the

bedrooms have an ocean view—slightly angled in some cases, but an ocean view nonetheless.

If you can't get a room in the inn, settle for the small motel in the garden. These rooms are compact, but you can always pretend they're cabins on a yacht; they all have balconies facing the ocean, and such unnautical equipment as "noiseless mercury switches" and "hydronic radiant heating," and they're "scientifically constructed against sound-conduction." The attraction of the dining room, besides the view, is the price—a lobster dinner costs only about $5, depending on the day's catch. You'll find golf, tennis, riding, boating and fishing nearby; Kennebunk Beach is within walking distance, or you can swim in the natural rock pools right in front of the inn.

Basically, a place for wave watching.

NAME: Seacrest Inn-on-the-Sea and Motel
INNKEEPER: John M. Somers (owner-manager)
ADDRESS: Kennebunkport, Me. 04046
TELEPHONE: 207-967-2125
DIRECTIONS: Follow the Maine Turnpike (Int. 95) to the Kennebunk signs, then follow State Highway 9a or 35 to Dock

Square in the center of Kennebunkport; then take Ocean Avenue, turn right at the sea and drive along the shore road until you come to the Inn.

RATES: EP—double bed-sitting room with private bath, $16.50 to $18.50 between July 1 and Labor Day, $11 or $13 April 1 to June 30 or Labor Day to November 30; double room near bath, from $5 to $10; motel room, $13 off-season to $22 on-season.

MEALS: Breakfast (to 9:30 a.m.), lunch and dinner (to 8 p.m.); no room service.

SEASONS: Open April 1 through November 30; peak season July 1 through Labor Day.

SHAWMUT INN
Kennebunkport, Maine

Throw open the curtains. Step out onto your balcony. Fill your lungs with brisk ocean air. Ahead of you the sun shimmers on the sea and the rocky shore. To your left, across Turbots Creek, the Vaughn Island wildlife preserve is already astir, and away on the horizon, Cape Porpoise Lighthouse peeps above the islands. If that doesn't have you hollering "Oh what a beautiful morning," it's because you're calling room service for breakfast. The location is great. To say nothing of the heated Olympic-size pool by the edge of the sea, the nine-hole three-par pitch-and-putt course, the badminton and croquet. Unfortunately, the inn itself is ho-hum. It started life as someone's summer home in the 1880s, and it became a hotel in 1914. Since then it's been enlarged, improved, renovated, and one by one most of the cottages on the surrounding estate have been taken under its wing. The rooms are comfortable, spacious, carpeted, they have tiled bathrooms and color TV and so on, but they could be anywhere (why not, for example, a print of a square-rigger

instead of that hackneyed etching of Rome's Piazza Navona?).
Wisely, the owners have put in picture windows everywhere so
that whether you're resting, drinking, loving or dining, you can
see the rocks and the sea.

There are 125 rooms in all, divided among the inn, the motel-
lodge and eighteen cottages. One of the small cottages near the
sea is your best bet, and the three rooms above the bar-lounge
your worst (they catch every amplified thump of the combo on
weekends, which can be very distracting unless you plan to
thump right back). But all the drawbacks fade away when you
sit on the rocks and watch the moon glisten on the sea. Oh,
what a beautiful evening.

NAME: Shawmut Inn
INNKEEPER: Frank Small
ADDRESS: Kennebunkport, Me.
TELEPHONE: 207-967-3931
DIRECTIONS: Leave the Maine Turnpike (Int. 95) at the Ken-
    nebunk exit, then follow State Highway 9a or 35 to the
    center of Kennebunkport, where you pick up Ocean Drive,
    which will lead you to the private road to Shawmut; by air,
    to Portland.
RATES: A complicated rate structure; they'll try to get you to
    take MAP but ask for EP (from $16 to $36 in winter, $36
    to $64 in summer) because the food doesn't match the
    view from the dining room, and you may want to sample
    one of the restaurants in Kennebunkport or Ogunquit down
    the coast.
MEALS: Breakfast (to 9:30 a.m.), lunch, dinner (to 9 p.m.; com-
    plete meals for $5 or $6, but lobster alone is $8); room
    service in summer, maybe in winter (depending on whether
    you talk to the owner or the waiter).
SEASONS: This is the only resort on the Maine coast that stays
    open all year; November through May are group and con-
    vention months, and the person who takes your reservation
    is supposed to tell you if there will be a group in the house
    when you're there, but ask anyway.

GREEN MOUNTAINS, WHITE MOUNTAINS

No, make me mistress to the man I love
If there be yet another name more free
More fond than mistress, make me that to thee!
\text{POPE}

15. The Inn at Sawmill Farm

16. The Old Tavern at Grafton

17. Bromley House

18. The Four Columns Inn

19. Chester Inn

20. Woodstock Inn

21. Hawk Mountain

22. The John Hancock Inn

23. The General Wolfe Inn

24. Wolfeboro Inn

25. The Inn at Steele Hill

26. Stafford's-in-the-Field

27. Farrell Lodge

28. Tecumseh Inn

THE INN AT SAWMILL FARM
West Dorset, Vermont

The old stable is now an airy lounge with a wall of window looking onto swamp maple and tamarack trees. The former stalls are bedrooms and the haymows are sleeping lofts. The cupola-crowned sugar house, where the farmer used to render the maple syrup, is now a summer card room by the edge of the swimming pool. The chess table in the bar was once a hand-cranked washing machine, and the planter on the dining room wall used to be a South Jersey cranberry rake.

Many people have converted barns; few of them have succeeded as nobly as Rodney and Ione Williams. What the Williamses have wrought is not so much a conversion as a metamorphosis. But then they started out with several advantages. Rodney Williams was, until a few years ago, an Atlantic City architect; Ione Williams was an interior decorator. The remainder of the family contributed muscle or encouragement during the transformation period, and they still play an enthusiastic part in running the inn—son and daughter help out in the kitchen and dining room, and Grandma makes the fresh tomato juice served at breakfast and the black raspberry pie with sugared crust at dinnertime.

Aromatic welcome

The inn gets its name from a sawmill that was erected here sometime in the late 1700s, where a branch of the Deerfield River funnels through a narrow rocky gully. You drive across this gully and up the hill a few yards to a small red building, softly floodlit by lamps artfully concealed in the stumps of trees. Step out of your car and immediately you notice the scent of apple trees and the whiff of a wood fire. Welcome to the Sawmill.

The inn's foyer is decked out like a farm shed, with yokes and harnesses, forks and hoes and all the impedimenta of a working farm. Go upstairs, and it's nothing like a farm. Nor a hotel, for that matter. It looks more like a classy antique store—an antique store where you can lounge and eat and drink and play.

The basic structure of the 80-year-old barn is still intact. All the hand-hewn weathered beams and barnboards are original; ditto the mellowed brick and textured fieldstone. None of the original timbers were discarded; when they weren't needed in their original position, they were salvaged and used elsewhere. There's nothing phony about Sawmill. Look up, for example, to the ceiling of the stable-lounge. Those hefty timbers are real. Note the balustrade along the library balcony—it's made from the stall dividers that once separated the cows from the bulls. There's a lot to admire in this lounge: the nonagenarian Elliot clock, the dainty Davenport desk, the copper-covered coffee table, the bronze telescope, the honest-to-goodness pans, pots, spoons, tongs and candleholders surrounding the big brick fire. All the colors of Vermont are here—from spring's celery-tinted walls and the lime-green upholstery to the russet and copper of autumn.

Escargots and Grandma's pies

Beyond the lounge you have a pair of dining rooms. The first is a formal jacket-and-tie sort of place, with overhead fans, walls lined with American primitives of young girls and old ladies, and chairs that are far too slender and elegant for a public dining room. The more popular dining room is a glass-enclosed patio overlooking the apple trees and the pool, a rustic room with flagstone floors, dark-brown barnsiding and directors' chairs to match. People drive for miles, through spring muds and winter snows, just for the pleasure of dining here: avocado stuffed with hot crab meat, escargots Bourguignonne, shrimp in beer batter with a pungent fruit sauce; crepes stuffed with chicken and served with spinach sauce, lobster Savannah, rack of baby lamb Persille (around $7 to $9). That's a lot of calories, but don't forget to leave room for one of Grandma's fresh-from-the-oven pies.

The inn's Pot Belly Bar is a calculated clutter of mustard and pepper tins, old biscuit tins, copper kettles, spirit lamps, antiquated ice skates, and pre-TV advertisements. It gets its name from a big old Franklin stove, but the focal point is actually a rollicking old player piano that plunks out any of a hundred tunes from "The Desert Song" to "When The Saints Go Marching In."

The Inn at Sawmill has only ten rooms, two of them "bedloft" rooms with extra twin beds (really for families, but they make an unusual change of pace if you can afford them). All ten rooms are decorated differently—Early American, Georgian, Victorian, Vermontian; but they all have delicate little touches, like washbasins recessed in copper-topped vanity tables, floral wallpapers and extravagant shower heads. Cow stalls were never intended to be soundproof, and you may still hear a hint of mooing and lowing from the adjoining rooms, but not enough to keep you awake.

Seasonal pleasures and pastimes

West Dorset is a pretty enough little old village, mostly white clapboard houses and a white church with a tall spire hiding behind a grotesquely ornate telephone pole. It's one of the oldest villages in Vermont, but it's not the sleepy backwater it seems to be—there are several bars, discotheques and restaurants in the neighborhood, including a cluster of them a few miles up the road at Snow Lake. However, a quick walk along the main street and you've seen West Dorset. In spring and fall, you can walk along miles of almost car-free byway, or explore the inn's twenty-five acres of woodland. In summer, you can swim in the pool or work up a tan on the sun deck. In winter, borrow a pair of snow shoes from the inn, or rent cross-country skis and follow a pair of four-hour trails (the Williamses will make up a picnic lunch with wine to sustain you); skate on the pond (bring your own skates); and, of course, you have a choice of downhill runs at Mt. Snow (a mile and a half to the north) and Haystack (two miles to the south). Let others shiver. I'll be sitting on the big sofa in the lounge, with my afternoon tea, and my feet on Rodney Williams' copper-topped table, watching the snow fall on the naked tamaracks and maples—a panorama of white.

NAME: The Inn at Sawmill Farm
INNKEEPERS: Rodney and Ione Williams
ADDRESS: Box 8, West Dorset, Vt. 05356
TELEPHONE: 802-464-8121
DIRECTIONS: On State Highway 100, 6 miles north of Wilmington, halfway between Brattleboro and Bennington, and 10 miles from the Marlboro Music Festival.
RATES: $22 to $35, MAP.
MEALS: Vermont breakfast; dinner served in two sittings—between 6 and 7, 8 and 9 p.m.; no lunch; afternoon tea between 4:15 and 5 p.m.; no room service.
SEASONS: Open year round; busiest in October and during the snow season, quietest in summer.

THE OLD TAVERN AT GRAFTON
Grafton, Vermont

This may well be the ultimate inn.

It's historic (it opened its doors in 1801), and it had a distinguished clientele (Daniel Webster, Nathaniel Hawthorne, Ralph Waldo Emerson, Ulysses S. Grant, Teddy Roosevelt and Rudyard Kipling, who stayed here so long one of the rooms is named after him). But historic inns often look their age, because

it takes so much money just to keep them from falling down. Not the Old Tavern at Grafton. There's enough petty cash here not just to keep it standing but to refurbish it from top to bottom. The secret is the Windham Foundation. This local philanthropic outfit has lavished thousands on restoring many of the old Colonial homes in the village, and particularly this proud old inn. Now it's virtually a brand-new 270-year-old inn, with modern heating, a fire detection system, sprinklers and an elevator. Kipling and Co. never had it so good.

When the inn first opened its doors, it was a much simpler structure than today's three-storied whitewashed building with twin verandas overhung by the third floor. There are two extensions at the rear—a kitchen and restaurant where the outhouses used to be, and a bar in the old barn; and across the street are a couple of old homes (also dating from the 1800s). The proprietors call this the "most elegant little inn in all New England." They're not kidding.

Step through the inn's main door and you're in the drawing room of a well-to-do squire—except that it's really the lobby and reception area. Its walls are chestnut and spruce green, with a portrait of George Washington above the mantelpiece. To the left is the Kipling Library, a blue parlor with shelves of books flanking an open fire, writing desks for dashing off *billets-doux,* and comfy sofas to settle back in with a volume of Kipling or Emerson or Hawthorne.

Upstairs in the guest rooms, you'll find the same impeccable taste. All the rooms are different, but they're all decorated with antiques and drapes and hooked rugs. Try one of the other rooms with tester beds—mini fourposters with cute embroidered canopies. If you need a lot of room for your frolics, ask for #8 or #9, both corner rooms with sofas and armchairs. The inn has thirty-five rooms spread over three buildings—fourteen in the old inn itself, the remainder in the Homestead and the Windham Cottage opposite. Normally, the words "across the street" might throw you into a tizzy. How dare they shunt you off to the annex! In this case, go. The rooms are delightful there, too. Karen's Room is all pinks and pastels, with bay windows and armchairs; Addie's Room, green and white, has a chaise longue where you can stretch out and watch the action down by the inn's swimming hole. There's another lovely old parlor in the Homestead, and a bar-like lounge with TV, fireplace and a discreet soft-drinks machine.

There's no air conditioning in the inn, but then up here in the mountains you don't need it except for maybe three or four days in summer.

One of the most convivial rooms in the inn is one Kipling and his cohorts never saw. It's the Tavern Bar, an austere corner of the barn, so snug you can't avoid clinking glasses before you drink.

On the other side of the bar's fireplace is the barn proper, with an even larger fireplace, puffy chairs and sofas; above it, the haymow has become a games room, with a piano, English bar billiards and a TV set tucked away in a corner.

Cranberry freeze and banana nut bread

This is another of those true-to-tradition taverns that lures travelers with the pleasures of its table—New England country fare (hearty roasts, stuffed turkey, duckling), with fresh-baked dinner rolls, banana bread, cranberry bread, and a succulent choice of twenty-two desserts. The two dining rooms are as attractive as the cooking: one is feminine and lacy, the other masculine and rustic, with big beams and a huge hutch stacked with pewter plates and decoy ducks.

Quiet corners, covered bridges

The Old Inn at Grafton is one of those places where you'll want to spend a few days. Just sampling all the quiet corners in the inn takes time: one morning writing postcards in the Kipling Library, an afternoon taking advantage of your luxurious room, cocktail hour in the Tavern Bar, an after-dinner drink in the Barn Lounge. Next day, a dip in the inn's private swimming pool in the meadow behind the Homestead. After lunch, a game of tennis. Or croquet. Or sit and rock on the porch, watching the automobiles go by every half hour or so. Or take a walk down the village street, past the antique shops, the art gallery, the general store and the lovely old homes, across one of Grafton's kissing bridges, and wander up the leafy lane on the side of the mountain. It's so peaceful you can almost hear the butterflies flap their wings.

NAME: The Old Tavern at Grafton
INNKEEPERS: Whitney and Joan Landon
ADDRESS: Grafton, Vt. 05146
TELEPHONE: 802-843-2375
DIRECTIONS: On State Highway 121, about ten miles from Bellows Falls and Interstate 91.

RATES: Room with twin beds $18 to $30, with double beds $18 to $28, EP.

MEALS: Breakfast (to 9:30 a.m.), lunch and dinner (to 8 p.m.); no room service; jacket and tie required at dinner.

SEASONS: Open all year (busiest during fall foliage weeks).

BROMLEY HOUSE
Peru, Vermont

Maybe I shouldn't suggest this place as an inn for lovers since it was originally built from the bricks and timber of a Methodist Church. You know how Methodists are.

When it opened in 1822 as a staging post for coaches going over Bromley Mountain, the inn was "indexed by the Bear, the old Oaken Bucket, and the First Built Open Outside Fireplace in the World." If you wonder what's so special about an outside fireplace, try standing on the porch on a wintry day waiting for the stagecoach to take you over Bromley. Peru is 2,000 feet up, Bromley 3,260 feet.

Bromley House stands in the middle of the village, on a grassy, tree-shaded triangle. Several additions have been tacked on to the original Methodist-brick structure, and it's now a three-story building with a veranda around the first floor and a square cupola on top (a potentially romantic little room, unfortunately, and unsportingly, the domain of the assistant manager). What the inn has going for it is the lounge—a room spacious enough for three big hooked rugs, a six-foot hutch, a white natural stone fireplace, three sofas and a library. It's a perfect place to sit and sip a sherry while you're waiting for a table in the dining room. There's another tiny bar, on the opposite side of the lobby, which aims at wood-and-wrought-iron period charm rather than the luxury of three sofas. There's more local color in the dining room—pine walls, tinted twelve–by–twelve peekaboo windows, a collection of antique flatirons, old paintings and prints. Robert

Frost used to drive over here from his home in Arlington for dinner. The meals are reputed to be something special, which is why you may have to wait for your table. Probably compared to the regular fare in these parts, they may be something special— breads fresh from the oven, relishes from a neighbor's garden, local ham cob-smoked by a friend, shrimp boiled in beer—but otherwise it's a basic menu. The wine list is restricted to seven items.

Old-time guest rooms

Upstairs, this old inn looks like an old inn. Wooden floors, scatter rugs, brass bedsteads. The two rooms facing the front have walls of exposed brick and their own fireplaces. There are eighteen rooms in all; a few of them have private bathrooms (with showers only); the others share several bathrooms with tubs the size of stagecoaches. The rooms are pleasant enough, it's just that they don't quite measure up to places like Grafton and Sturbridge. A philanthropic foundation could work wonders here.

Not that you're likely to be spending much time in your room anyway. There's plenty to turn your mind to beyond the peeka-boo windows.

The inn has its own swimming pool, out back where the stables used to be, and you can also swim in a small mountain lake at Hapgood Pond Park, a short walk away. You can go hiking on the Long Trail (two miles from the inn and part of the Appalachian Trail), or riding through the pine and spruce forests. There are auctions, antique shops and two summer theaters in the neighborhood. If it happens to rain, nip down to the basement and have a sauna (open until 11 p.m.), or a game of table tennis or billiards (you may have to dust off the table first). There's even a TV set down there. Peru itself is about as quiet as a village can be before it's declared a ghost town—except in winter, when the crowds gather to ski the Big B. Then you can rent a pair of snowshoes from the inn and go stomping among the snow-trimmed spruce and pine trees.

NAME: Bromley House
INNKEEPERS: Janice and Jack McWilliams
ADDRESS: Peru, Vt. 05152
TELEPHONE: 802-824-5511
DIRECTIONS: On State Highway 11, in the Green Mountain National Forest, about 10 miles east of Manchester Depot in Southern Vermont.
RATES: Twin-bedded room with bath $16, with sink $14, in summer (June 20 through the foliage season); $18.50 and $16.50 respectively in winter (mid-December through mid-April), all EP.
MEALS: Breakfast and dinner only (dinner is served from 6 to 7:30 p.m. in winter, to 9 in summer, but make reservations); no room service.
SEASONS: Closed mid-October to mid-December and during the Mud Season—mid-April to mid-June.

THE FOUR COLUMNS INN
Newfane, Vermont

At some point on your trip, probably close to lunch or dinner, you may decide how marvelous it would be if Vermont had one of those great little inns like they have in France.

It does. *Voilà*. The Four Columns.

Poke your head into the restaurant here and you might think you're in Burgundy. Have dinner here and you may still think you're in Burgundy. The reason is, of course, that Rene Chardain, *le patron,* comes from France (from Champagne, rather than Burgundy), and Anne Chardain from French Canada. What they've created is an almost-typical French auberge in Vermont.

The France-in-Vermont ambiance runs all the way through. None of the fourteen rooms are alike, and though the antique

and not-so-antique furniture comes from auctions around Vermont, the print wallpapers, the curtains and the bedspreads collectively have a look of France about them. All the rooms have private baths, and most of them have air conditioning.

The name comes from the four white columns decorating the slightly pompous facade of Kemball Hall, a house built for a Mr. Marshall Kemball back in 1830. It sits well off the main road, behind the Newfane Inn, the village green and the county courthouse. It's in two parts—the old white house at the front, and a red barn at the rear—the two connected with a sheltered patio where you can drink and dine in summer. The restaurant, bar and half the rooms are in the barn. At the rear, a footbridge leads across a pond, with a flock of cantankerous geese, to a trail leading up the hill (affectionately known as Mont Chardain) behind the inn.

Pheasant and candlelight

This is no grab-a-snack joint. It's a place where you dawdle until the last drop of Burgundy is sipped, where you plot an entire evening that begins with a *kir* and ends with a kiss. The dining room greets you with a huge fireplace, a wall with subdued splashes of roses, a pheasant on the mantelpiece, a stag's head on the wall; the gentle lighting comes from sconces and candles; and copper pieces hanging from the dark, beamed ceiling glitter in the candles' glow. It's a mellow atmosphere. And *très intime.* No rush, no bustle. Just that quiet, unobtrusive service you get in a restaurant where the food is more important than the maitre d'.

The dishes are served up with that little extra care you associate with France, and the plate itself is carefully garnished; the waitress sweeps away the bread crumbs between courses, the plates appear and disappear without clatter.

The portions, *hélas,* are mountainous, and, doubly *hélas,* delectable to the last morsel. M. Chardain's specialties are duckling Bigarade flambée, rack of lamb, filet mignon Poivre Vert flambée, lobster with crab meat stuffing, trout (live from the tank or the pond), pheasant from their own farm, filet Wellington. A meal here is expensive, say $20 to $25 for two, with wine. That's the way French food is. The question is, is it worth it? That depends on who's with you.

M. Chardain's skills have been highly praised in *Life, Holiday, Vogue* and *Esquire* (in each case when he was running the Newfane Inn across the green). Naturally, the wine list is also compiled with a little more care in such a place, and you can toast *l'amour* over Batard Montrachet ($13), Chateau Lafitte Rothschild ($28) or Gevrey Chambertin ($10)—or, if you don't let her see the prices, a modest Brouilly or Medoc (for $5), or a St. Julien or Pouilly Fume (both $5.50).

After all that, there's nothing for it but to stumble upstairs to bed.

NAME: The Four Columns Inn
INNKEEPERS: Rene and Anne Chardain
ADDRESS: Newfane, Vt. 05345
TELEPHONE: 802-365-7713
DIRECTIONS: On State Highway 30, 15 miles northwest of the

Brattleboro exit on Interstate 91 (a superb highway, by the way).

RATES: EP, $18 to $25, year round.

MEALS: Lunch, dinner, Sunday dinner (1 to 8 p.m.); in winter, there's no lunch and Sunday dinner is from 4 to 8 p.m.; no room service; jacket and tie at dinner.

SEASONS: Open year round, except Mondays in summer (end of May through October), and Tuesdays in winter (end of December through April).

CHESTER INN
Chester, Vermont

After a while it gets to be like a movie scenario. Young couple gets fed up with big city, moves to country, buys old inn, lives happily ever after. In this case, the big city was New York, the young couple Jim and Audrey Patterson, and the inn the 19th-century Chester Inn in southern Vermont. The Pattersons have upgraded it, painted it and added, oddly enough, a touch of Manhattan as modish as their clothes. Or as they put it—"old-fashioned in comfort, young in spirit."

The Chester Inn is a stubby three-story building, sitting well back from the main street on the village green. It's now colored pale salmon (or is it trout?), trimmed with blue; guests from the big city can sit and rock on the porch and watch a day in the life of a small Vermont town. Gorgon the St. Bernard (he came with the hotel) is usually harrumphing around somewhere between the porch, the kitchen and the big fireplace in the lounge. Join him in front of the fire. The Chester Inn's spacious lounge has liberal supplies of sofas, armchairs, magazines—and warmth. Just beyond it, behind the beaded glass screen, you step into the ambiance of Manhattan in the inn's cocktail lounge—green plaid carpets, green walls, leather padded bar, black leather stools, oak paneling, banquettes and a piano with a blessedly restrained pianist.

The dining room next door continues the subdued decor with impeccable stemware, candles and roses on the tables.

Upstairs, things haven't achieved quite the same style—at least, not yet. The inn's thirty rooms are vaguely "motel," with fitted carpet and bath or shower, decorated more or less in uninspired browns, but comfortable and perfectly adequate for an overnight stay. Some of the rooms have TV.

The inn has its own pool, and Vermont's oldest summer theater is only a few miles away, at Weston.

NAME: Chester Inn

INNKEEPERS: Jim and Audrey Patterson

ADDRESS: Chester, Vt. 05143

TELEPHONE: 802-875-2444

DIRECTIONS: On State Highway 103, 15 miles northwest of exit 6 on Interstate 91.

RATES: EP—$19.50 to $27.

MEALS: Breakfast, lunch and dinner; no room service; jacket and tie at dinner.

SEASONS: Closed late November through mid-December, early April to June.

WOODSTOCK INN
Woodstock, Vermont

What the world needs is more Laurence Rockefellers, conservationists who have the wherewithal to put their money where their hearts are, men who'll put up beautiful inns like this one and then spend $3 million of their own money to bury telephone poles around the village green. Even before the poles went under, Woodstock was one of "the five most beautiful villages in America." It has an elliptical village green ringed with Colonial homes, four sets of Paul Revere bells in its church steeples, and a brand-new kissing bridge across the Ottauquechee River. The green, the bells, the bridge and the river are circled by a protective bowl of hills where people ski in winter and hike in summer.

There's been an inn on this same spot on the village green since 1793, but all that remains of the earlier hostelries is the great handcarved eagle above the portico of the 1969 inn— guardian of the inn's tradition of two hundred years of New England hospitality. Someone really cared about the details in the Woodstock Inn. Look around your room before you hop into each other's arms; note the jaunty handmade quilts, the brass hinges on the doors, the evocative photographs on the walls, the custom-designed oak furniture and the bedside table with the discreet AM/FM radio (the TV, alas, is not so discreet). There are a hundred of these rooms, including a few suites (which are merely elongated rooms with dormer windows, very nice, but the regular rooms are so comfortable there's no reason for paying the extra $15).

You spend your public hours in equally tasteful, restful surroundings, with ten-foot stone fireplaces, weathered Vermont timbers, a neat coffee shop, a cocktail lounge/piano bar and an elegant blue-red-and-white dining room. In the rear, there's a broad terrace where you can dine beneath the awnings or sit in a rocker and admire the garden while readying your appetite for avocado bisque, roast leg of lamb Flamande and Washington pie; but take your time over the decision because it's so pleasant rocking, listening to the birds twittering their evensong and the Paul Revere bells chiming the hour, as the shadows lengthen across the lawn.

Adder's tongue, dutchman's breeches

Woodstock is a nice place to be any time of the year, but every lover has his favorite season. Come here in the spring and you can follow woodland trails, stepping lightly through the wild-flowers—adder's tongue, dutchman's breeches, cowslip, blood-root and jack-in-the-pulpit; in fall, you're sitting inside a golden bowl, and in winter you can go jingling through the streets in a one-horse open sleigh. Spring, summer and fall you can swim in the garden pool (but no diving, it's only four feet deep); or play tennis and golf at the country club (one of the oldest courses in the country); or rent a bike ($4 a day) and go riding off down the backroads.

NAME: Woodstock Inn

INNKEEPER: George Pynn

ADDRESS: Woodstock, Vt. 05091

TELEPHONE: 802-457-1100

DIRECTIONS: By car, from New York, take Interstate 91 to the White River Junction exit, then go 14 miles west on Vt. 12 (driving time 5 hours); from Boston, follow Interstates 93 and 89 to U.S. 4, then go west 10 miles (driving time 2½ hours); by air, scheduled flights to Lebanon, N.H. (an $8 cab ride per couple from Woodstock).

RATES: EP—$25 to $40 from June 1 through October 31, $20 to $35 the remainder of the year.

MEALS: Breakfast (any time), lunch, dinner (to 9:30 p.m.); room service (to 11:30 p.m.); jacket and tie in the dining room in the evening, informal in the coffee shop.

SEASONS: Open all year; busiest July, August and October; small top-echelon groups most of the year, but the meeting rooms are all downstairs and you may never know there's a group in the house.

HAWK MOUNTAIN
Pittsfield, Vermont

Turtledove Mountain would be more like it, because there's a love affair going on up here, a love affair between people and trees. "The nice thing about Vermont," as one young Vermonter once remarked, "is that the trees are close together and the people are far apart." And that's the way it is on Hawk Mountain. You have complete, unruffled seclusion (you rent homes, not rooms) among the pine, spruce and maple trees, where kingbirds and tree swallows swoop and sing as if they're happy to be here. You'll have a terrace among the branches of the spruce and maple, and if you're here in warm weather you may find yourself spending most of your time there: brunching on the terrace, snoozing on the terrace, reading on the terrace, sunbathing on the terrace, sundowners on the terrace, dinner on the terrace, love on the terrace with the moonlight of Vermont filtering through the leaves.

Hawk Mountain is a place for two people who are happy just being with each other. There's no action. You enjoy simple pleasures here—a swim in the spring-fed pond, a walk to the top of the mountain for stunning views of wave after wave of green-clad slopes (you're surrounded on three sides by the Green Mountain National Forest); walks around the common grounds in fall to pick armfuls of apples, blackberries and raspberries.

Timber houses, fieldstone fires

Hawk Mountain is neither a resort nor a hotel, and to say it's a housing development is like calling Yehudi Menuhin a fiddler. At Hawk Mountain people buy lots, build vacation homes, and put them into a rental pool when they're not in use. You're the big winner—because for a few nights or a few weeks you have all the advantages of living in a smart vacation home in the forest without owning it. They're no ordinary vacation homes either: only eighty-five houses on 265 acres; one acre in five is common land; all houses are completely screened from each other and from the driveways by trees; all houses must be built of timber and finished with a stain only (no paint); even the "garbage houses" have to match the homes. All the homes have complete kitchens, terraces, fieldstone fireplaces, rustic summer-home decor (some more imaginative than others), firewood, electric heating, picture windows filled with trees, a few cobwebs if they haven't been used for a day or two. A few homes have two bedrooms, but most of them have three or four (the rates are not much different, see below). You can have maid service if you want it, none if you don't want to see any living creatures except the kingbirds and swallows.

Hawk Mountain is the brainchild of a Harvard-graduated architect, Robert Carl Williams, and a doctor, Hugh Kopald, who grew up together in the Great Smokies of Tennessee, discovered they shared the same concern for man and nature, and found the perfect spot for turning their ideas into reality along Route 100 in Vermont.

Route 100 is known as the "Ski-way," because of Killington and a dozen other ski slopes. Which brings you to two of the advantages of Hawk Mountain—it's a year-round hideaway, and if you do decide to rejoin the world for a few hours, you'll find golf, tennis, riding, fishing, sailing, hiking, dining and dancing within a short drive of your terrace. You'll also find billboards, litter, gas stations, junkyards and traffic. It's nicer up on the mountain. Stay there, and enjoy your love affair with the trees.

NAME: Hawk Mountain
INNKEEPERS: Robert Carl Williams and Hugh Kopald
ADDRESS: Route 100, Pittsfield, Vt. 05762
TELEPHONE: 802-746-5171
DIRECTIONS: 260 miles from New York, 155 from Boston, 18 from Rutland; from Interstate 89, take Bethel exit, then go west on Vt. 107 to Killington Ski Area where you go north on Vt. 100; from Interstate 87 take exit for N.Y. 149, then

follow U.S. 4 east to Vt. 100. By air, to Rutland, White River Junction or Montpelier.

RATES: Very complicated, depending on the house, the day of the week and the week of the year, but here are some samples for a two-bedroom house—$20 weekdays, $25 weekend or holiday night, $40 for weekends, $70 for short weeks (Sunday to Thursday) in June and September; the same figures for the same period for a three-bedroom house are $25, $30, $50 and $90; in November, the comparable figures are $15, $20, $30 and $50 for two bedrooms, $20, $25, $40 and $70 for three bedrooms; small additional charge for maid service.

MEALS: None.

SEASONS: Open all year; busiest during ski weekends (December through April, sometimes May), July and August, and the foliage season (late October, early November); in May you'll be up to your ankles in mud—a good reason for staying indoors.

THE JOHN HANCOCK INN
Hancock, New Hampshire

Hancock is reputed to be, quote unquote, one of the six prettiest towns in New Hampshire. That's one reason for going there. The other is the local hostelry, which has been luring travelers off the highway long before anyone ever thought of such things as prettiest villages.

The John Hancock Inn has been standing tall and stately since 1789, on a street of fine Colonial buildings, a few yards from the village green and a meeting house with bells forged by Paul Revere. Hancock himself never actually saw the place; apparently the Declaration of Independence wasn't the only document Hancock signed—he was also a land-speculator and put his quill to a title deed buying up several hundred acres of property in this neighborhood. Some of his local admirers voted to name the village after him (when he turned down an invitation shortly afterwards to visit the town, the snubbed villagers tried to have the name changed).

If Hancock never dined here, Daniel Webster did, and over the generations a host of notables have walked through the heavy hospitable red door of the inn—Peter, Paul and Mary, Nelson Rockefeller, Ted Williams and Tony Bennett among them.

Patchwork quilts, itinerant painters

Much of the inn's decor is authentic, some of it dating from the days of John Hancock, Esquire. The fifteen rooms are decked out with braided rugs, wide floorboards, fireplaces (but no fires), wash stands, half tester beds, pencil post beds, slatback chairs with footstools, travel trunks or patchwork quilts. The most unusual room in the inn (in fact, one of the most unusual anywhere) has walls depicting a blue-green lake-and-forest setting, painted by an itinerant and evidently third-rate artist, who paid for his room and board with this work.

The Hancock's Coach Lounge is the snug sort of room you look forward to finding in a country inn (but the TV on the bar is *not*). The seats are tufted leather benches from old buggies, the tables blacksmiths' bellows, and there's a big roaring brick fireplace in one corner. Businessmen drive from miles around to have lunch here, but most diners continue through to the rear and one of three pleasant dining rooms. One is an enclosed patio overlooking the garden at the rear, another a quiet blue-hued den with only four tables. The Hancock's cuisine is basically New England country fare, with an occasional bow to Continental cuisine. The New England seafood casserole in sherry sauce is as tasty a way as any to wind up an evening. Dinner here, with a carafe of wine, will cost you about $15 for two, slightly more if you order a Medoc or Margaux.

Canoeing and sailing

Hancock is in a region known as Monadnock, which local people sometimes call "The Currier and Ives Corner of New Hampshire," a succession of quiet towns and uncrowded winding roads. But you don't have to walk farther than the meeting house for your recreation—to Norway Lake, a private lake for the residents of the town and guests of the hotel. It has lifeguards, and you can rent a Sunfish or a canoe.

Hancock is also close to several ski runs—Onset and Crotched Mountain to the east, Temple Mountain to the south, Pat's Peak to the north. In winter, of course, you'll probably find yourself sitting around the blazing fire in the Coach Lounge, sing-songing along with skiers and a cumbersome player piano that regales with 150 reels.

NAME: The John Hancock Inn
INNKEEPER: Glynn Dells
ADDRESS: Hancock, N.H. 03449
TELEPHONE: 603-525-3318
DIRECTIONS: On State Highway 137, a few miles from U.S. 202 (between Hillsborough and Peterborough) and about 20 miles from Keene (if you arrive by air at Keene, the inn will pick you up).
RATES: EP—$18.90 all year round (including tax).
MEALS: Breakfast, lunch and dinner; no room service.
SEASONS: Open all year, busiest in fall.

THE GENERAL WOLFE INN
Wolfeboro, New Hampshire

Wolfeboro claims to be the oldest resort in America. It's still a town with a year-round population of only 3,500 residents, but in summer the population swells to ten times its basic 3,500. Most of the visitors troop into motels, but a few lucky ones stay at one of the town's two inns. Lucky Wolfeboro, to have *two* fine old inns.

The General Wolfe is on the edge of town, surrounded by the seventh and eighth fairways of the Kingswood Golf Course; it is a restored 250-year-old farmhouse which was converted into a hotel in 1902, with a big barn at the rear, and additional rooms in what was once the old carriage house. It came under new management in 1972, and although you may not agree with everything Dick Faulkner, a 27-year-old ex-airline pilot, is doing with the place, you can't expect instant perfection from someone who had to completely rewire an old inn, rip down walls, put in a new kitchen, and do all the chores that crop up in these circumstances.

The decor and furnishings are a melange of Colonial, Empire, Early American, Country Chintz, a bonanza of bric-a-baroque. The overstuffed lounge has a pair of modern leather armchairs and a sofa, the dining room windows are clustered with potted plants, jugs, vases, pineapple lamps and parrots; but there's a coziness and homeyness here you don't always find in some of the more "classical" Colonial inns. The guest rooms are mostly furnished with antique rockers and desks, with old prints on the walls and quilts on the beds. All the rooms have private bath-shower combinations. There are seventeen rooms in the main building, plus another four in what is called the "motel wing"— unfairly, because it's a former carriage house, the rooms paneled in pine, with screen-enclosed verandas overlooking the fairways, the forest and the distant Belknap Mountains. You can even have your meals served up on your own private veranda.

There are two dining rooms, one piney and candlelit, the other an enclosed patio for summer dining. No escargot or duckling Bigarade here—just good wholesome country fare, with occasionally a beef Stroganoff or veal parmigiana thrown in for variety. It's not expensive either—about $5 to $6 for a meal. The wine list is almost exclusively all-American, except for a solitary Chablis and a solitary Mateus.

"The swingingest place in Wolfeboro"

The newest innovation from Dick Faulkner is the transformation of the big barn: it has now acquired a gallery, a stage and a dance floor. You can have drinks or a snack—and listen and dance to country-and-western or rock-and-roll orchestras. This is reputed to be the liveliest place in town in summer—in fact, the only spot of its kind. (The rumpus affects only one guest room in the hotel, and Faulkner and his mother won't rent it when there's a dance in the barn; if noise upsets you, you may have more problems with the taped music in the dining room.)

300 miles of lake shore

The General Wolfe is a convenient place to stay if you want to sample the pleasures of Lake Winnipesaukie and its 300 miles of shoreline. You can take a four-hour ferryboat trip on the "Mount Washington," or sail a Sunfish in and out of the bays. If you feel like a swim you can take a dip in the lake, or in the inn's own pool (at the back of the inn, but it doesn't give you much privacy from drivers on the fairways on one side, and drivers on the highway on the other).

In winter, The General Wolfe is a snowmobile center. For some reason, it has become an unofficial headquarters for ski-dooers, who leave their machines there all winter. This isn't much fun if you've come up for a quiet vacation away from the pneumatic drills of the big city. Be warned. Try to come *during* the week, although even then you can't be sure of unruffled quiet.

NAME: The General Wolfe Inn
INNKEEPERS: Dick Faulkner and Fran Dugan
ADDRESS: Wolfeboro, N.H. 03894
TELEPHONE: 603-569-1911
DIRECTIONS: On State Highway 28, on the east side of Lake Winnipesaukie.
RATES: In winter, room with double bed and private bath $15.50 EP, with twin beds and private bath $12.50 EP, *without* bath $10.50 EP; and in summer, from $15.50 to $19.50; rates in the motel are $18 double in winter, $23.50 in summer.
MEALS: Breakfast (to 9:30 a.m.), lunch and dinner (to 9 p.m.); room service; informal.
SEASONS: Open all year (closed possibly for a couple of weeks between Labor Day and Christmas).

WOLFEBORO INN
Wolfeboro, New Hampshire

There probably aren't too many Colonial inns in New England with four dented Saabs in the back yard; but then there aren't too many Colonial runs by retired hot-rodders. That's no qualification for an innkeeper, of course, but Paul McBride also spent a long time with the Sheraton chain before coming here ten years ago—and that is.

The Wolfeboro Inn, which dates from 1891, has thirteen bright-and-breezy rooms, all decorated with period furniture, all with private bath or shower. Three of them have double beds, three have fireplaces.

When he wasn't denting Saabs, McBride was scouring the auctions of New Hampshire for antiques for his inn. He tracked down some beauties. The parlor has a fine set of "Praying Mantis" andirons—whirls and swirls of wrought-iron patterns crafted in Cape Cod in 1731. The huge hooked rug, on the other hand, is no antique: it was hooked a few years ago by Mary McBride. The other rooms are chock-a-block with bellows, pewter, silverware and copperware (at least they were on a recent visit, but if guests continue to pocket the pewter there may not be much left by the time you get there).

The inn's restaurant is a 130-seater, a new extension tastefully designed (by Paul McBride) to blend in with the overall decor and atmosphere, but if you don't want to eat with the crowd there's also a charming little dining room at the front of the main house.

The inn's hefty meals are welcome after a day in the fresh air on Lake Winnipesaukie. The shortest route to the lake is through the back yard, past the Saabs to the inn's private beach—only ten feet of the lake's 300 miles, but enough to introduce you to the refreshing waters. You can also borrow one of the inn's two Sunfishes and sail away across the lake.

And if you get to know Paul McBride he may take you for a hair-raising spin in his mighty racing boat. Once a hot-rodder, always a hot-rodder.

NAME: The Wolfeboro Inn
INNKEEPERS: Paul and Mary McBride
ADDRESS: 44 North Main Street, Wolfeboro, N.H. 03894
TELEPHONE: 603-569-3016
DIRECTIONS: On State Highway 28, on the eastern shore of Lake Winnipesaukie.
RATES: Room with private bath $16 at the rear, $18 at the front, EP.
MEALS: Breakfast and dinner only (to 9 a.m., dining room closed on Mondays); main dishes from $3.75 to $8; no room service; informal.
SEASONS: Open all year, except for part of March.

THE INN AT STEELE HILL
Laconia, New Hampshire

The setting is exhilarating.

The inn perches between Steele Hill and heaven with 500 acres of forest on three sides, and a sixty-mile vista of Lake Winniesquam and the Belknap Mountains. Everything plays second fiddle to the setting. The architecture blends in perfectly: a chalet-like design, built in 1941 from hand-hewn cedar shakes (originally timber felled by the great hurricane of 1938), milled right there on the spot.

The public rooms are basically picture windows, enclosing a rustic restaurant or a lounge with log fire, Wurlitzer organ and a Steinway baby grand piano. The wide veranda is for rocking and enjoying the view, and even when you're lounging in the sun by the swimming pool your horizon is sixty miles wide.

In some ways this is an ideal hideaway. If you want to lounge around and do nothing, you can. If you want to keep active, you certainly can. If you want to join civilization for a few hours you can drive down to Laconia and its resorty bustle. Besides swimming in the pool (unheated) or playing a rather lopsided game of golf on the inn's hilly nine-hole course, innkeeper Jerry Walker can put you on a horse, a trailbike, a hiking trail, a badminton court. There are billiards, table tennis and hayrides. In winter the golf course becomes a ski slope (the inn has its own 600-foot tow rope, which is free, and an instructor), crosscountry ski trails, ice skating, ice fishing. And since it's an informal shirt-and-jeans place you never have to worry about wandering through the lobby in your sporting duds.

That's not to say that the accommodations are primitive. The guest rooms are bright little nests, with sunny decor and country furniture, and private baths or showers. There are sixteen rooms in the inn, plus another nine in forest-hugging cottages. If you want your own little Hansel-and-Gretel nook, rent the Hobby House, a small honeymooners' hideaway cottage above the main lodge; it has a lounge and bedroom in rough-hewn pine walls and beams, a few antiques, a tiled bathroom and a small kitchen. You can't get anything much quieter than this without disappearing into the forest.

NAME: The Inn at Steele Hill
INNKEEPERS: Nancy and Jerry Walker
ADDRESS: Laconia, N.H.
TELEPHONE: 603-524-0500
DIRECTIONS: Going north on Interstate 93, take exit 20, drive east on U.S. 3 (direction, Laconia), then follow the signs (after about 6 miles) to Steele Hill.
RATES: AP preferred—$40 and $44 a night; special mid-week rate, except on holidays, from Sunday evening to Friday morning—$170 to $210.
MEALS: Breakfast (to 10 a.m.), light lunch (by the pool in summer), dinner (to 8 p.m.); no room service; informal.
SEASONS: Open all year, busiest in peak summer and peak winter.

STAFFORD'S-IN-THE-FIELD
Chocorua, New Hampshire

If a guest absolutely must watch the ball game on TV, he can— in the scullery. That's where the set's been relegated, because most people who come here (professors, writers, musicians, doctors and so forth) usually prefer the joys of the countryside. And there are plenty of joys here.

This is White Mountain country. Stafford's-in-the-Field tops a knoll above a gravelly back road, near a lake, beneath a mountain; a long, grayish-green farmhouse next to a big barn. If it looks more like a farm outside, it feels more like a home inside. It's run by the Stafford family from California. Fred Stafford is tall, gangling and amiable; his wife, Ramona, is the chef (the first words you usually hear about the hotel are "the food is terrific"); daughter Momo, 19 years old and pretty as spring, is the pastry chef and baker; sons Fritz and Hansel help out with the hard work. Bebe, the monumental St. Bernard, is captain of the guard. They all trekked east from San Diego eight years ago because they hankered after something old and "New England." They got it. The oldest part of the family's inn dates back to 1784, and as Hayward's-in-the-Field it took in its first paying guests in 1894. They added more of their "New England" with antiques—a collection of milk churns, an unusual butter washer, a boudoir desk, rocking chairs, a blacksmith's bellows for a coffee table. They have only seven rooms in the main building (there are cottages for three dozen guests at the rear, but most of them are too large for couples), decorated the way you expect rooms in a country inn to be—with cheery wallpapers and some of their antiques. Three of the rooms have double beds, but only two have private baths (the others share four baths). The rooms are charming, especially the small ones on the top floor, with corner windows looking straight into the upper branches of the trees— it's almost like living in a tiny tree house.

The largest room in the inn is the dining room, yellow and bright, with a big open fire on one wall, a Franklin stove on another, and a musical corner with player piano, ancient Victrola and a grand piano. Sometimes the younger Staffords entertain the guests with madrigals and folk songs. Dinner is served family style, everyone seated at one table, Fred Stafford at the head. One sitting—beginning somewhere between 6:30 and 7 p.m., which gives you an expansive evening afterwards for rocking on the porch, or snuggling up before a log fire in the parlor.

The menu is determined not so much by what's in the local stores as by the guests; if Ramona Stafford feels they look like they'd enjoy Mexican food she'll serve up carne asado. Another time it might be a curry, or maybe Fred will roast a joint of lamb on a spit before the fire. All the dishes are prepared from scratch, the vegetables are fresh; all the bread—white, rye, pumpernickel, French or dinner rolls—are home-baked by Momo, and in summer she goes out and gathers fresh blueberries for her blueberry pie. Even the maple syrup served with breakfast is tapped from their own maple trees, and during summer you can usually have your breakfast outside in the garden, beneath the same maples. (One problem: the Staffords don't have a liquor license, but you can bring along your own bottles; if you want wine with your meal, better bring a bottle of white and a bottle of red since you don't know what's on the menu.)

Spring-fed pool, chamber music in the barn

After you've downed your breakfast, then what? Wander down to the lake for a swim, or rent a canoe (the lake's private, and power boats are prohibited). Climb Mount Chocorua. Disappear into the woods to the natural pool for a swim *au naturel* (the water's warmer than the lake because it's spring-fed).

In the evenings, you can take in a play at one of the three summer theaters in the region; sometimes Fred Stafford, Innkeeper, becomes Fred Stafford, Impresario, and puts on a recital of chamber music in the big barn (apparently, it has a superb acoustic), and most Thursdays during the summer there's a barn dance.

In winter, borrow a pair of snow shoes and trudge around the countryside; or rent a pair of skis and tour cross-country (send your size to the Staffords and they'll rent a pair of skis and boots for you and have them waiting when you get here). By order of the obviously influential people who live in these parts, there are no snowmobiles to disturb the serenity of the snow-muffled countryside.

NAME: Stafford's-in-the-Field
INNKEEPERS: Fred and Ramona Stafford
ADDRESS: Chocorua, N.H. 03817
TELEPHONE: 603-323-7766
DIRECTIONS: Chocorua is on State Highway 16, between Lake Winnipesaukie and the White Mountain National Forest, about ten miles from Conway; the inn itself is a few miles from the village on State Highway 113.
RATES: MAP—from $26 without bath to $30 with bath.

MEALS: Breakfast and dinner only (light lunches or picnic lunches can usually be arranged on request); no room service; meals are served only to the inn's guests; informal.

SEASONS: Open all year, except between October 20 and December 26; busiest July until late October.

FARRELL LODGE and TECUMSEH INN
Waterville Valley, New Hampshire

The Lodge and the Inn appear in these pages by the grace of the White Mountain National Forest. By themselves they're unexceptional, but the setting is, and you have to have *some* place to stay.

The valley first.

The Mad River flows through a gap between Tecumseh, Snow and Osceola mountains. In spring, when the snows are melting and impatient, the river lives up to its name, but in summer and fall it's not even sulking. The river is 1,500 feet above sea level, the surrounding peaks 4,000 feet and more. Between the two are unbroken forests of spruce and pine. This is Waterville Valley. It's still very much nature's country. Only in the past half dozen years has it been developed, and then respectfully.

One of the new developments is a ski community called Waterville Valley Resort—an enclave of condominiums, lodges, restaurants and sports facilities. In winter they're noisy with the clomping of ski boots; in spring, summer and fall, something of the camaraderie remains but the crowds and the ski boots have gone.

The scenery is, well, magnificent, and you could spend days walking and hiking here without passing the same tree twice. You can play a leisurely nine-hole golf course that weaves among the spruce and firs. There are five topnotch tennis courts,

and countless secluded mountain pools where you can peel off
and plunge in.

Great outdoors, average indoors

This is the great outdoors as it used to be. You'll probably have
to drag yourself away from the pine-scented mountain air. That
being so, you can make allowances for the average indoors.
Farrell Lodge and Tecumseh Inn are contemporary chalets of
weathered pine, and the Lodge in particular has an interesting
interior of angles and glass and beams, and a multi-level lobby
overlooking an indoor/outdoor heated pool (which is open, by
the way, until 11 p.m.). But the rooms at both are only one
polystyrene cut above a good motel, with tiny bathrooms, small
TVs, and blah furniture. Farrell Lodge has an edge, since every
room has a balcony (though not every balcony has a view). If
you want something with more style (and space) you might consider renting an apartment in one of the condominiums. It will
come with either modern or rustic decor, full kitchens, log fires
(the management will supply the logs) and "concrete sound control in floors and walls."

The Lodge and the Inn (and the other two lodges that make
up the community) are relatively quiet, since all the fun and
games, drinking and eating and dancing take place in the adjacent
Fourways Restaurant. This is a big timber-and-candlelight
restaurant, with a Swiss chef, good food (you can have a meal
for two for under $10), a cocktail lounge and a "beer cellar"
where you can listen to overamplified country-and-western
groups.

Six miles down the valley, at Six-Mile Bridge, there's another
condominium development where you can rent an apartment; it
has a circular heated indoor pool, tennis courts, a stable, and a
restaurant that's reputed to serve the best food on that side of
the White Mountains—the Gateway Restaurant, French cuisine
by candlelight in a hundred-year-old farmhouse.

NAME: Farrell Lodge
INNKEEPERS: Sara and Dave Farrell
TELEPHONE: 603-236-8336
NAME: Tecumseh Inn
INNKEEPERS: Cynthia and Tod Baldwin
TELEPHONE: 603-326-8366
ADDRESS: Waterville Valley Resort, N.H. 03223
DIRECTIONS: Take Interstate 93 to Exit 28, then State Highway 49 six miles to Waterville Valley Gateway, 12 miles to Waterville Valley Resort—2 hours from Boston without a single traffic light.
RATES: All four lodges charge the same—$16 EP in summer, $28 in winter; a condominium apartment rents for $30 in summer, $40 in winter.
MEALS: The inns serve free coffee round the clock, but no meals; no room service; breakfast, lunch and dinner in the Fourways Restaurant.
SEASONS: Open all year (although one or another of the lodges may close for a week or two in the off-season); busiest in the ski season, more or less uncrowded the rest of the year.

IN AND AROUND THE BOSKY BERKSHIRES

O, my luve's like a red, red rose
That's newly sprung in June;
O my luve's like the melodie
That's sweetly play'd in tune . . .
BURNS

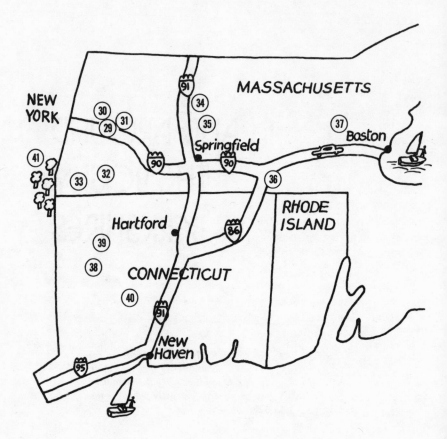

29. Red Lion Inn

30. Blantyre Castle

31. Orpheus Ascending

32. The Flying Cloud Inn

33. Stagecoach Hill Inn

34. Old Deerfield Inn

35. Lord Jeffery Inn

36. The Publick House

37. Longfellow's Wayside Inn

38. The Mayflower Inn

39. Kilravock Inn

40. Harrison Inn

41. Swiss Hutte

RED LION INN
Stockbridge, Massachusetts

Stockbridge has one of the prettiest main streets in America, and it's getting prettier every day; so is the Red Lion. The venerable lion, a spry centenarian, was renovated a couple of years ago; it now has a courtyard cafe where you can nibble brook trout beneath a huge oak tree and a new tavern where you can dine on chateaubriand in a pubby atmosphere, as well as an elegant main dining room with prim silverware and linen; you can now spend blissful nights in canopied beds or brass beds or beds with handcarved headboards, and then dally over breakfast in a window alcove, perched on a Victorian love seat. By day you can lounge around the inn's pool; play golf or tennis at the local country club; wander along the pretty main street looking for antiques and paintings; or drive a few miles along Route 183 to Alice's new Alice's Res-tau-rant.

The Red Lion is a white clapboard inn fronted by a veranda with a dozen wicker rockers—very much in the New England tradition of country inns. The original Red Lion was built in 1773 to serve the stagecoaches between Boston and Albany; in 1862 it was bought by the Plumbs, who added all the 18th-century furniture, Staffordshire china and antique pewter that decorates the lobby; it was destroyed by fire in 1896, and rebuilt more or less in its present form in 1897. Recently it was bought again, by Jack and Jane Fitzpatrick, a Stockbridge couple who run Country Curtains (a flourishing mail order company that ships orders all over the world), and taken in hand by a new manager, Henricus G. A. Bergmans, an enthusiastic Dutchman who's been riding bikes all his life and still doesn't own a car.

Through the years the Red Lion has hosted everyone from Hawthorne and Longfellow and a galaxy of Roosevelts, to Otto Preminger, Marlo Thomas and Thornton Wilder, who's been coming here so often he considers room #101 *his* room.

Let him have it, there are ninety-nine others. They've all been spruced up with period wallpapers from an old mill in North Adams, and, of course, curtains in all their variety—in muslin, gingham, organdy, with ruffles, tiers, tiebands, knotted fringes and pompon trims. Rooms #212 and #112 are big corner rooms with lots of windows—one with rose-patterned wallpaper and matching upholstery, wicker headboards, marble-topped coffee table; the other with pink paper, floral carpets, twin beds, rockers and wing back chairs and lots of daylight.

No two rooms are identical, but they all have air conditioning and room phones, two-thirds of them have private baths, and one-third of them (the thirty-odd rooms that stay open in winter) have TV. Winter's becoming a more popular season up here. There's good skiing in the neighborhood, ice skating, good long tramps in the snow; but many people come just for the Christmas card setting, like something from the cover of an old McCall's—which it was, since Norman Rockwell lives around the corner and painted the Red Lion many times. Take a walk in the frost or snow, wrap your arms around each other to keep warm, then hurry back to the Red Lion for a drink in the wood-panelled warmth of its new Widow Bingham's Tavern.

NAME: Red Lion Inn
INNKEEPER: Henricus G. A. Bergmans
ADDRESS: Stockbridge, Mass. 01262
TELEPHONE: 413-298-5545
DIRECTIONS: Five miles southwest of Exit 2 on the Mass. Pike, at the junction of U.S. 7 and Mass. 102.
RATES: EP—$16 to $24 from Labor Day through June 30,·$16 to $40 from July 1 through Labor Day.
MEALS: Breakfast (to 10:30 a.m.), lunch, dinner (to 10:30 p.m.); room service; informal.
SEASONS: Open all year; busiest during July, August and October, and on weekends during the skiing season.

BLANTYRE CASTLE
Lenox, Massachusetts

Turpentine, plain fifty-cents-a-can turpentine, built this manor house in a Berkshire parkland. A Scotsman by the name of Robert W. Paterson came to this country sometime in the 1800s, became "the turpentine king of the south," and then settled in the Berkshires and in 1902 built a replica of a castle he had admired back in his native Scotland—the Hall of Blantyre.

The pitted driveway up through the park suggests that a parsimonious Scot is still in charge, but in fact the estate changed hands in 1968 and the castle was converted into a hotel—one of the most unusual, most delightful hostelries in a part of the country that isn't exactly short of fine old inns and hotels.

It's a rambling, rather somber stone structure, overgrown with ivy, with an impressive porte cochere and heavy oak doors leading to a full-bodied baronial hall—hand-carved mantel and stair-case, carved wooden wall paneling, beamed ceilings with heraldic designs, petit-point chairs, and French windows leading to the terrace. The grandeur overflows into the Jacobean dining room, which extends into a glass-enclosed terrace in what was once the conservatory (you can also dine on the terrace in summer, and expect to pay $20 to $30 for a meal for two).

Upstairs you can live more or less in the style of the turpentine king's house guests—and some of the Victorian fabrics look like they did service in those days. The fourteen rooms here are spacious and high-ceilinged, with funny old bathtubs, antique chests, a few brass beds, print draperies and armchairs; they all have TV and telephone, and most of them have air conditioning. You can live in a completely different style in sixteen newer rooms in the carriage house, a two-minute walk from the main building; the rooms here are contemporary, with bold bright colors, floor-to-ceiling windows opening onto small patios, small kitchens with coffee-making machines, heat lamps in the bathrooms, and beds that fold out of the wall. Three suites have identical decor but with sleeping lofts you reach by spiral stairs.

Cucumber trees, scallop-and-lobster pie

Blantyre Castle sits in an eighty-five–acre estate, planted with pine, oak, copper beech, black walnut, Chinese chestnut and cucumber trees, surrounded on three sides by a golf course, and atwitter with the love songs of chickadees, starlings, larks, partridges and pheasants. You can swim in a pool in what used to be the formal garden with a view of several rolls of the rolling Berkshires; there are four tennis courts in the garden (free to the guests) and miles of walking trails among the pines and oaks. You can play golf on the surrounding course, which belongs to the Cranwell School. The castle is only minutes from the Tanglewood and Jacob's Pillow summer festivals, but think for a minute of Blantyre's attractions as a winter hideaway: ice skating, cross-country skiing; lunching in the conservatory looking out at the snow on the trees; afternoon naps in brass beds; long walks in the snow, then soaking in the big bathtubs to warm up again; drinks before the crackling fire in the lounge; New England scallop-and-lobster pie, nutbread caramel custard or Scottish sherry trifle for dinner; cheek-to-cheek dancing in the lounge, or the hip-shaking variety downstairs in the discotheque.

Amazing, isn't it, what turpentine can do?

NAME: Blantyre Castle
INNKEEPERS: Sam LaGrotteria and Paul Rothenstein
ADDRESS: P.O. Box 995, Lenox, Mass. 01240
TELEPHONE: 413-637-0475
DIRECTIONS: The castle is 2 miles southeast of town on U.S. 20, and 3½ miles north of Exit 2 on the Mass. Pike.
RATES: EP—$22 to $26 for rooms, $36 for suites, except in July and August when the rooms are $45 to $49, and suites are $59; all with Continental breakfast.
MEALS: Breakfast (to 11 a.m.), lunch, dinner (from 5 to 9 p.m. in winter, 5 to 10 p.m. in summer); room service; jackets in the dining room in the evening.
SEASONS: Open all year, busiest July, August and October; small groups and seminars at other times.

ORPHEUS ASCENDING
Stockbridge, Massachusetts

Orpheus and Eros and Bacchus—they're all ascendant here, a jovial trio who make this a welcome newcomer, because there's never been anything around the Berkshires with quite the same casual sophistication, the same Broadway-weekending-in-the-Berkshires atmosphere. The OA's guest list includes the Norman Mailers, Leonard Bernstein, and members of the Boston Symphony, who often drop by for dinner after their concerts.

Orpheus Ascending gets its unusual ambiance from its owner,

Stephen Citron, a pianist/composer who used to be Piaf's accompanist in Paris. While he lived in the land of *haute cuisine,* he learned to play pots and pans as well as the piano, and when he returned to this country he bought a Christmas-tree farm and modulated it into a French-style country inn with a piano bar, where Citron plays Citron, except when his show biz friends decide to entertain *him.*

This 140-year-old farmhouse is an unlikely backdrop for such goings-on—a small white clapboard house with yellow shutters, low ceilings and lurching floors, surrounded by pines and lawns. It barely manages to squeeze in ten guest rooms on the second floor and in the attic, all but two of them with private showers, most of them with cheery wallpapers, a sprinkling of antiques, a dash of Salvation Army, but very home-like and charming. (They're also rather tiny and not too private; if you usually make love like a pair of boisterous buffalos you may find yourself inhibited here.)

The rooms are almost an afterthought, because the inn is basically a restaurant, and the menu is, not surprisingly, French —crepe de volaille, crepe de crevettes, le porc-chop Maxim. After a feast of escargots Bourguignon, filet mignon flambée au Calvados, coupe aux marrons and a jug of Sangria (it's made with brandy), you'll probably be grateful you can ascend Orpheus Ascending and plop right into bed—even if the room *is* tiny.

Next morning, you can have breakfast and *The New York Times* in bed, and then look forward to a day of idleness. The inn's six acres of lawns and pine trees are laced with walking trails, and there's a secluded pool in the garden, within wafting distance of the tantalizing smells from the kitchen. You don't even have to get up to get your crepes—lunch is served by the pool.

The only problem with Orpheus is scheduling: in summer, you have to stay a minimum of four days, and in winter the inn is open only on weekends. It may require some effort to get here, but Orpheus, Eros and Bacchus are worth the trouble.

NAME: Orpheus Ascending

INNKEEPER: Stephen Citron

ADDRESS: Route 7, Stockbridge, Mass. 01262

TELEPHONE: 413-298-4700

DIRECTIONS: Halfway between Stockbridge and Lenox, 2½ hours by car from New York, slightly less from Boston; from New York take the Taconic Parkway to U.S. 23, then drive 17 miles to U.S. 7 and north 10 miles; from Boston, take the Mass. Pike to Exit 2 (Lee), go north on U.S. 20 to U.S. 7, then south 4 miles.

RATES: MAP from June 1 through September 15—$50 with private bath, $47 with semi-private bath; EP in winter—$25 with private bath, $20 with semi-private bath; minimum stay of four days in summer, two in winter.

MEALS: Breakfast (to noon), lunch (poolside service), dinner (to 10 p.m. officially, but usually to 1 a.m. on Tanglewood weekends); room service (breakfast is served in bed unless you ask for it otherwise); informal.

SEASONS: Open all year, but only on weekends (Friday through Sunday nights) in winter.

MISCELLANEOUS: "Due to its dedication to the care and comfort of sophisticated adults, Orpheus Ascending is sorry to have to refuse accommodations for children under ten."

THE FLYING CLOUD INN
New Marlboro, Massachusetts

Most of the old Colonial inns in New England are smack dab on the village green or main street, but here's a Colonial retreat far out in the country at the end of back roads leading to byways, surrounded by a couple of hundred acres of pine, Japanese dog-

wood, tamarack and half a dozen types of apple trees. You wake with the lark, go to bed with the owl, and the big bad world never intrudes on your peace. No phones, no TV.

You spend your days simply—swimming in a spring-fed, unpolluted pond; wandering through the pine and birch in search of beavers and otters and muskrats; picnicking in a stand of hemlock in the southwest corner of the property; or riding a bike along the new trail to the beaver pond. There are tennis courts a dozen paces from the back door, with a ball machine, pro shop and one of the finest views in the Berkshires; ping-pong in the barn, badminton on the lawn. Come here in winter and you can go cross-country skiing, sledding, snowshoeing or ice skating, or just sit in front of the fire and roast chestnuts. At the Flying Cloud, you're part of a world detached in time and place, but if you want to sample civilization you're only a short drive along the byways and back roads from Tanglewood and Jacob's Pillow. Only a Mozart or Margot Fonteyn could lure you away from a spot like this.

The Flying Cloud was originally a farmhouse, built in 1771 by New England shipwrights, a white clapboard cottage with plank floors and hand-wrought oak and chestnut beams. No more than twenty guests can stay here at one time, so in the festival and fall foliage seasons your problem is not crowds but reservations. All ten rooms are different, all furnished with fine antiques.

Six of the rooms have private baths, and the other four share a couple of baths. Take a stroll through the house and pick out your bed—with muslin canopies, with pencil, pineapple or acorn knobs, or a bed made from five different types of wood. All are charming places to spend loving nights, and in the morning you'll discover David Schwarz has thoughtfully installed opaque window shades "for late sleepers."

The Flying Cloud tends to be a convivial place at times, and the guests usually gather for pre-dinner drinks in the lounge before the fire, or out on the screened porch; but the Shaker-styled dining room has candlelight and tables for twosomes who want to be twosomes. Menus feature good, wholesome food, with vegetables (broccoli, squash, lettuce and beans) fresh from the garden, soups made from stock, roast lamb or beef, and occasional Continental dishes like daube a la Provençale or zucchini casserole (there's no choice of entree), followed by muskmelons or strawberries fresh from the garden. The wine list is exceptional for a small country inn—from half-bottles of Beaujolais around $2.75 or a 1964 or 1966 Pichon Lalande which still sells for its pre-devaluation price of $9 a bottle, to a 1957 Mouton Rothschild that was $30 when last heard of. Maybe the weekend you're here they'll be having one of their wine-tasting sessions. Even if they're not, start reserving one of the ten rooms now.

NAME: The Flying Cloud Inn
INNKEEPERS: David R. Schwarz (owner), Michael and Sindy McCarthy (managers)
ADDRESS: Box 143, Star Route, New Marlboro, Mass. 01230
TELEPHONE: 413-229-2113
DIRECTIONS: By car from New York, take Interstates 684 and 84 to Conn. 8, then go east on U.S. 44 to Mass. 183 and go north 14½ miles; from Boston, the Mass. Pike to Exit 2 (Lee), then go south on Mass. 102 and U.S. 7 to Mass. 23 and Mass. 57, where you fork right (about a mile beyond the New Marlboro village green) and follow a tiny sign to the Flying Cloud; or by private or charter plane to Great Barrington.
RATES: AP—$25 without bath, $30 with private bath, May 12

through October 31; slightly less remainder of year; rate includes gratuity and use of all facilities (except bikes—$2 a day).

MEALS: Breakfast (to 9:30 a.m.), lunch, dinner (at 6:30 p.m. in summer, 7 in winter); no room service.

SEASONS: Open all year, except the months of April and November; busiest in July, August and October.

STAGECOACH HILL INN
Sheffield, Massachusetts

¢

For candlelight dinner in the Colonial dining room, you can choose blackbird pie or Alderman's Carpetbag, polished down with a tankard of Watney's Red Barrel; when you've sated yourself, wander through to the timbery Tap Room, settle down before the fire and sample a rarity from the inn's Locked Scotch Cabinet or Locked Brandy Cabinet—say, a 20-year-old Royal Reserve by Arthur Bell, or a Biscuit Debouche Extra Cognac. From the Tap Room it's only a few steps through the pine-scented garden to your room.

The Stagecoach Hill Inn is something of a curiosity—an old coaching house that was also the village poorhouse, and now billing itself as "the English Inn in the Berkshires," a red-brick building hidden by a clump of maple trees. Behind the inn is a two-story red shingle cottage, the former poorhouse, with the four best rooms in the inn; beyond that are the lawns, and two three-room chalets with plasticky motel furnishings (the new managers plan to upgrade them in a style more in keeping with the inn). The best rooms are #10 and #11 in the Poorhouse, under the eaves, with chintz curtains and pretty but uninspired decor. But chances are you won't be in a mood to analyze the decor after you've feasted yourself in the dining room, which is what you come here for in the first place. Scotty Burns and Wilbur Wheeler have made a gallant attempt to get away from the standard steak and lobster fare; in addition to the blackbird pie and Alderman's Carpetbag (it's a sirloin with a "secret pocket" stuffed with half a dozen oysters) their menu lists steak and mushroom pie, veal a l'Estragon and chicken livers Rumaki. Prices are in the $6 range, except for the Carpetbag, which carries a $8.50 tag.

Stagecoach Hill could be a terrific little spot if the owners get around to fixing up all the rooms; meantime, it's a place to come and gorge yourself (if you can overlook the background music) and stop over between trips to Tanglewood, Jacob's Pillow, Music Mountain, the Music Barn and all the other summer lures of the Berkshires. When there's racing at Lime Rock, sports car buffs come here and paint the inn red.

NAME: Stagecoach Hill Inn

INNKEEPERS: Scotty Burns and Wilbur Wheeler

ADDRESS: Route 41, Sheffield, Mass. 01257

TELEPHONE: 413-229-8585

DIRECTIONS: On Mass. 41, a scenic winding highway that doesn't really go anywhere and seems to be in no particular hurry to get there, 10 miles south of Great Barrington.

RATES: EP—$15, $18 and $20 for rooms, $25 for a suite, year round.

MEALS: No breakfast (coffee machines in the rooms), no lunch (except on Sunday when the dining room is open from lunch through dinner), dinner (to 10 p.m.); no room service; informal.

SEASONS: Open all year, except Christmas Day.

OLD DEERFIELD INN
Old Deerfield, Massachusetts

When they buried the telephone cables here a few years ago the villagers had a party, and when they finally had to chop down the 300-year-old elm tree in front of the Asa Stebbins House some of the old-timers wept. Old Deerfield is that kind of village.

And Old Deerfield Inn is that kind of inn. Where else can you dine off polished mahogany tables with silver candelabras and English antique cutlery? Or sleep in guest rooms with reproductions of 18th-century wallpapers? The inn was built in 1884, and although it's been tittivated in recent years, it still has the feel of a coaching house. The twenty rooms are divided between the second and third floors. Most of them have private baths, and all except one have twin beds. Room #3, at the rear, has a lovely plush love seat in a corner by the windows, surrounded by lacy curtains. All the rooms on the second floor have electric blankets —while all the tiny attic-like rooms on the third floor have rope ladders in case things get *too* hot. Rooms on the third floor share bathrooms and they're smaller, but quite charming—and cheaper.

Bye, bye, twentieth century

The inn has a sunny veranda lounge with lots of windows and a view consisting almost exclusively of a gigantic catalpa tree, whose branches seem as eager to grow down as up, fringed in spring with orchid-like blossoms. Through the blossoms you get a glimpse of the white clapboard walls of the Joseph Stebbins House, built in 1774, and a foretaste of what's in store if you can coax yourself out of your Hitchcock chair to go for a stroll.

The Street (that's what they call it—simply The Street) is lined with elms and maples and more than fifty fine old houses from the 18th and 19th centuries. Most of them have been restored, but instead of being mere museums (more than a hundred period rooms are open to visitors), they're actually people's *homes*. Some people call this the prettiest street in all America and they may be right—just elms, maples, houses, gardens and Deerfield prep school on the Common. No neon, no telephone poles.

The Street wasn't always so peaceful. At dawn on February 29, 1704, a band of Indians crept into town, burned homes, killed forty-nine settlers, and then marched the remaining 109 through the snow to Canada, 200 miles away. One of the local museums still exhibits a door axed by a tomahawk.

Deerfield Academy was founded in 1799 with the motto "Be Worthy of Your Heritage," but since then the entire village seems to have adopted the sentiment. And back in 1952 a well-to-do couple by the name of Flynt fell in love with the place and set up the Heritage Foundation to preserve the village in its unspoiled state. Hence the spic-and-span Old Deerfield Inn, where you can nod off in Colonial bliss and not have to worry about the Indians sneaking in.

NAME: Old Deerfield Inn

INNKEEPER: James Venetos

ADDRESS: The Street, Old Deerfield, Mass. 01342

TELEPHONE: 413-773-3838

DIRECTIONS: *OLD* Deerfield is just off U.S. 5, three miles south of Greenfield, which in turn is at the intersection of U.S. 2 (the Mohawk Trail) and Interstate 91.

RATES: $22 and $24 EP on the 2nd floor, $10 and $12 on the 3rd floor.

MEALS: Breakfast (to 9:30 a.m.), lunch and dinner (to 7:30 p.m., choice of only two main dishes, complete dinner $5); one of the few inns that serves afternoon tea (25¢ with biscuits); dining room closed on Mondays; small snack bar downstairs serves sandwiches and soups every day of the week; no room service.

SEASONS: Open all year, except for three weeks at Christmas and New Year's; overrun at Parents' Weekend (usually around Mother's Day) and Graduation (one proud grandfather already has his room booked for *1983*).

LORD JEFFERY INN
Amherst, Massachusetts

The innkeeper here has a degree in German Socialism, and half the waiters and waitresses have degrees in something or other, including a pair of Ph.D.'s. That's no qualification for running an inn, but sample the friendly, efficient service here and you may decide that all innkeepers, waiters, and waitresses should have degrees.

The Lord Jeffery has the look and the feel of an old New England inn, with its Colonial furnishings and beamed ceilings, but in fact it was built in 1924 by Amherst College; two years ago, the inn was refurbished, and the college decided to go back to running it (rather than leasing it to a hotel chain as they used to). Hence the literate staff. Hence the big improvements in the amenities.

The inn is a white-going-on-red building on a corner of the village common, an oasis of maples and elms in the bustle of a college town that's grown into a sort of supermarket of learning (the University of Massachusetts' ultra-modern Amherst campus is one of the largest in the country). It gets its name from Lord Jeffery Amherst, a young general and friend of the Duke of Cumberland, who trounced the French Army at Cape Breton in 1758, thereby earning the respect and gratitude of the Colonists. His namesake is a credit to his lordship.

Take a tour. When you enter the lobby, you're surrounded by gleaming oak, with period sofas and armchairs spread out before a big fire; to the left is an elegant library with shelves of leather-bound volumes, and a fireplace with a window. Beyond the dining room with the literate waitresses (and inexpensive menu), you come to the Jeffery Tavern, an L-shaped room with carriage lamp, tiled floors and steps leading to the loveliest part of the inn—the garden. The sheltered garden has been spruced up, decked out with tables and umbrellas among the maples and crab apple trees, and planted with red and white impatiens. Eight of the inn's forty-six rooms have balconies overlooking the garden, and they're the ones you should ask for. (All the other rooms have been redone with period furnishings, American primitive prints, telephones, television and air conditioning. They're okay.)

Guests are allowed to play on the college's twenty tennis courts, a short walk away, but you're more likely to use the Lord Jeffery as a center for touring the surrounding Pioneer Valley and the Mohawk Trail. After a day on the road, the Lord Jeffery is a nice place to spend the night.

NAME: Lord Jeffery Inn
INNKEEPER: Frans Wetterings
ADDRESS: On the Common, Amherst, Mass. 01002
TELEPHONE: 413-253-2576
DIRECTIONS: By car, take Interstate 91 to the exit for Mass. 9 (at Northampton), then drive east 10 miles.
RATES: EP—$17 to $25 for rooms, $36 to $43 for suites (the rooms facing the garden are $25), including Continental breakfast.
MEALS: Breakfast (to 10 a.m.), lunch, dinner (to 9 p.m.); room service; informal.
SEASONS: Open all year; busiest in April, May, September and October.

THE PUBLICK HOUSE
Sturbridge, Massachusetts

Lafayette once warmed his *derrière* before the huge open fireplace in the taproom. The taproom is now the dining room and you can feast yourself before the same fire—on onion popovers, baked lobster pie or beef turnover, cranberry bread or pumpkin bread.

The Publick House was first established as a coaching tavern in 1771, by Colonel Ebenezer Crafts, a legendary innkeeper who could lift a barrel of cider and drink from the bunghole. He also equipped and drilled a company of cavalry on the Common opposite the inn, and marched them off to help Lafayette in some of his skirmishes. The tavern did a hefty business because of its location at one of the busiest crossroads in the Colonies. "The old fordway at Tantiusque" was the route taken by the Indians when they carried corn to the Pilgrims in Plymouth; in turn, the first white settlers traipsed over the same route on their first ventures westward. Later, the Old Colonial Post Road ran through Sturbridge. Ben Franklin traveled along it when he was deputy postmaster of the thirteen Colonies and made a field trip to most of his post offices.

This is the era you still breathe when you step beneath the lantern and through the door of the Publick House.

Apples on the bedside table

If Lafayette had stayed the night he would have slept in a room that hasn't changed much to this day. He might not recognize the wallpaper on the landing but it's so jolly and patriotic it would probably have sent him off to bed with his heart as warm as his *derrière*. The period furniture and lurching floors have been joined by discreet concessions to the 20th century—like tiled bathrooms, cuddly towels, telephones, air conditioning and a sprinkler system. There are twenty-five rooms in the old inn, plus another six rooms, not quite so "period," in a newer wing. They all welcome you with a bowl of apples on the bedside table. But don't spoil your appetite. Your innkeeper has some tasty dishes waiting downstairs.

Popovers in the barn

The Taproom restaurant, with its big fire and curtained windows, is a pleasant enough spot, but lovers will probably prefer the inn's Barn Restaurant, where the hand-hewn beams and timber stalls make quiet nooks for diners who want to look into each other's eyes while dipping into their onion popovers.

You can round out your dinner with a cognac in the cocktail lounge downstairs, another cozy low-ceilinged spot. But be warned—the combo may be playing, amplified, and you can bet your bottom dollar they're not playing "Let tyrants shake their iron rod . . ."

If you're here on a Yankee Winter Weekend (January through March) the inn will also entertain you with hot buttered rum, roast chestnuts, roast venison and mincemeat pie, square dancing, sleigh rides through Old Sturbridge Village, and sugaring-off parties; then wake you next morning with the aromas of an open-hearth breakfast—hickory-smoked bacon, porridge with maple syrup and hot apple pan dowdy.

Pick your own apples, chew penny candies

In spring, the county's orchards are fluffy with apple blossom; in the fall, you can visit the orchards, pick your own McIntoshes, and then wander off, hand-in-hand, away from the village and the highways, and find yourselves a leafy glade for an afternoon of munching, drowsing and daydreaming.

Or you can visit Old Sturbridge Village. It's a corny, touristy sort of thing to do, but do it anyway if there aren't too many people around. Old Sturbridge Village is a 200-acre re-creation of a New England country town of the late 18th, early 19th centuries—forty fully-furnished homes, shops, a meeting house, and costumed hosts and hostesses to show you around and demonstrate how your ancestors used to spin, weave, make pottery and brooms and grow herbs. Hop on the horse-drawn carry-all wagon for a jaunt around the village, and buy your sweetheart old-fashioned penny candies at the General Store.

NAME: Treadway Publick House
INNKEEPER/MANAGER: Treadway Inns & Resorts
ADDRESS: On the Common, Sturbridge, Mass.
TELEPHONE: 617-347-3313
DIRECTIONS: A few miles from the intersection of Interstate 84 and the Massachusetts Turnpike, about an hour's drive from Boston.
RATES: $22, $24 and $26 EP (two dollars less in winter, November 1 through April 30).
MEALS: Breakfast (any time), lunch and dinner (to midnight); no room service; informal.
SEASONS: Open all year (busiest during the fall foliage weeks).

LONGFELLOW'S WAYSIDE INN
South Sudbury, Massachusetts

"As Ancient is this Hostelry/As any in the Land may be . . ." So rhymed, precariously, Henry Wadsworth Longfellow.

He wrote and set his *Tales of a Wayside Inn* in this very hostelry. Alas, this makes it super-historic, and a place that many Americans feel they ought to see, even if they've never managed to get beyond "Listen, my children, and you shall hear/Of the midnight ride of Paul Revere." They come out from Boston by the coachload. This puts you, the guests, almost in the category of exhibits in a museum, not much fun for most lovers unless they're the kind that fancies an audience.

Still, the Wayside Inn is such a delightful old place it's worth bucking the busloads; in any case, during the off-season (October through June) there's only a scattering of day-trippers. Then you have the place practically to yourself because there are only ten guest rooms to begin with (it must have been a tight squeeze when King Ibn Saud and his retinue dropped in). They're not the most elegant in Massachusetts, but they're charmingly furnished with period pieces, and they all have phones, air conditioning and private baths. Most of them were tacked on a long time after Longfellow rhymed, but two of them are authentically ancient: room #9, with its plank floors, pine walls, low beamed ceiling, sconces, sideboards and armchairs; and room #10, which is smaller, with tiny windows, red curtains and antique tables (but no phone).

This is just the right sort of atmosphere in which to stretch out and think about the history of these old beams and planks, and to invent your own tales of lovers and elopers who've slept within these bulging walls.

Patriots, poetasters and teamsters

This inn is so old it goes back to the days *before* stagecoaches. The original two rooms were built in 1686—the date that led Longfellow to rhyme his lines claiming it as the oldest inn in the country. In those days guests came galloping up on horseback or lumbering up by oxcart; they warmed themselves in the tap room and then retired upstairs to a sort of dormitory, now known as the Drovers' Room, where there were five beds for the teamsters. The inn was built by a David Howe and called the Howe Tavern, but by the time of the Revolution it had become the Red Horse. It was still owned by a Howe, Colonel Ezekiel, who gathered a group of Sudbury farmers in his tap room before marching them off to the field at Concord. When the fracas got properly under way, the Colonel dined here with George Washington, who was on his way to Boston to take command of the army. The inn got its present name, of course, from Longfellow, who actually spent only two weekends here.

The inn stayed in the Howe family until the turn of the century, when it started to decay. Henry Ford bought it in 1920 and fixed it up (some say *over*fixed). He stayed there many times, and often invited his friends over for a few days—Edison, Firestone, the Prince of Wales. In 1953, the inn caught fire, but fortunately on a freezing morning; when the firemen poured on water it turned to ice and froze the fire. Otherwise, the entire inn might have been destroyed. It was restored in 1958 with a grant from the Ford Foundation, and the inn is now run by its own foundation dedicated to preserving it as an historical and literary shrine. It's non-profit; any money you spend there goes to keeping the place in tiptop condition. The maintenance bill alone is $20,000 to $30,000 a year, yet surprisingly the inn pays its way.

You can tell the money isn't wasted the minute you set eyes on its neat, russet-colored clapboard exterior, rather like the shape of a haystack, and the trim lawn guarded by two tall oaks. It's set back a hundred yards from the main road on a twisting country lane, or as Longfellow put it, "A region of repose it seems/A place of slumber and of dreams/Remote among wooded hills . . ."

On your right when you go through the door is the Old Bar Room—an austere, timbered room with the original settle, pewter sconces, hutch tables and chairs. Across the hall is the Longfellow Parlor, one of the rooms where Longfellow supposedly wrote and recited some of his tales. It's still furnished with authentic period items, including "the first spinet in Sudbury," and other items mentioned in the poem. The Longfellow Bedroom upstairs is preserved as an example of the sort of room people used to stay in back in the 18th century, with pencil post bed, Spanish footchairs and a 1710 highboy. The old Drovers' Room is still there, but in its post-Ford form when it was Edison's favorite room, with two rather than five beds.

Most of the trippers who visit the inn stop off for lunch or dinner in the big Colonial-style dining room at the rear, but the Red Horse Room is cozier, a pub-like sort of place with hovering beams, slat-backed chairs and wooden tables. The menu is basically New England, but with something for everyone— Yankee beef broth with barley, roast Massachusetts duckling, baked fresh scrod, ribs of beef, filet mignon. Complete dinners cost from $3.95 to $7.25, lunches from $3. You've read of many inns that bake their own bread, but the Wayside Inn goes one better—its rolls and muffins are made from flour and meal stone-ground at the inn's own grist mill, down the road.

Coow Woows and Stonewalls

The Old Bar isn't normally used for serving drinks, but after the crowds have gone for the day you can probably persuade the innkeeper to serve you a drink before the crackling fire. Try one of the inn's specialties from the old days—a Coow Woow (pronounced coo-woo), a 17th-century drink made with ginger brandy and rum on crushed ice; or a Stonewall, which is a century older—gin and applejack over ice cubes. They may not inspire you to write a poem, but they're sure to put some kind of ideas into your head.

NAME: Longfellow's Wayside Inn
INNKEEPER: Francis J. Koppeis
ADDRESS: Sudbury, Mass. 01776
TELEPHONE: 617-443-8846
DIRECTIONS: On U.S. 20, the old stagecoach route, midway between Boston and Worcester, and an easy drive to places like Concord, Lexington and Sturbridge.
RATES: All rooms, all year, $17 EP.
MEALS: Breakfast (to 9:30 a.m.), lunch and dinner (to 8 p.m.); no room service, except breakfast if you make arrangements with the front desk the night before. The Red Horse Room is informal, but men must wear jacket and tie and ladies must wear dresses (no pant suits) in the main dining room Sundays, evenings and holidays.

SEASONS: Open all year; May through October are the day-trip months; winter is quietest (the inn has its own snow ploughs, but if you prefer to be snowed in, the obliging staff can probably arrange it).

THE MAYFLOWER INN
Washington, Connecticut

"Live, Love and Laugh" is the official motto here—but all in a low-key sort of way. Don't come here for roistering; come instead for tranquility, in a setting of gardens and streams, in one of the loveliest Colonial villages in the state.

The shingled, steeply-roofed Mayflower crowns a knoll on thirty acres of gardens and woodlands—a fragrant place to idle away a few days. Lounge on the manicured lawns. Picnic in the ash grove. Feed the swans in the brook. Tip-toe among the garden's forty-eight varieties of flowers (pride and joy of a greenthumb with the unlikely name of Howard Johnson). Wander among the maples and pine, and the beechnut trees that like the place so much they've grown to twice the size of normal beechnuts. Or hike the woodland trail up to the Steep Rock Reservation—20,000 acres of private wildlife preserve donated to the town of Washington away back in the 1800s.

Your base camp for all this bosky frolicking is a relatively young inn with all the traditional charm of an old New England Colonial inn.

From three R's to three L's

The Mayflower was built about a hundred years ago as a school, and it continued to teach the three R's until 1920, when it was bought by a Washingtonian, Henry B. van Sinderen, who

had earned fame and fortune on Wall Street. He wanted to share his good fortune with his home town, so he converted the school into an inn. Since he was a genial and generous host, most of the guests were his personal friends, but the Mayflower's reputation began to spread, the guest list expanded, and by the time he died in 1968 van Sinderen was able to bequeath a successful hostelry to his local alma mater, the Gunnery School (which has nothing to do with artillery, by the way). The inn is still owned by the school's board of trustees, and since it's considered something of a memorial to van Sinderen, the inn is still geared to his amiable philosophy of the three L's— Live, Love and Laugh. As a memorial it sure beats a statue.

The inn's make-yourself-at-home approach creates a friendly, relaxed atmosphere. Where would you like to have your drink— in the paneled library, before the fireplace in one of the sitting rooms, on the porch or out on the lawn? Would you like to dine in the Captain's Cabin (supposedly a replica of the dining salon on board the seagoing Mayflower), in the Gallery (where you can admire the works of local artists), or in the enclosed Sun Room porch (a popular spot for breakfasts)? When it's time for bed, the Mayflower offers you a choice of rooms in the main lodge or in a couple of cottages in the garden; they all have period furniture and private bathrooms, some have porches, and ten of them have working fireplaces. In the main lodge, ask for the Blue Room or the Green Room; in the Coulton Cottage ask for the downstairs room overlooking the garden and the brook, with spacious sitting room, white pine walls and an enormous carved stone pictorial fireplace—and when you leave in the morning you're greeted by the sounds of birds and brook and the scents of the gardens.

The Mayflower sounds like a marvelous place to visit in summer. It is. But it's also marvelous in the fall, when the maples and the fireplaces are blazing; in spring, when you can play a bracing game of golf or tennis at the local country club; or in winter when you can go skating on the pond or trudging through the snow. You can play, live, love and laugh here any time of the year.

NAME: The Mayflower Inn
INNKEEPERS: Tristram and Ki Gaillard
ADDRESS: Washington, Conn. 06793
TELEPHONE: 203-868-7411
DIRECTIONS: Washington (not to be confused with its neighbor, Washington Depot) is in the northwestern corner of Connecticut, about halfway between U.S. 7 and Conn. 8, 25 miles from Danbury, 90 miles from New York; and the inn is 4 miles south of town, near the junction of Conn. 47 and Conn. 199
RATES: EP—$14 to $26 year round.
MEALS: Breakfast (to 10 a.m.), lunch, dinner (to 8:30 p.m.); no room service; informal.
SEASONS: Open all year, busiest in fall; small groups throughout the year.

KILRAVOCK INN
Litchfield, Connecticut

Louis Ripley, the railroad tycoon, built this multi-gabled, half-timbered manor in 1905 as a wedding gift for his bride, who came all the way from Scotland to marry him. Kilravock (pronounced, apparently, Kil-rook in Scotland) is a replica of her home in the Highlands. A house built for love, it's now a place for lovers.

Kilravock became an inn only in 1972, when it was taken over by the Hoyts (Philips Hoyt was a stockbroker until then, but he graduated from Cornell Hotel School). When you drive through the park-like gardens to the Hoyts' great stone front door, you'll probably be greeted by Nippy and Brandy, the West Highland terriers; and when you open the heavy wooden door you step into Act I, Scene 1 of a comedy set in a country house somewhere near London—a baronial hall with carved walnut paneling, a carved balustrade climbing three floors, an oak table laden with magazines and a basketful of apples, a huge fireplace with inglenook seats, a grand piano, and French doors leading

out to the garden. Stage left rear is the library, a dignified paneled room with three walls of shelves gleaming with leather-bound copies of Balzac, Hawthorne and Dumas, and the inn's sole television set (until 9 p.m. only, and never on Sunday).

Follow the balustrade upstairs and pick out your love nest. There are only sixteen rooms in the inn, and of those, only eleven are doubles (no double beds, however, at the moment); the most romantic are probably #23, a blush of dusty pinks, with wooden floor, shag rug and fireplace; #26, with fireplace, a pair of acorn-knob beds, chaise and a nifty bathroom with a mammoth tub; #21, big, sunny, with white drapes and bed-spreads, an upholstered chaise longue by the window and a private porch. Rooms #35 and #36 are connecting singles occasionally pressed into service by illicit connecting doubles who have to check in separately in case of telephone calls from colleagues or spouses. (There are also a dozen rooms in two adjoining cottages, which were dormitories when Kilravock endured a few years as a girls' school; they don't have the charm of the rooms in the main house, but they're adequate if there's nothing else left.)

Meadow, cornfield and home-made manicotti

From Kilravock's bedrooms you look out on unspoiled views of countryside, beginning with the inn's own 146 acres, a topiary garden and fountain, a cornfield, meadows where you can lie in the grass all day listening to the bees and blinking at the sun, woodlands where you can disappear on long thigh-to-thigh walks. A few steps from the French doors you'll find *four* tennis courts and an unheated swimming pool where you can sun yourselves and think of the beautiful Colonial mansions you could see if you could stir up enough energy to drive a mile into Litchfield.

When the sun starts dropping behind the cornfield, head for the inglenooks and sip a sherry while you're waiting for one of Maria the cook's masterpieces. Maria is from Rome, and she believes that manicotti and tortellini should be home-made; one forkful will carry you all the way back to Trastevere. On Sundays the menu shifts to Copenhagen for Lis Hoyt's Danish smorgasbord. Consider yourselves lucky Mrs. Ripley isn't still around or you might be sitting down to haggis.

NAME: Kilravock Inn
INNKEEPERS: Philips and Lis Hoyt
ADDRESS: Litchfield, Conn. 06759
TELEPHONE: 203-567-8100
DIRECTIONS: Take Conn. 8 to Torrington, then go west on Conn. 25, through Litchfield to the edge of town where you'll see the Kilravock signs.
RATES: EP—$20 to $35 in the main house, $25 in the two cottages, year round.
MEALS: Breakfast (to 10 a.m.), lunch (Monday, Tuesday, Thursday and Friday only), dinner (to 8:30 p.m., except Sunday—when Danish smorgasbord is served from 12:30 to 3 p.m.); no room service; informal.
SEASONS: Open all year, delightful at any time.

HARRISON INN
Southbury, Connecticut

Put this down as a possibility for a windy, wintery weekend. You can curl up in snug rooms that look like pages from a California homes and gardens magazine: cedar walls, rattan chairs, handwoven wall hangings and blow-ups of photographs, custom-designed wood-block closets, a bath-and-a-half, and stereo and TV. Without ever venturing beyond the inn's cedar-sided walls you can soak in a sauna, work out in an exercise room, play pool, listen to Dixieland, watch old movies, shop in one of the most unusual bazaars this side of Ghirardelli Square, and dine in a pubby restaurant.

If you come on a mellow day you can swim in the heated pool, or sit in the gazebo and look at the gardens and listen to the stream. There are a pair of all-weather tennis courts, a golf course on the other side of the stream, and bikes and horses to take you through the countryside.

All this sounds like a pleasant country inn, and that's how Harrison Inn promotes itself, but it's really nothing like a traditional New England country inn. It's part of a community for old people called Heritage Village, and it's geared to seminars and groups of executives from all those corporations proliferating around Hartford and in Westchester. That doesn't sound too romantic, but the truth is that the elderly inhabitants seem to keep to themselves, and the executives all go home on weekends, when the inn is taken over by a youngish, moderately swinging clientele. And it is an interesting inn.

NAME: Harrison Inn
ADDRESS: Heritage Village, The Village Green, Southbury, Conn. 06488
TELEPHONE: 203-264-8255
DIRECTIONS: Take Interstate 84 to exit 15, then drive to Conn. 67 and follow the signs.
RATES: EP—$30 to $36 for rooms, $60 and up for suites, year round.
MEALS: Breakfast (to 9 a.m.), lunch, dinner (to midnight); room service; informal.
SEASONS: Open all year; seminars throughout the year, but mostly midweek.

SWISS HUTTE
Hillsdale, New York

Behind the lodge, a steep hill struggles up to the highway; facing the lodge, across the meadow, is Catamount. The view is everything: you see it from the balcony of your room, when you're dining on the patio or outdoor terrace, when you're relaxing in the two wooden armchairs on the jetty by the pond. Even the Rode Gluckel Bar has its windows angled to take in the mountain view.

The Swiss Hutte lodge was a farm before the Breens converted it into a lodge and tacked on a motel wing. There's nothing grand about the Hutte; it's rustic in a yodelly sort of way, a pleasant, friendly place in a sheltered setting. You can swim in the spring-fed pond by the edge of the meadow, or in the heated pool; walking trails wind up into the forest and lead you miles away from everyone. In winter you can skate on the spring-fed pond, ski cross-country along the trails you hiked in winter, or ski the slopes of Catamount.

The rooms are so-so (all with TV, private bath/shower, individually controlled heating or air conditioning, balcony but no phone), but the lodge itself has a piney, flowery atmosphere that puts you in the mood for a hearty meal—the inn's specialty: scampi Dijonnaise, roulade de porc Cordon Bleu, that sort of thing, with a few items such as schnitzels and steaks in the $7 and $8 bracket. Any of the Swiss Hutte's dishes tastes more scrumptious on the terrace surrounded by pine, crabapple and honey locust trees, with the stars over Catamount and the brook trickling by beyond the pond.

NAME: Swiss Hutte Inn & Motel
INNKEEPERS: Tom and Linda Breen
ADDRESS: Hillsdale, N.Y. 12529
TELEPHONE: 518-325-3333

DIRECTIONS: On NY 23, 3 miles east of Hillsdale, 7 miles east of the Taconic Parkway, and 30 minutes from Tanglewood or Jacob's Pillow.

RATES: MAP—$52 in the motel, $44 in the lodge; 20% less in spring, fall and winter, and on weekdays you can probably arrange to have EP only, $24 a room; 15% service charge added for gratuities.

MEALS: Breakfast (to 10:30 a.m.), lunch, dinner (to 10 p.m.); no room service; informal.

SEASONS: Open all year, except April and November; quietest months are May, June, September and October.

FROM
THE SHAWANGUNKS
TO
THE ALLEGHENIES

How silver-sweet sound lovers' tongues by night,
Like softest music to attending ears . . .
SHAKESPEARE

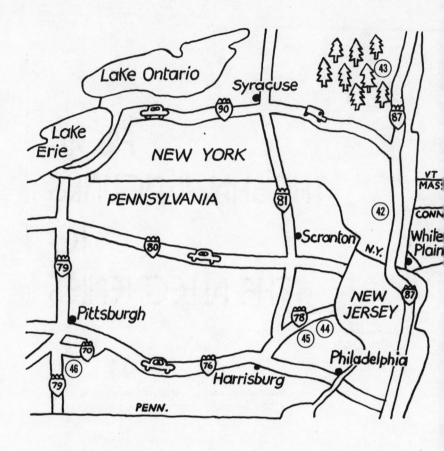

42. Mohonk Mountain House

43. Auberge des Quatre Saisons

44. 1740 House

45. Tulpehocken Manor Farm

46. Century Inn

MOHONK MOUNTAIN HOUSE
Mohonk Lake, New York

It's eye-boggling. A rambling, gabled, turreted, eighth-of-a-mile long Victorian chateau, 1,250 feet up in the mountains, with a lake at its doorstep and 7,500 acres of wilderness all around. From a distance it looks like a medieval Nuremberg, from close up like a Disney fantasy elongated for Cinemascope. Inside it's even more stunning: walls and balustrades of intricately carved birch, square columns with carved capitals, leaded and textured glass, pierced-wood screens, "Sultan's Corners" with plush banquettes, bentwood settees, velvet-covered love seats, a pair of five-foot Japanese cloisonné vases flanking a parlor organ and a Steinway concert grand. This is just where you take afternoon tea; wait until you see the dining room.

"Forever wild"

The whole massive anachronism is the cherished preserve of a family called Smiley. The first Smileys started it all back in 1869, when they built a summer house for their friends; hence the word House rather than Hotel, because the fourth generation of Smileys still like to think of it as a private country house (some country house, with 305 rooms and 150 fireplaces), and love to show guests around the gardens or entertain them with a recital on the Steinway. They're Quakers, and you have to put up with a few eccentricities: no smoking in the dining room or main parlor; no drinking in public places except for one hour during dinner (you can tipple in your room if you like, and the hotel will supply

97

you with set-ups); you may not play the piano in the lounge between two and five in the afternoons; you won't find TV or room phones in the uncompromisingly Victorian rooms; but you can forgive these trivia when you see what else the family has done for you. A few years ago they turned over 60 percent of their land (a tidy $10 to $15 million worth of real estate) to the Mohonk Trust to ensure that the mountain wilderness will be "forever wild."

Forever wild, and forever enjoyed, because the Smileys have set things up so that you can fill your days with unpolluted pleasures. Sun yourself on the sandy beach (that's right, sand even at 1,250 feet). Paddle a canoe across the lake. Put a dime in a dispenser for a handful of fish food to feed the trout. Ride horses along forty-five miles of woodland trail lined by spruce, birch and beech. Wander hand-in-hand through the gardens of red salvias, snapdragons, asters and zinnias; sniff the mignonette, heliotrope and shrub roses. All over the gardens and up the side of the mountain, the Smileys have built tiny gazebos (about 150 of them) of weathered hemlock with thatched roofs where you can rest, kiss, and admire the view across the Shawangunk Mountains and Rondout Valley to six states. You can go sightseeing by horse-drawn carriage, play golf or tennis, or sit on a veranda and rock the hours away to dinner time; in winter you can go skiing, cross-country skiing, snowshoeing, sleigh riding or skating. There's something for everyone, although Mohonk Mountain House may not be everyone's cup of afternoon tea. But for those who enjoy something unique, a hangover from bygone days, Mohonk offers magnificent surroundings, crystal clear air and hour after hour, mile after mile of Quaker quiet.

NAME: Mohonk Mountain House

INNKEEPERS: The Smiley Family (owners), Ben Matteson (resident manager)

ADDRESS: Mohonk Lake, New Paltz, N.Y. 12561

TELEPHONE: 914-255-1000 (in New York, direct dialing: 233-2244)

DIRECTIONS: The hotel is 6 miles west of New Paltz, about 90 from New York City; by car, take the N.Y. Thruway to Exit 18, then follow New Paltz's Main Street until you come to the bridge over the Wallkill River, then turn right and follow the signs for Mohonk; by rail to Poughkeepsie, where you can arrange to have a Mohonk car meet you; by air, to Stanton Airport, 10 minutes from the hotel.

RATES: AP—$26 without private bath, $38 to $45 with private bath, from May 24 through October 23; slightly lower remainder of year; also special Midweek Package Plans of $292 for two from Sunday evening through Tuesday afternoon, or Monday through Friday.

MEALS: Breakfast (to 9 a.m., later in the old-time ice cream parlor), lunch, afternoon tea, dinner (to 8 p.m.); room service; jacket and tie for dinner; no bar, but cocktails are served for one hour before lunch, and wines with meals.

SEASONS: Open all year, busiest in summer; small groups during remainder of year.

AUBERGE DES QUATRE SAISONS
Shandaken, New York

Lie on the lawn, with the birds singing and the brook chuckling, and let the cooking smells that wisp past your noses lull you to Burgundy. Walk into the dining room and everything confirms that you're in a small French provincial inn—the pine walls, the checkered tablecloths with white napkins, the French accents, the way the wine appears on the table before the food. Even the new chalet wing wouldn't look out of place in the Haute Savoie. Your map tells you you're in the Catskills, but a long way from the Catskills in spirit. This is France, from the aperitif on the porch to the first sip of Beaujolais, from the *soupe a l'oignon* to the deliciously gooey *profiterolles.* You come here to eat, and between meals you can frolic in the pool, sun yourselves on the lawn, play volleyball, ping-pong or tennis—all within sniffing distance of the kitchen. You can take long lonely walks through sixty-five acres of woods behind the hotel, or just sit on the porch and watch the big white cat chase a chipmunk.

The Auberge is a mile or so from busy Route 28 on unbusy Route 42, a dark-shingled lodge on a tiny hill surrounded by a hillside of trees. Its rooms, too, are more Burgundian than Catskill—piney walls, lino floors with skimpy rugs, and so small you have to embrace every time you turn around. Most of the rooms in the lodge don't have private baths; if you want that kind of extravagance, and room to move around without getting into a clinch, take a room in the chalet. Twice the space, but half the charm.

As if it weren't enough to have the birds, the trees, the brook, the tennis, the Frenchness and the *profiterolles,* the Auberge keeps its most endearing quality when it presents your bill—what you'd normally pay for just a room in most inns buys you room *and* breakfast *and* dinner at the Auberge.

NAME: Auberge des Quatre Saisons
INNKEEPERS: Annie and Dadou Labeille
ADDRESS: Shandaken, N. Y. 12480
TELEPHONE: 914-688-2223
DIRECTIONS: About 120 miles or 2 hours and 15 minutes from New York by N.Y. Thruway to Exit 19 (at Kingston), then U.S. 28 to N.Y. 42; or by Palisades Parkway to Thruway Entrance 9, then to Exit 19.
RATES: MAP in summer and winter—$28 without private bath, $32 with private bath in lodge, $40 in the chalet; slightly less in spring and fall.
MEALS: Breakfast (to 9:30 a.m.), lunch, dinner (to 9:30 p.m.); no room service; informal.
SEASONS: All *quatre,* busiest during summer and ski seasons.

1740 HOUSE
Lumberville, Pennsylvania

Lumberville slumberville—this small village drowses alongside the Delaware River and the Pennsylvania Canal, about three miles upstream from the Stockton Bridge. This is the place where Harry and Janet Nessler decided to build their dream inn when they gave up the real estate business in New York a few years back.

The 1740 House is a warm, friendly place, right on the edge of the canal and surrounded by sycamores, pines, oaks and box-wood, and banks of asters, roses and rhododendron. River Road runs by on the other side, almost as silently as the canal. This is what peace is all about. "The folks who feel insecure without color TV in the room and a piano bar in the cocktail lounge should stay away," says Harry Nessler. "They'll hate it here." In fact, not only is there no TV or piano, there's no bar either. The

1740 part of the 1740 House is an old stable, but most of the inn is a modern timber structure, blissfully at one with the surrounding trees. You wake to nature, you dine with nature, you play in nature. The inn has acres of windows; each of its twenty-four rooms overlooks a panorama of river and woods and canal, and if that's not enough step out onto your own patio and take in the whole depth of the scene—the greenery, the scent of the forest, the chirping of birds, the swish of a canoe along the canal.

On summer evenings, dinner is served in a brick patio surrounded by peach, apple, walnut and dogwood trees, where you can dine on fresh seafood Lamaze or pâté in aspic, duckling a l'orange or sliced porterhouse steak with sauce Bearnaise, mousse au chocolat with whipped cream or rum creme cake.

Afterwards you can take a turn along the towpath or retire to your patio overlooking the canal, sip a nightcap, listen to those mysterious night sounds on the river and count stars.

Breakfast is served in a small dining room filled with camellias, hibiscus, ivy, a lemon tree, gardenias and begonias, overlooking the river. It's buffet style—great pitchers of orange juice, pots of coffee, heaps of freshly baked croissants, rolls and cold cereals.

After breakfast, tiptoe down the rickety steps with English ivy growing all over them that look as though they've been there since 1740, untie one of the two canoes or the rowboat and go for an expedition along the canal. You won't have to worry about rapids and white water here—the most ruffled the water gets is when a mosquito flits down for a drink. The inn has its own small pool, and there are golf, tennis and fishing in the neighborhood. In winter, someone lowers the level of the water in the canal so that you can go ice skating or ice boating.

Beamed ceilings, sparkling baths

The rooms, in fact the entire inn, are handsomely furnished with antiques. Bucks County is a region of fine old family homes and when someone dies the antiques go up for auction; a lot of them have ended up here. The reading table that holds the register, for example, is a copy of one found in the Governor's palace in

Williamsburg. Two of the rooms are in the old part of the structure—Room #2, with thick stone walls and beamed ceilings, was once the stable; and Room #23, with a cathedral ceiling and wide oak beams, was once the hayloft. Otherwise, all the rooms are new, with wall-to-wall shag carpeting, individually controlled central heating and air conditioning, and sparkling bathrooms with tubs and showers. The original house, which was formerly an antique store, is now the sitting room. Here you'll find lurching floors and old ceiling boards, with comfortable antiques and a big wing chair, as well as Mariah, a Labrador retriever, and Molly, a long-haired dachshund, in front of the log fire. The Nesslers' motto is "If you can't be a house guest in Bucks County, be ours." Be theirs.

NAME: 1740 House
INNKEEPERS: Harry and Janet Nessler
ADDRESS: River Road, Lumberville, Pa. 18933
TELEPHONE: 215-297-5661
DIRECTIONS: On State Highway 32, just north of New Hope and
    U.S. 202, about 30 miles from Philadelphia.
RATES: EP (but including the buffet breakfast) $25; on weekends between April 1 and November 30, and on holidays at
    any time of the year, $30.
MEALS: Breakfast (to 10:30 a.m.) and dinner (to 8 p.m.) only;
    no room service, no liquor license, but the inn will provide
    ice and setups if you want to bring your own.
SEASONS: Open all year.

TULPEHOCKEN MANOR FARM
Myerstown, Pennsylvania

Go easy as you drive around the big barn because the ducks may be sitting in the middle of the road. And if no one answers the doorbell, it's probably because Jim Henry is out mending the

east fence; he'll be back soon, so just pull up one of the fourteen chairs on the veranda and enjoy the shade of the two tall maple trees.

Tulpehocken is a working farm that also takes in a few tourists and sightseers because it's old, unique and historic; it was built about the same time as the Republic, by a German settler who quarried his own limestone and cut the timber from the family's own groves of walnut trees. The original two-story building has had several additions, including a mansard roof, a third story, and an ornate two-story veranda. The other buildings on the property are unique for this part of the world—they're built Swiss-style over a groundfloor walk-through archway.

The farm was bought up about ten years ago by the Nisslys and Jim Henry, who've restored it and filled the bedrooms with furnishings of the period. Filled? Stuffed. Clogged. Like the creation of a benign Charles Addams. You squeeze your way to bed past a jumble of Victoriana, Belgian glass doors, handcarved walnut banisters, painted slate mantels, handcarved yellow pine doors, brass table lamps, Hitchcock chairs, Windsor chairs. One of the rooms has a four poster bed and matching chest of drawers, another a bed with a headboard over eight feet tall and weighing between 500 and 600 pounds (the man who designed that must have been quite a performer—or a braggart). The farm has twenty-seven rooms in all; nine of them are in the adjoining cottages (with kitchenettes and private baths, but with nothing like the personality of the manor rooms). The eighteen rooms in the manor house share three bathrooms (a fact that didn't faze some Rockefellers, who stayed there a few months ago), and they all have ugly little plastic TV sets— except one.

The Room

The exception is the room sightseers pay to see. The Room George Washington Slept In. I've tried to avoid that chestnut all the way through this guide, but in the case of Tulpehocken it's justified, because Washington slept here not once but three times. You should know this, because if you happen to rent the room he slept in (first floor, front, left) you'd better be prepared to rise early or be caught *in flagrante delicto* by a family of sightseers from Ponca City.

Get up, then, and take a look around the farm. Count the cattle (fifty-nine registered Angus), or take a walk along quiet paths that follow streams and a stretch of the old Union Canal. Tulpehocken is a lazy place, a place to lie on the grass, chew a blade of grass and dream dreams, or in winter a cozy place to curl up with a good book or something. It would be the ideal hideaway if you didn't have to leave the place every time you want a coffee, Coke or chocolate chip cookie; if only Miss Nissly could be persuaded to leave a jug of juice or a pot of coffee on the sideboard for breakfast. If the ducks don't get out of the way and let you drive to the local diner you may not get breakfast at all.

NAME: Tulpehocken Manor Farm
INNKEEPERS: Miss Esther E. Nissly and her father John S. Nissly, and James W. Henry

106

ADDRESS: R.D. #2, Myerstown, Pa. 17067

TELEPHONE: 717-866-4926

DIRECTIONS: In Pennsylvania Dutch Country, 5 miles east of Lebanon, on U.S. 422; to get there from the Pennsylvania Turnpike, take the Lebanon/U.S. 72 exit, and from Interstate 78, take the exit for Pa. 501, follow 501 to 422, then go west 2 miles.

RATES: EP—$8 to $20 for rooms, more for cottage rooms with kitchens.

MEALS: None.

SEASONS: Open all year; busiest in July, August and October.

CENTURY INN
Scenery Hill, Pennsylvania

Route 40 used to be the National Pike, which was the main east-west route in the early days of the Union. Century Inn opened for travelers and stagecoaches a few months after Washington began his second term, and by the time his old buddy Lafayette passed this way on his Grand Tour of 1825, the massive stone walls already had a covering of ivy. Other guests in the coaching days included Andrew Jackson, the James K. Polks, General Zachary Taylor, and Chief Black Hawk, on his way to Washington as a prisoner of war. An historic little spot, it hasn't changed character much since those days. Its rooms are almost like antique shops: walls are draped with odd bits and pieces—giant corkscrews, copper utensils, prints, duck decoys; a five-by-seven-and-a-half-foot fireplace in the small dining room is festooned with pots, pans, skillets and ovens; the main lounge has not one but two brick fireplaces, an 18th-century cherry highboy with scroll top, and a collection of rare glass from the once-famous Albert Gallatin glass works down the pike. The inn has only six guest rooms, and of these the prettiest are #3, #9 and #11 (which has a connecting door with the adjoining room). All three have private tub-showers. No TV (there's one in the lounge).

The inn's two-and-one-half-story facade has a big, white veranda for rocking on, and there's a garden at the rear for lounging in. Otherwise, there's nothing to keep you here by day. The village of Scenery Hill belies its name in a shamelessly nondescript manner, but the countryside to the south is Pennsylvania at its pastoral best. Spend a couple of nights here; breakfast early, and then drive off to a quiet glade or stream for a picnic, and don't come back until the setting sun has cast a facelifting glow on Scenery Hill; have an aperitif in the inn's snug bar, and dine on baked stuffed pork chops or breaded shrimps or the inn's famous roast turkey (most entrees are priced around $4). The main dining room is a bright, cheerful place with fresh flowers on the table, but ask for a table in the two-table room with the massive fireplace. It's more *intime,* as Lafayette would say.

NAME: Century Inn

INNKEEPER: Mrs. G. F. Harrington

ADDRESS: Scenery Hill, Pa. 15360

TELEPHONE: 412-945-6600

DIRECTIONS: Take Interstate 70 (the Pennsylvania Turnpike) to Exit 917 and follow Pa. 917 to U.S. 40, then go east a couple of miles to the village of Scenery Hill.

RATES: EP—$10 without bath, $14 with bath, year round.

MEALS: Breakfast (to 10 a.m.), lunch, dinner (to 8 p.m.); no room service; informal, but jacket and tie preferred in the evening.

SEASONS: Open all year, except from 3rd week in December to Palm Sunday or thereabouts; busy in summer, very busy in the fall foliage season, but a great place to visit in the quiet of winter, when you can spend your days with a good book before a roaring fire, and your evenings over a leisurely meal.

IN AND AROUND
THE CHESAPEAKE BAY

Omnia vincit Amor: et nos cedamus Amori . . .
VIRGIL

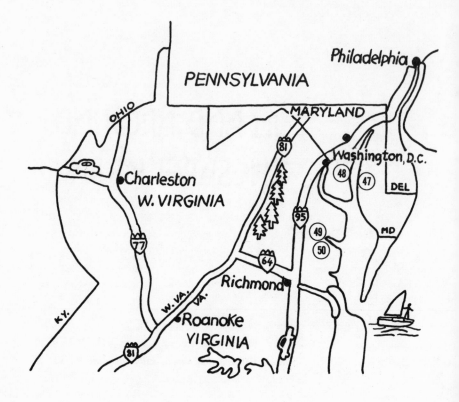

47. Robert Morris Inn
48. Maryland Inn
49. The Tides Inn
50. The Tides Golf Lodge

ROBERT MORRIS INN
Oxford, Maryland

Robert Morris was a prominent English merchant who met with a curiously unheroic end in the Colonies when he was fatally wounded by the wadding from a gun firing a salute in his honor. The Robert Morris *you* might have heard of was his son—a close friend of George Washington and fund-raiser for the Continental Army.

The inn was built as a private home in the earliest days of the 18th century by ships' carpenters using the techniques of ship-building—wooden pegged paneling, fourteen-inch square beams and pilasters fastened with hand-hewn oak pegs, that sort of thing. The house was purchased for Robert Morris Senior in 1730; it first became an inn at the time of the Civil War, and since 1970 it's been owned by George White, a Baltimore lawyer and Spiro Agnew's campaign manager. The inn sits by the edge of the Tred Avon River, just by the 200-year-old ferry ("the oldest U.S. ferry not attached to a cable") that hauls cars and people across the estuary. It's still very much a Colonial-style inn. Four of the rooms have the original handmade wall paneling; the fireplaces were built of brick made in England and used as ballast in sailing ships; the mural panels in the dining room were made from wallpaper samples printed 125 years ago on a screw-type press using woodcuts carved from orangewood.

The inn has twenty-one rooms, all with air conditioning, but otherwise they're very basic—no phones, no TV, and only five of them have private bathrooms. Your best bets are room #1, which has both a bath and a view, and #15, which has a pencil post bed so high you need a set of steps to get up to it. There

are seven more rooms (and three bathrooms) in the Lodge—
a big Victorian house a few yards along the bank of the river,
with spacious lawns and verandas overlooking the Tred Avon
traffic.

The public rooms at the inn are plusher—the delightful River-
view Lounge with the original wood-pegged wall panels, one of
the old brick fireplaces and an antique grandfather clock. The
dining room is decked out with silk drapes, chandeliers and
Hitchcock chairs; and the beamy Tap Room, where you can sip
a hot toddy or buttered rum before a big brick fire, is all wooden
and nautical. Since so many people come to the Robert Morris
for dinner, the owner recently installed a gleaming new $50,000
kitchen; but all that newfangled gadgetry doesn't faze Laura
Horsey, a venerable lady who's been fixin' the crab cakes that
have headed the inn's list of specialties for generations, regard-
less of who happens to own the place at the time. The menu's
pièce de résistance, however, is a gluttonous Special Seafood
Platter—$7.45 worth of chilled gulf shrimp and lump crabmeat,
deep-fried crab cake, shrimp, clams, stuffed shrimp, and broiled
crab imperial and filet of rockfish. Too much? Try the crab and
shrimp Norfolk, another local dish. Ask Maitre d' John Miller
(from Oxford, England, to Oxford, Maryland, by way of Clar-
idge's in London and Luchow's in New York) to recommend a
wine from his well-stocked cellar.

Munging and jousting

The Robert Morris Inn sets the atmosphere nicely for Colonial
Oxford and its surroundings, and it's a perfect base for dis-
covering the oddities of Chesapeake Bay—Baymen "munging"
for terrapin; "gunkholes," or creeks, with names like Canoe
Neck or Ape Hole or Antipoison; the skipjacks and bugeyes—
the last working fleet of sailing vessels in the entire country; the
jousting tournaments over in Talbot County. In summer there
are several regattas. When you hear a starting gun go off—
duck. The wadding can be dangerous, remember?

NAME: Robert Morris Inn
INNKEEPER: Ken Gibson
ADDRESS: Oxford, Md. 21654
TELEPHONE: 301-226-5111
DIRECTIONS: From the Delaware Memorial Bridge, take Mary-
    land 13 south to Maryland 301 and Maryland 50 to Easton,
    then go west on Maryland 333; from the Chesapeake Bay
    Bridge, follow highways 50, 301 and 50 to Easton; from
    the Chesapeake Bay Bridge Tunnel, take U.S. 13 north to
    Maryland 50, go west to Easton, then take Maryland 333
    to Oxford; by sea, follow the Choptank River to the Tred
    Avon River and tie up at the protected anchorage at Town
    Creek.
RATES: EP—$10.40 and $12.48 without bath, $14.56 and
    $20.80 with bath in the inn; $16.64 to $22.88 with bath in
    the lodge (all prices include tax).
MEALS: Breakfast (to 11 a.m.), lunch, dinner (to 9 p.m.);
    dining room closed on Monday; no room service; informal in
    the Tap Room, jacket and tie in the dining room.
SEASONS: Open all year; busiest in summer and during the hunt-
    ing season when the generals come over from the Pentagon
    to show everyone they're real soldiers who know how to
    handle a gun; also check ahead for local events and regattas.

MARYLAND INN
Annapolis, Maryland

Wassail, Black Velvet, Sideboard Toddy, roast grapevine goose and corn pudding are served up here on special weekends when the inn whisks you back to the heady early days of the Republic. The inn is on Church Circle, one of the more historic spots in the nation: the Maryland State Capitol is the oldest existing capitol in the country, and its old Senate Chamber was the place where a tearful George Washington resigned as Commander-in-Chief of the Continental Army. It's just possible that the tearful senators filed out of the chamber and across the circle to salute the emotion-charged ceremony in wassail or sideboard toddy or whatever senators were sipping in those days.

This "elegant brick house adjoining the Church Circle, in a dry and healthy part of the city" is a forty-four-room, four-story wedge of red brick, with an afterthought of a white two-story veranda at the entrance. The lobby has marble floors and fifteen-foot ceilings, and the guest rooms still have some of the flavor of Colonial/Victorian times, even with the addition of window air-conditioning units and television; all the rooms have private baths or showers, and heavy masonry walls that block out the senatorial snores from adjacent rooms. The most attractive rooms are probably #301, #401, #314 (which has four windows and three views—the Capitol, the harbor and the roof-tops), and the Hyde Suite on the second floor (original timbers, rocking chairs, fireplace, writing desk, wing back chairs, and bedroom with shower).

Earl "Fatha" Hines and Charlie Byrd

The Maryland Inn was also "a house of entertainment, for which purpose it was originally intended." In 1974 it's once again a house of entertainment, of a kind that would have boggled the minds of those early senators—Earl "Fatha" Hines, Charlie Byrd, the Hal Posey Jazz Quintet and occasional singers of ballads, folk songs and sea shanties. This is one of the innovations by the inn's new host, a former actress by the name of Anne Pearson May, to get young Annapolitans interested in the old inn when the senate shuts up shop and the legislators rumble off to their constituencies. The musical evenings (mostly weekends, music charge of $2.50) take place in the King of France Tavern, a handsome room with stone and brick walls, wooden beams, church pew seats and tables made from whiskey barrels; it looks as mellow as the old Capitol but was actually built a couple of years ago.

The "ordinary," or dining room, is another old-time room (authentically old in this case), and even if the roast grapevine goose and corn pudding aren't on the menu, you can still dine well on local specialties like crab cakes ($4.95) and Maryland crabmeat Norfolk (which is backfin crabmeat sauteed in butter with Smithfield ham—$4.75); and even if you can't have your wassail, you can sample a local wine. From *Maryland?* Wine? It's called Boordy. It comes from the Riderwood Vineyards, it's only $3 a bottle and it beats wassail as a companion to Crabmeat Norfolk.

NAME: Maryland Inn
INNKEEPER: Anne Pearson May
ADDRESS: Church Circle & Main, Annapolis, Md. 21401
TELEPHONE: 301-263-2641
DIRECTIONS: By car, from U.S. 2 (north and south), or U.S. 50/301 (east and west), then all the way into the center of town.
RATES: EP—$16 to $20 for rooms, to $36 for suites, year round.
MEALS: Breakfast, lunch, dinner (to midnight); room service; informal.
SEASONS: Open all year, but more or less monopolized by state senators in the first three months of the year.

THE TIDES INN
Irvington, Virginia

Some inns treat you to hayrides or sleigh rides, but the Tides Inn welcomes you with cruises aboard its yachts—the "whiskey run" at sunset, or a dinner cruise by moonlight, from Carter's Creek into the Rappahannock River and then out to the Chesapeake Bay, on the Stephens family's private yachts—which range from forty-six feet to the stately hundred-footer, "Miss Ann."

Everywhere you turn here, you see water. The creek surrounds the inn on three sides; lounges, terraces, dining rooms and most of the guest rooms look out over water; lunch is served in a gazebo above the water; there's a seaside heated pool, and a tiny beach with swivel-and-tilt wicker sunchairs; the inn's second "parking lot" is a marina where waterborne guests tie up for the summer.

The Tides Inn sits on a low hill overlooking the creek, surrounded by twenty-five acres of lawns, Virginia pine and crepe myrtle, with the Virginia scents of magnolia and azalea competing with the salty tang of the water. (They also have piped music humming from the trees, which may be therapeutic for the trees but doesn't do much to enhance the quiet atmosphere.)

The setting, in other words, is superb; and the hotel itself is not far behind. A bit stuffy maybe (you can't set foot in the lobby after six without a tie), but its other blessings more than make up for that: the ninety rooms range from elegant and simple (in the four-story lodge) to elegant and luxurious (the semi-suites in Lancaster House and Windsor House); and there's plenty of pleasant activity to keep you going until it's time for the whiskey run.

By gondola to the golf course

You can rent pedalos and sailboats, play tennis for free; and if you want to play golf, you walk down to the water, board the

"Gondola" and cross the creek to The Tides Golf Lodge (see next listing). Evenings you can dance in the Chesapeake Club (a bottle club open to guests, because the inn doesn't have, and doesn't want, a liquor license). Most of the staff, like Curtis Sampson, has been with the inn since it opened twenty-five years ago, and they all perform with the friendly, dignified service you expect in Virginia. Even in the Northern Neck of Virginia. Irvington is on that patch between the Rappahannock and the Potomac, a relatively uncrowded but historic corner of the state: Route 3, which takes you to the inn, is known in these parts as Historyland Highway because George Washington, Robert E. Lee and President Monroe were born nearby, just in case you get bored swiveling and tilting on the beach.

NAME: The Tides Inn

INNKEEPER: Robert L. Stephens (president and manager), Curtis Sampson (resident manager)

ADDRESS: Irvington, Va. 22480

TELEPHONE: 804-438-2611

DIRECTIONS: By car from the north, take U.S. 301 south from Baltimore to Va. 3 (a few miles after you cross the Potomac) and follow it east for about an hour to Irvington; from Richmond, take Interstate 64 and Va. 33 to West Point and Saluda, then turn right to the Rappahannock River Bridge and The Tides Inn.

RATES: AP—$50 to $66 for rooms, $68 and $70 for semi-suites, $100 and $110 for suites; from November 26 through January 2, $20 less.

MEALS: Breakfast (to 9:30 a.m.), lunch, dinner (to 10 p.m.); room service; jacket and tie in the evening.

SEASONS: Open all year, except from January 2 through March 12 (or thereabouts).

THE TIDES GOLF LODGE
Irvington, Virginia

Toss the word golf into the creek and you're left with a secluded location, up a creek, miles from anywhere, on a peninsula surrounded on three sides with water and on the fourth with a golf course; a modern two-story lodge with edge-grained fir siding hemmed in by mountain laurel and wild flowers, where you can breakfast on a private balcony and watch the morning mists rise and the early birds swooping for the early fish. Even if you never set foot on the first tee (and it's a shame if you don't because the green fees are only $4.50), you can fill your days with sailing and outboard boating, tennis, putting, swimming in a heated pool, fishing, lounging in hammocks strung out among the trees, or cruising in the lodge's sixty-five-foot yacht.

The Tides Golf Lodge is kid brother (it was opened in 1969) to The Tides Inn, above; it's owned by the same family and shares most of the other's facilities, but it's operated as a separate entity and has a personality all its own—amiable, relaxed and less formal than the inn. The lodge's forty rooms all have balconies with views of the water, color TV, room phones, and so much tartan decor that going to bed here is almost like cuddling under a kilt.

The tartan is in honor of Sir Guy Campbell, the revered golf course architect from St. Andrews, who helped design the lodge's links; he also has a tartan-splashed lounge named in his honor, where you can drink a toast to his memory before dinner. The pubby dining room features local delicacies—Rappahannock soft shell crabs, Chesapeake Bay shad roe or roast Urbanna duckling. If you're ever up the creek, this is as nice a way as any to go.

NAME: The Tides Golf Lodge
INNKEEPER: E. Stephens
ADDRESS: Irvington, Va. 22480

TELEPHONE: 804-438-2233

DIRECTIONS: Same as for The Tides Inn, but branch off a few miles farther west from Va. 3.

RATES: MAP—$48 to $52 from March 12 through November 26, $42 to $46 remainder of the year (when green fees are included in the rate).

MEALS: Breakfast (to 10 a.m.), lunch, dinner (to 9 p.m.); room service (breakfast only); jacket with or without tie in the evening.

SEASONS: Open all year; *spring* is the busiest season, summer is reasonably quiet; occasional small groups (meetings are held ' in a room away from the regular lodge fun and games, and no name tags are allowed in the lodge).

THE SHENANDOAH VALLEY – UP HILL AND DOWN DALE

We'll gently walk, and sweetly talk,
Till the silent moon shine clearly . . .
BURNS

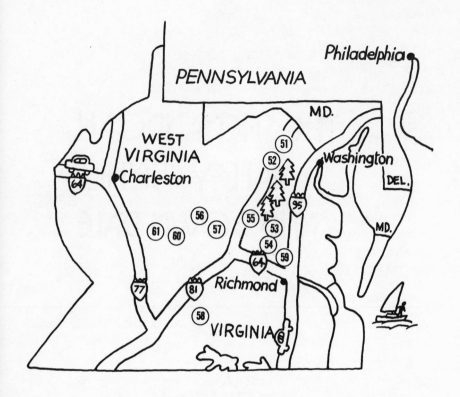

51. Wayside Inn

52. Narrow Passage Inn

53. Skyland Lodge

54. Big Meadows Lodge

55. Sky Chalet

56. The Homestead

57. Valley View Inn

58. Peaks of Otter Lodge

59. Boar's Head Inn

60. The Greenbrier

61. Pipestem Resort

WAYSIDE INN
Middletown, Virginia

The Wayside Inn has known the sighs of lovers for 175 years but it still greets you with the charm and low-ceiling, lopsided elegance of those early days when Virginia dandies rode up in their coaches with sweet Southern belles. The inn has just been through a ten-year refurbishing, courtesy of Leo Bernstein, a D.C. banker and avid collector of Americana, who drove past the inn one day, liked what he saw and bought it within an hour. (If that isn't avid collecting, what is?) Since then he has decked it out with close to a million dollars' worth of Americana and, here and there, Britannica; the two lounges alone are almost museums —with George Washington looking down from above the fireplace on a Beau Brummel commode, an early Blickensdorfer portable typewriter, an English coin sorter, a petit-point chair and leather scroll footrest. Leo Bernstein's great hero is George Washington, and you can't go anywhere in the Wayside without G.W.'s beady eyes looking down on you from an engraving, painting or statuette—sometimes alone, sometimes with Martha.

You'll find them upstairs in the guest rooms, too. Especially in room #16, a big green room with a pair of canopied double beds, a tallboy, chest of drawers, and half a dozen prints of G.W. Room #1 has a canopied double bed, fireplace, braided rug, circular commode, and a few steps leading down to a real bathroom (all of the inn's rooms have private bathrooms and air conditioning, but no TV); room #10 is known, *sotto voce,* as the Red Velvet Whorehouse—a flamboyant nest with red velvet bedspreads and drapes, twin mahogany beds with gilt embellishments, and a hefty curlicued dresser; since the room is at the rear,

it's quieter than its decor. All fourteen rooms are different, and your preference will probably depend on your taste in antiques.

You can't escape Washingtons even in the kitchen, where the cooking is in the hands of the fourth and fifth generations of a family called Washington—Irene and Herman, and daughter, Pat. They bake their own sweet rolls and Shenandoah apple pie, cook a special peanut soup and their own version of Virginia country ham with red-eye gravy. Prices are in the $5 region for main dishes and the house wine is only fifty cents a glass, which makes the inn a popular spot for people to visit for a meal, and the Wayside has had to expand to six dining rooms. Don't get caught up in the bustle. Grab a couple of the seven white rockers out on the veranda and listen to the birds in the bushes until the throngs have gobbled their ham and trotted off to the theater.

Summer theater, winter film festival

A few yards down Main Street you come to the 259-seat, air-conditioned Wayside Theater (another Bernstein project) where you can see professional productions of plays, musicals and revues in summer (the '73 repertory included *Butterflies Are Free* and *The Miser*); in winter, the theater hosts festivals of historic and unusual movies. Beyond Main Street, all the pastoral prettiness of the Shenandoah Valley is at your pleasure. Try some of the quiet back roads that wind up into the Shenandoah Mountains—they haven't changed much since the days of Virginian dandies and Southern belles.

NAME: Wayside Inn
INNKEEPER: Larry Jones
ADDRESS: Route 11, Middletown, Va. 22645
TELEPHONE: 703-869-1797
DIRECTIONS: Take Interstate 81 to Exit 77, drive west a mile to U.S. 11, then go left into Middletown's Main Street.
RATES: EP—$16 to $25, year round.
MEALS: Breakfast (to 10 a.m.), lunch, afternoon tea, dinner (to 9 p.m.); no room service; informal.
SEASONS: Open all year; busiest during the Apple Blossom Festival in spring, and in July, August and October.

NARROW PASSAGE INN
Woodstock, Virginia

The narrow passage in this case is a limestone ledge between two streams; Indians used to ambush settlers here, and during the Valley Campaign Stonewall Jackson set up camp here on several occasions. The limestone ledge is now U.S. 11, and one side is this limestone lodge, built in 1927. It's basically a restaurant, with a big fireplace at one end, a beamed ceiling with medieval designs overhead, and unusual antiques all around. Part of the limestone wall has been replaced with floor-to-ceiling windows so that you can admire the view while you're dining—a bend in the Shenandoah River, a tree-shaded farm, an old swinging

bridge, and meadows spreading across the valley to the Massa-
nutten Mountains. There are only four guest rooms in the inn;
try to get one of the two at the rear—not so much for the view as
to escape the traffic. The Narrow Passage is owned by the Wayside Inn in Middletown (see above) and the menus are similar
—but a meal at the Narrow Passage costs a dollar or two less.

NAME: Narrow Passage Inn
INNKEEPER: Joseph Renggli
ADDRESS: Route 11, Woodstock, Va. 22664
TELEPHONE: 703-459-4770
DIRECTIONS: Woodstock is a mile east of exit 72 on Interstate
81, and the inn is 2 miles south of the town on U.S. 11.
RATES: EP—$14 to $16.
MEALS: Breakfast, lunch, dinner; jacket and tie in the evening.
SEASONS: Open all year, busiest in July, August and October.

SKYLAND LODGE
Shenandoah National Park

Chase a white-tailed deer through the hickory and pignut. Take
a deep breath and sing "Oh Shenandoah, I long to hear you"
into the wind. Scramble over the rocks for a picnic beside a
waterfall. Lie on the grass and tickle each other's ears with
columbine, while you read Spenser "Bring hither the Pink and
purple Columbine/With Gillyflowers/Bring Coronation and
Sops in wine/Worn of Paramours./Strew me the ground with
Daffadowndillies . . ." All around you are 300 square miles
of wildlife preserve, rustling with deer, black bear, woodchuck
and gray fox; meadowlarks and indigo buntings skim through
the staghorn sumac and chokecherry; and in spring, lousewort,
bebb's zizzia and columbine paint the meadows.
    The location is close to beatific—the highest point on the Sky-

line Drive, that marvelous ambling highway that snakes along the spine of the Blue Ridge Mountains. Skyland's 160 rooms are spread out among lodges and cottages with names like Bushytop, Raven's Nest, Hemlock and Wildwood, scattered among the pines and hemlocks, and all on different levels so that every room seems to have a view across the shimmying Shenandoah. The rooms are so-so, but at least they're piney and rustic; they all have private bathrooms, but no room phones. And no TV, so you'll just have to look at the stars.

BIG MEADOWS LODGE
Shenandoah National Park

A ninety-two room, stone-and-timber brother of Skyland Lodge, also operated by the Virginia Sky-Line Company. Like Skyland, its main attraction is its peaceful, nature-loving location on top of the Blue Ridge Mountains, screened from the traffic by pine and hemlock and lawns. Big Meadows is nine miles south of Skyland; otherwise, all the information below applies to both.

NAME: Skyland Lodge, Big Meadows Lodge
ADDRESS: P.O. Box 191, Luray, Va. 22835
TELEPHONE: 703-599-2211
DIRECTIONS: Don't let the address fool you—they aren't in Luray itself (a bit like saying Central Park is at Coney Island), but up on the Skyline Drive, 10 miles south of the Thornton Gap Entrance, which is intersected by U.S. 211.
RATES: EP—$15 to $20.
MEALS: Breakfast (to 10 a.m.), lunch, dinner (to 8:30 p.m.); no room service; informal.
SEASONS: Early April through October or early November; avoid weekends, holidays and fall foliage weeks, and make a res-

ervation well in advance and *always* before you go up onto the Highway, because with a 35 m.p.h. speed limit it takes a long time to get back down.

SKY CHALET
Mt. Jackson, Virginia

"Haven't served a loaf of bread from a store in twenty-five years" claims Mrs. Wright, who runs this friendly place practically single-handed. You get home cooking up here, roast beef and things, and home-baked desserts, served in a rustic dining room with big circular windows looking out over great expanses of virgin Virginia.

The chalet is on a ridge, with undisturbed views of the Shenandoah Mountains to the west and the Blue Ridge Mountains to the east. The small pool, the verandas, the binoculars and the rockers face the Shenandoahs; you have to stand up to see the Blue Ridge Mountains. There are no sounds up here but the sounds of nature, no lights at night except the stars. No television, no telephones. You can play ping-pong or pool, or borrow a book from the library. You can drive back down to the main road and do a spot of sightseeing or picnicking along the Shenandoah Valley. Or you can just lounge in hammocks among the trees, or make friends with the birds that flutter onto the porches.

There are only six rooms in the lodge itself, with another nine in a cottage farther along the garden. Take the lodge rooms; they all have private bath, homey furniture, and a couple of them (#1 and #2) are downstairs on the pool level with separate entrances to the garden.

Sky Chalet has no liquor license, but you can bring your own; technically, you're supposed to drink only in your own room because of the antiquated liquor laws of holy-rolling Virginia. A shame. Because Sky Chalet's porch might almost have been designed for a leisurely pre-dinner drink as the sun goes down over the Shenandoahs and Mrs. Wright prepares to serve her home-baked bread for the umpteenth time in twenty-five years.

NAME: Sky Chalet
INNKEEPER: Mrs. Joseph A. Wright
ADDRESS: Star Rte., Mt. Jackson, Va. 22842
TELEPHONE: 703-477-2236
DIRECTIONS: It's actually about 12 miles from Mt. Jackson, west on Va. 263, and about 10 miles west of exits 68 and 69 on Interstate 81.
RATES: AP—$24 to $34.
MEALS: Breakfast (to 9 a.m.), lunch, dinner (6 to 6:30 p.m.); no room service; informal.
SEASONS: Open all year; busiest July, August and October, and on weekends during the ski season.

THE HOMESTEAD
Hot Springs, Virginia

Back in the unhurried, unruffled days before the Civil War, Virginian high society whiled away its summers on a grand tour of the mineral springs in the Allegheny Mountains—from Warm in the north, southward to Hot to Sweet to White. A week here, a week there. Nowadays they head straight for Hot Springs and the magnificent Homestead.

The Homestead sweeps you up into a mountain world where 17,000 acres of forests and streams and meadows blot out the humdrum and the mediocre. You can go riding here day after day, mile after mile, and never trample the same soil twice; you can take leisurely strolls through the gardens, or rugged hikes that will leave you massaging thighs for therapeutic rather

than aphrodisiac reasons; you can relax in mineral baths or saunas, take buckboard rides, play a set or two of tennis on a dozen courts, or a round of golf on three beautiful pine-lined courses; you can float in an outdoor or an indoor pool—and how many mountain resorts treat you to a sandy beach for sunning yourselves?

Chamber music and afternoon tea

The Homestead is one of America's great classic resorts, built on a scale you don't see too often these days—a towering chateau of 615 rooms that looms over the forest and rooftops of Hot Springs. When you enter The Homestead, you find yourselves in the Great Hall—a nave of sixteen pillars and fourteen chandeliers, great log-burning fireplaces, a solarium and a string orchestra playing chamber music during afternoon tea. That's just the Great Hall—you've still to visit the lobbies and lounges and shopping arcade. Everything at The Homestead is on the grand scale, and if you start to wonder why a hotel like this manages to survive in this day and age, wander down to the lower level of the brand-new $8-million South Wing where you'll see suites of meeting rooms to house the conventions that keep those 615 rooms busy throughout the year. The Homestead is now one of the nation's classic convention hotels—a description which should instantly eliminate it from this guide; but the truth is that even with half a dozen conventions and seminars in the house, there's no overcrowding, and no hint of strained service.

The Homestead was geared to mollycoddle the mollycoddled, and the emphasis is still on service that takes everything in its well-ordered stride even if they no longer have waiters who dance with stacked trays on their heads. In return, it expects a little class from its guests, and the hotel's brochure reminds you that "gentlemen must always wear coats when dining"; and even with "young ladies can wear contemporary bathing suits" this is clearly no place for people who like to spend their vacations lounging around in stained jeans. You come to The Homestead to show off a beautiful woman in beautiful gowns, to make an entrance in the dining room, to command attentive service from maitre d', head waiter, waiter, wine steward and busboy.

On the other hand, if you don't want to go through the fuss of dressing up every night, slip into a robe and order up room service. The Homestead has the right kind of rooms for casual, bathrobe evenings, with soothing pastel colors and comfortable furniture. The most coveted rooms have parlors and big, screened porches high above the gardens; the quietest rooms are in the eleven white clapboard cottages in the garden; and the plushest rooms are the penthouse duplexes in the new South Wing, with spiral stairs leading to bedroom balconies. Up in that cozy love nest you're light miles from the conventions and the fol-de-rol.

NAME: The Homestead
INNKEEPER: Thomas J. Lennon (president), William E. Worsham (general manager)
ADDRESS: Hot Springs, Va. 24445

TELEPHONE: 703-839-5500

DIRECTIONS: On U.S. 220, 80 miles north of Roanoke, 15 miles north of Interstate 64; by air, to Ingalls Field 17 miles away (daily scheduled taxi flights); or by Chessie System to Covington, where you'll be met by the hotel limousine.

RATES: AP—$83 to $93 for rooms, $55 to $70 for parlors, $93 for room with balcony in the new South Wing, $110 for a duplex suite in the new South Wing, $188 for a cottage from April 1 through November 4; lower rates rest of year.

MEALS: Breakfast (to 10 a.m.), coffee shop, lunch (indoor, outdoor), afternoon tea, dinner (to 1 a.m.); room service; men are expected to wear jackets at all meals, jacket and tie at dinner (and a lot of guests wear black tie on weekends).

SEASONS: Open all year; busiest in April, May, June, September and October; conventions most of the year; in winter, you can ski, skate or go on sleigh rides.

VALLEY VIEW INN
Hot Springs, Virginia

"It's amazing how many of our guests just sit around and watch the cows and horses," muses innkeeper Scheiber, a young exiled Austrian with a Carolinian wife. "Or else they go for walks through the forest—there's a seven-mile path up there, a bit overgrown but natural."

If Hot Springs sounds like a nice place to visit, but The Homestead sounds too expensive or too formal, consider the simpler pleasures of Valley View Inn. It's only three miles up the road from The Homestead, on top of a knoll, surrounded by white picket fences. Valley View is not so much an inn as a farmyard, with shingle cottages, a tumbledown barn, and a big red villa. The guest rooms are simple and unpretentious, comomas Jefferson, for that

ennis courts, swimming
 Sports Club with more
orm tennis courts and a
ub for $5 a day.
leasant enough, relaxing
 exploring the attractions
xquisite and fascinating
e University of Virginia.
d weekends and holidays.
e Old Mill Room at the
ekends, and you have to
you're a guest, despite the
om says *No Reservations*
 Colonial britches, "that's
 lists items like escargots
it when the chef sticks to
e does well. But remember

ville, Va. 22901

ypass, 2 miles beyond the
y air, scheduled service, to

s, $40 and $44 for suites.
nch, dinner (to 9:30 p.m.);
nner.
July, August, October; check
 and business conferences."

fortable, a bit frayed here and there, and not too private; but they're being refurbished by Stefan Scheiber ("I'm cook, butcher, painter and plumber around here") with Colonial-style furnishings, sort of, and a few feminine touches supplied by Nancy Scheiber, a painter. Nine of the rooms have private baths, and the best bets are probably #1 and #3, both in the main villa, and both with screened porches.

The inn's dining room is a pleasant rustic porch, with more valley views, a mixed Continental/American menu, and prices ranging from $2.95 to $5.95. Some evenings the menu features complete Austrian dinners prepared by the plumber/painter/ butcher/cook, and during the busiest weeks and weekends you can grab a snack in the folksy, homemade Tiroler Keller downstairs (usually accompanied by live or jukebox music). If you want to do more than look at the cows and the horses, you can lounge around the pool and work up a tan; or drive down to the Homestead and use their tennis courts and riding stables, or over to Warm Springs to wallow in a mineral bath.

NAME: Valley View Inn
INNKEEPER: Stefan and Nancy Scheiber
ADDRESS: Hot Springs, Va. 24445
TELEPHONE: 703-839-2725
DIRECTIONS: Three miles north of The Homestead on U.S. 220.
RATES: EP—from $14 to $18 for rooms, $21 for cottages.
MEALS: Breakfast (to 9:30 a.m.), lunch, dinner (to 9 p.m.); no room service; wine and beer only; informal.
SEASONS: Open all year—busiest July, August, October, and weekends during the ski season.

PEAKS OF OTTER LODGE
near Bedford, Virginia

Here's another dreamy location—by the edge of
across from Sharp Top, Flat Top and Harkening
Shenandoah National Park. In spring the meadows
with merrybells, trilliums and columbine; in fall
weed, goldenrod and bottled gentian. You can follo
mile of hug-and-cuddle trails through sweet birch, b
pignut, pines and oaks; or find a quiet spot to w
meadowlark, chickadee or white-breasted nuthatch.
ning, elk and white-tailed deer sometimes wander d
lake for a sundowner. This is strictly a place for
nature and love. There's no swimming pool, no tennis
unspoiled, unhurried nature.

And the Virginia Peaks of Otter Company has t
trouble to erect a rustic lodge that harmonizes with the s
ings—rough-hewn pine walls, slate-topped dressers an
cane-backed chairs, acres of glass for admiring the viev
of lawn for lounging by the lake, and all the rooms with b
or patios facing the lake. The main lodge has an open
and a glass-enclosed lounge facing the lake, a downsta
and a raftered dining room with tables for twosomes
window. You can dawdle over Allegheny Mountain tr
Virginia country ham, while you watch the sun set ove
Top and the moon slip past Sharp Top. (Meals here
bargain, by the way—from $2.75 to $6.50.)

Get to bed early, but leave the balcony door open and
can be awakened by the meadowlarks and chickadees.

NAME: Peaks of Otter Lodge
INNKEEPER: Carl E. Vause, Jr.
ADDRESS: P.O. Box 489, Bedford, Va. 24523
TELEPHONE: 703-586-1081 (winter: 703-586-0122)
DIRECTIONS: On the Blue Ridge Parkway at the junction w

well than William Shakespeare. Or The
matter.

Besides the nine-hole golf course,
pool and sauna, there's a Boar's Head
tennis courts (including indoor), platf
squash court. Inn guests can join the c

On the whole, the Boar's Head is a
inn, but it is less a resort than a base fo
of this part of Virginia—Jefferson's
Monticello, his elegant campus for th

These are places to savor, so avoic
And that advice applies equally to th
Boar's Head. It gets crowded on we
make a reservation for dinner even if
fact that the brochure in your bedro
("Oh, that," says the maitre d' in his
all wrong"). The restaurant's menu
a la Provincial, whatever that is, bu
tavern-like dishes such as roast beef,
to make a reservation.

NAME: Boar's Head Inn
INNKEEPER: David Plymire
ADDRESS: Ednam Forest, Charlottes
TELEPHONE: 804-296-2181
DIRECTIONS: Follow the U.S. 50 b
intersection with U.S. 29; or b
Charlottesville.
RATES: EP—$24 and $26 for room
MEALS: Breakfast (to 11 a.m.), lu
room service; jacket and tie at di
SEASONS: Open all year; busiest in
for "select, top-level seminars

THE GREENBRIER
White Sulphur Springs, West Virginia

There's a touch of *Last Year at Marienbad* about The Greenbrier: a string trio plays for afternoon tea, chandeliered corridors lead you to more chandeliered corridors, couples stroll arm in arm across acres of lawns. Occasionally, someone sips a glass of the mineral water from the sulphur spring, and some of the old-timers may be reminiscing about the day the Prince of Wales sat in with the orchestra during a gala ball.

More likely the guests are trying to recall names and faces not from last year's spa, but from last year at the insurance executives' conference, or the convention of ad biggies; because The Greenbrier is another classic resort, like The Homestead, that now keeps its aristocratic head above water by filling most of its rooms with conventioneers. They haven't taken over completely, because fortunately a lot of people still recognize that The Greenbrier is a great spot to vacation.

Champagne and watermelon

The Greenbrier owes its fame and fortune to a spring with water that tastes and smells something like a hard-boiled egg that's been lying in the bottom of a rucksack for a week. The Indians knew of its curative powers; then a Mrs. John Anderson came along in 1778 and from that point on White Sulphur Springs became one of America's great spas. Robert E. Lee spent a lot of time here, riding Traveler around the estate and admiring the gaggles of South'n belles and the budding beaux who regaled them with champagne and watermelon. They've been followed through the years and social upheavals by tycoons, dukes, lords, princes, shahs, sheiks—and now conventioneers. The Greenbrier is one of the largest resort hotels in the world, and there are a lot of well-heeled and well-traveled types who'll tell you it's one of the best. Marienbad would probably have to look a long way back in its memory book to match the present opulence of The Greenbrier.

Its palatial facade gleams in the clear mountain air, white and massive against the dense green of the pine-clad mountains all around. Across the park-like garden, the hilltop Presidents' Cottage reminds you that no fewer than nineteen U.S. Presidents have visited White Sulphur Springs, and the rows of piazza-fronted cottages running from either side take you back to the days of Robert E. Lee. (One of the rows actually houses an artists' colony, where you can buy hand-woven tweeds or a batik scarf with your own name in an original design.)

The Chesapeake & Ohio Railroad, which built it, didn't stint on The Greenbrier: the hotel has 650 rooms, and no two are alike; the ashtrays at the entrance are antique Chinese rice bowls (and every time they're cleaned out the porter imprints the sand with The Greenbrier's special script-type logo); it has its own fire department, and every room is linked directly with a warning control panel in the firehouse; forty-nine gardeners and groundsmen tend the lawns and the fifty-four fairways; thirty-three chefs whip up everything from scrambled eggs to Tête de Veau Tortue; the golf pro is a legend, and the swimming coach has more gold medals than Mark Spitz.

Lover's Leap

Don't let all this abundance turn you off. The Greenbrier is *so* big you can easily escape to quiet corners. Take a walk, for example: you have a choice of thirteen trails, from a quarter mile to ten miles (one of them ominously named Lover's Leap). You're not going to find too many conventioneers up there; in fact, you're not going to find too many anythings up there except shagbark hickory, big tooth aspen, Virginia pine and staghorn sumac. If you decide to go riding on some of the hotel's 200 miles of private trails, you don't even have to go to the stables to pick up your mounts; the groom will deliver them "at the appointed hour" in the riding circle by the north entrance.

When you get back from your ride, stop off in the clubhouse terrace overlooking the golf courses and sample the sumptuous buffet lunch. You have something like ninety dishes to nibble from.

You can pamper yourself silly in a place like this, and you can leave feeling like a million. Of course, it helps if you *arrive* with a million. Elegance doesn't come cheaply these days.

NAME: The Greenbrier

INNKEEPER: E. Truman Wright (vice president), Wesler T. Keenan (general manager)

ADDRESS: White Sulphur Springs, W. Va. 24986

TELEPHONE: 304-536-1110

DIRECTIONS: By car, take Interstate 64 to the White Sulphur Springs exits, then U.S. 60 ½ mile west of town; by train, daily Amtrak service practically to the doorstep; by air, daily scheduled flights or charter to Greenbrier Airport.

RATES: AP—March 31 through November 15, $85 to $95 for rooms, $105 to $170 for suites; November 16 through March 30, $70 for rooms, $90 to $145 for suites; a few cottages are also available (rates on request); maids' and chauffeurs' quarters, $12.

MEALS: Breakfast (to 10 a.m.), lunch (dining room or magnificent buffet on clubhouse terrace), afternoon tea, dinner (to 8:45 p.m.), supper (to 1:45 a.m.); room service (to 1:45 a.m.); jacket and tie at dinner (black tie optional).

SEASONS: Open all year; busiest in summer and fall; conventions all year, but generally fewer in winter (when there are plenty of indoor activities, including a heated pool, to keep you amused).

PIPESTEM RESORT
Hinton, West Virginia

This is the poor man's Greenbrier. However, if you're looking for a room with a view, you'll see more trees and more mountains from the lodge at Pipestem than you could see if you climbed the flagpole at Greenbrier. Pipestem is a state park high in the Appalachians. It gets its name from *spiraea alba,* a hollow-stemmed plant that the Indians used for making peace pipes. The hills around here are covered with this *spiraea alba,* as well as forsythia and dogwood and blooming redbud, and pines and firs.

The main lodge is an overpowering, seven-story timber-and-stone lodge perched on the edge of the hill. Its rooms are motelly, but who cares with that magnificent view out there beyond your balcony. All 113 rooms in the lodge have private bathrooms, room telephones, television and individually controlled heating. There are also cottages snuggled among the trees, but even with fireplaces and porches they're more suitable for families than lovers.

Canyon-bottom lodge

The most unusual feature of Pipestem is Mountain Creek Lodge. This is a two-story complex of thirty guest rooms 1,000 feet down in Bluestone Canyon, at the edge of a winding mountain stream. The only way you can get down to the pleasant, comfortable motel-type rooms is by a 3,600-foot aerial tramway (it's free, and runs more or less at your convenience). There's also a cafe/restaurant down there, so you have no reason to surface.

All the facilities of the lodge take advantage of the superb view—even the indoor swimming pool has windows two floors high, so you can frolic around in the pool even in winter and enjoy the layers of mountains covered with snow-like mounds of whipped cream. As a guest of the resort you have access to the state park's sporting facilities—miles of walking and riding trails, a nine-hole and an eighteen-hole golf course (green fee $5), tennis courts, archery ranges and an outdoor theatre. But nothing they perform there can be as dramatic as that view.

NAME: Pipestem Resort

INNKEEPER: Philip Garett

ADDRESS: Pipestem, W. Va. 25979

TELEPHONE: 304-466-1800

DIRECTIONS: Complicated. It's on W. Va. 20, about 16 miles from Hinton or Princeton (the southern end of the West Virginia Turnpike); or about 50 miles southwest of White Sulphur Springs and Interstate 64, along a very slow winding country road where the school bus stops at every shack; by air to Bluefield.

RATES: EP—Main Lodge $21 to $26 in winter, $24 to $28 in summer; Mountain Creek $22 in summer (closed in winter); cottages by the week, $145 to $210 in winter, $195 to $275 in summer.

MEALS: Breakfast (to 11 a.m.), lunch, dinner (to 10 p.m.); no room service; informal.

SEASONS: Open all year, busiest in summer and fall; check for conventions throughout the year.

FROM
THE CAROLINAS
TO THE KEYS

It is the hour when from the boughs
  The nightingale's high note is heard;
It is the hour when lovers' vows
  Seem sweet in every whisper'd word . . .
                                        BYRON

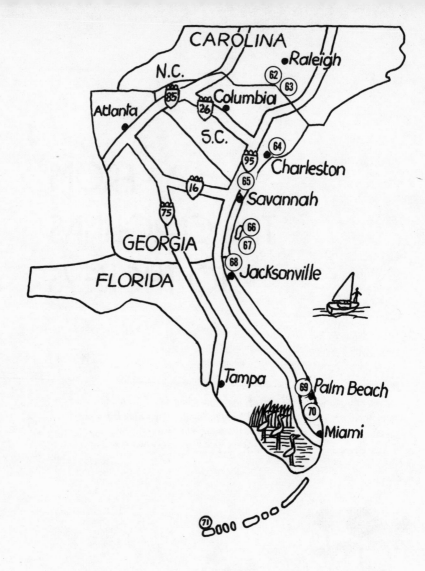

62. Holly Inn

63. The Carolina Hotel

64. Mills Hyatt House

65. Hilton Head Inn

66. The Cloister

67. King & Prince Hotel

68. Greyfield

69. The Breakers

70. Boca Raton Hotel and Club

71. Pier House

HOLLY INN
Pinehurst, North Carolina

There's this little white inn in a sleepy village where azaleas and peach blossoms grow among the longleaf pines; then there's this gung-ho resort development company that's just bought up the village and the inn from a family that bought the place a hundred years ago for a dollar an acre. For now, it's a stand-off, and you'll just have to assume that the promised new shopping mall and town center will indeed be an improvement, and go there anyhow because Pinehurst is a delightful piney-fresh place. Its white clapboard, three-story inn is half-hidden behind a three-story holly tree, surrounded by leafy streets filled with boutiques, antique shops and restaurants. The eighty bed-chambers are furnished with Victorian trappings that might have been put there when the inn was opened seventy-five years ago, and some of them have those luxurious big bathtubs you could almost have a picnic in. But maybe, instead of building a shopping center, the new owners could be persuaded to buy a few pots of paint to spruce up the corridors.

There's a secluded kidney-shaped swimming pool at the rear, not much larger than the bathtubs, but your best bet here is to grab a tandem and go cycling off along the pine-lined lanes. The countryside is glorious.

NAME: Holly Inn
INNKEEPER: Chris Schweitzer
ADDRESS: Village Green Road, Pinehurst, N.C. 28374
TELEPHONE: 919-295-6161
DIRECTIONS: By car, it's just a few miles west of U.S. 1 and 1 mile west of N.C. 15/501; by air, to Pinehurst Southern Pines Airport; by train, to Hamlet.

145

RATES: MAP—$44 to $48 from October 1 to November 30, $48 to $52 from March 1 to May 31, $40 to $44 the remainder of the year.

MEALS: Breakfast (to 9:30 a.m.), snack bar for lunch, dinner (to 9 p.m.); room service; jacket and tie in the evening.

SEASONS: Open all year, but fall and spring are the most popular seasons (winters, however, are relatively mild—mild enough for tandem rides).

THE CAROLINA HOTEL
Pinehurst, North Carolina

Any hotel with *five* golf courses on its doorstep can't be all bad. But apparently, in this case, it wasn't all good either, because the old faithfuls stopped rolling up in their wheel-chairs and there weren't enough young people rushing to take their places. So, the owners sold out to the Diamondhead Corporation, who put something like $5 million into rejuvenating the 300 guest rooms—which means flooding the place in deep pile carpeting, hanging new drapes, installing air conditioning and color TV, and so on. It's now closer in spirit to Miami than the stately Carolinas, but there's no denying it's a comfortable, roomy, well-equipped hotel, and if you're looking for sporting facilities, few hotels anywhere are geared up like this one: besides the five golf courses mentioned above, Pinehurst also has a Saddle Club, a Gun Club (including two lighted skeet fields), a Tennis Club (eight courts) an olympic pool (with three life*girls*), sauna and gymnasium. And you play all year.

And as if that weren't enough, the new management plans an ice skating pavilion, a new swimming and racquet club, a new health spa, bowling alleys, and a whole new hotel and bungalows on the fairways. Maybe they'd be better off trying to straighten out the haphazard service and lukewarm food in the dining room first. Still, even with all the new plans, there are lots of quiet spots hidden away on the hotel's 13,000 acres of pine and sycamore, among the camellias and azaleas and wisteria and magnolias.

NAME: The Carolina Hotel
INNKEEPER: Bill Hall
ADDRESS: Pinehurst, N.C. 28734
TELEPHONE: 919-295-6811
DIRECTIONS: Same as for Holly Inn, page 145.
RATES: MAP—$50 to $66, from February 15 through May, lower remainder of the year; EP also available.
MEALS: Breakfast (any time), lunch, dinner (to 10 p.m.); room service; jacket and tie in the evening.
SEASONS: Opened all year round for the first time in 1972/3; busiest in summer, but watch out at other times for conventions and golf tournaments.

MILLS HYATT HOUSE
Charleston, South Carolina

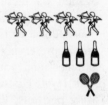

"Bathing rooms for gentlemen are fitted up in good style, convenient to the barber's pole . . ." wrote a local newspaper on the opening of Mills House in 1853; and it was probably such style and convenience that persuaded Robert E. Lee to establish his quarters there when he commanded the Charleston garrison. Now, 120 years and a $6-million facelift later, there are private bathing rooms for gentlemen *and* their ladies, fitted up in tiled and gleaming style, and hop-and-skip convenient to the canopied beds. What you have at the Mills Hyatt House, in fact, is something unique—one of the oldest hotels in the country looking like it was built yesterday. Which is more or less what happened.

A group of Charlestonians who were proud of their heritage (and few people are prouder of their heritage than Charlestonians) got together to buy the venerable but rather dilapidated

Mills House. They planned to spend half a million dollars re-painting it and installing private bathrooms. But the local fire department, proud of *its* heritage, said nix, it's a fire hazard. So the gallant group then decided to raze the innards and rebuild virtually from the ground up. The bill came to something like $6 million. But it was worth it—at least from the point of view of guests who only have to put up $30 or so for all this luxury.

Gaslight, garden patio

If Robert E. Lee came clattering down Meeting Street today he'd recognize the old place—wrought-iron balconies, gas lamps, the elegant tripartite doors, a mansion-like lobby with a sweeping double staircase, a garden patio with a three-tiered fountain. He'd feel at home in the interior but he might not recognize the individual decorations. One of the prime movers behind the ren-ovation was a successful Wall Street bachelor, Dick Jenrette, who fell in love with Charleston, bought one of the stately town-houses down by the waterfront, and got involved with his neigh-bors in preserving the aristocratic feel of the city. He's a lover of antiques, and you'll now find an impressive collection in the Mills Hyatt House—a Regency-styled zebrawood table, Chinese Ming portraits, French clocks, Empire candleholders, a black lacquered Dutch bombe chest and a pair of mirrors from a Viennese hunting lodge, all from the early 19th century. You even sign in on a marble-and-brass inkstand on a marble reg-istration desk.

The room you check into is furnished in a style that suggests rather than re-creates the 1800s—canopied (but squeaky) beds in fabrics that match the drapes, leather Queen Anne wing chairs, footstools, silver and copper table lamps, and such mod-ern touches as princess telephones, individual temperature con-trols and color TV. All 240 rooms are attractive, but the eight poolside rooms ($27) have French doors leading to little wrought-iron porches next to the pool. If you want the best in the house, ask for the Mary Boykin Chestnut Suite (if you can't remember that mouthful, it's the one on the seventh floor).

Mirrored alcoves, Chateau Lafite-Rothschild

There are many beautiful things in the Mills Hyatt House and one of the most beautiful is the Barbados Room, a forty-table dining room with small alcoves in mirrored arches just big enough for two, fresh flowers on the table, candles in brass candlesticks, pewter plates, ceiling fans, rattan chairs, and an overall atmosphere redolent of the Caribbean island that gives the room its name (another touch of heritage—many of the first settlers in Charleston came up from the islands). Even breakfast can be something special here: papaya lightly flavored with fresh lime juice, shrimp *pâté* and grits, waffles with creamed chicken, beaten biscuits, honey and muscadine jelly. The menu will introduce you to some of the dishes that distinguish Carolina cooking: conch stew, conch salad, oyster pie, Myrtlebank lump she crabmeat cocktail, Charleston she crab soup, langouste Calhoun (lobster, mushrooms, in cream and sherry sauce, served in the shell—$6.75), roast duckling Carolina (with peaches and baked apple), Huguenot tort and strawberries Mills House (marinated in Grand Marnier and served with ice cream, cognac and creme chantilly).

They've really created one of the country's prettiest restaurants here, which is hard luck on the staff because in a less beguiling setting the service probably wouldn't remind you of Joe's Corner Cafe. There is, for example, a surprisingly good wine list, from Beaujolais Village at $2 for the half bottle to a Chateau Lafite-Rothschild at $42; but if you have any respect for good wine you'll order the Beaujolais rather than watch a superb burgundy being whirled and twirled and juggled like a drum major's baton. Fortunately, the Beaujolais happens to be rather good for the price.

Candlelight, wine, music

Don't let the few failings in service put you off coming here. The Mills Hyatt House would be worth visiting even in Gary, Indiana. As it is, it happens to be in one of the loveliest cities in the South—one of those places that people always want to call "a grand old lady." There's still enough of the aristocratic Charleston left to let you savor the atmosphere of the antebellum South. The promenade down by the waterfront, lined by more stately townhouses than you could raise a top hat to, is one of the most handsome cityscapes in America—particularly when the mist comes rolling in from Fort Sumter like candy floss. The Mills Hyatt House will rent you a map and cassette recorder (for $4) if you want to take a walking tour past the homes, Catfish Row (the one that inspired *Porgy and Bess*), and the old Slave Market (farmers' market on weekdays, flea market on weekends). Around Easter you can take a tour through the interiors of half a dozen of these historic homes and gardens; some evenings also feature galas in the houses, with candlelight, wine, chamber music or concerts of spirituals. Dinner in the Barbados Room, chamber music in the Nathaniel Russell House, love in the Mary Boykin Chestnut Suite—that's not such a bad way to spend an evening anywhere.

NAME: Mills Hyatt House
INNKEEPER: Edward Rabin
ADDRESS: P.O. Box 1013, Charleston, S.C. 29402
TELEPHONE: 803-577-2400
DIRECTIONS: Follow the downtown signs to the junction of Meeting and Queen streets, near the waterfront; also by scheduled air and Amtrak service direct to Charleston.
RATES: EP—$24 to $30, suites $50 to $100, year round.
MEALS: Breakfast, lunch, dinner; room service (to 11 p.m.); jacket and tie in the evening.
SEASONS: Open all year; busiest months are March through May (when the gardens of Charleston are abloom and the homes are open for tours); small conventions throughout the year.

HILTON HEAD INN
Hilton Head Island, South Carolina

Not Conrad—William. William Hilton was the English sea captain who discovered the island. It used to be an authentic old plantation island, forty-five square miles of rice and cotton and loblolly pines. Now the southern tip of the island is a 5,200-acre resort community surrounded by four miles of white beach, criss-crossed by marsh and lagoons, and looking properly tropical under shady cypress, live oaks with mossy whiskers, palmetto and bamboo. The plantation has forty miles of cycling and riding trails lined with magnolia and dogwood, and the air, sometimes, is rich with the scent of jasmine and tea olive; the 572-acre forest preserve is home to a gallimaufry of winged creatures—hawks, eagles, quail, dove, egret and ibis. There are hammocks under the trees, environmental beach walks, no industry, no hot dog stands, no high-rises.

Sports galore

Jack Nicklaus designed one of the plantation's three courses, Arnie Palmer is designing a fourth, and the Harbor Town links was described by one magazine as "one of the ten greatest tests of golfing skill in the world." (Green fees—$7.70 to $10.) There are (count them) two dozen tennis courts (some with coin-operated floodlighting), and a pro shop headed up by champion Stan Smith. (Rates $3 a day—a bargain.) Sailboats and power boats rent for $15 a half day, horses for $5 a half hour, bicycles for $1 an hour.

All of which sounds wonderful, except for one snag: Hilton Head Inn is only one quarter of the Sea Pines Plantation resort community, and the 250 guests of the inn may be sharing all these facilities with the residents or guests of 400 condominium apartments and villas. The plantation may be a better place to live than visit, because not everyone wants to show a pass to armed guards every time they want to golf or sail; and sometimes the dining facilities can't cope with the diners (as one waiter put it, "when it gets crowded like this it takes an awful long time for everyone to get served").

Rooms, suites, villas, tree houses

The Hilton Head Inn was the first hotel on the island, built between 1959 and 1965 (and still being remodeled). It's a series of brick and weathered-cypress two-story villas facing the pool, the gardens or the beach. It has *two* fresh-water pools, a dining room, a bar that sells Heineken beer for $1.40 a bottle, boutiques, and rooms that are not very distinctive but decidedly comfortable. They all have wall-to-wall carpeting, television coffee machines, patios, individual heat and air-conditioning controls; the Cottage Suites have bedrooms, sitting rooms that convert into bedrooms, refrigerators and wet bars. The 400-odd condominium apartments or villas are also available for rentals; most of them have cypress or cedar siding and contemporary decor. The most romantic are the tiny circular tree houses tucked away, more or less, among the pines on Deer Island (which isn't an island but a peninsula); the most unusual are apartments in Harbour Town, a circular harbor on the Inland Waterway, inspired by Riviera fishing villages and Charleston mansions. All the villas and apartments were built in the past ten years, and all have air conditioning, kitchens, refrigerator-freezers, stoves and dishwashers, and most of them also have washers, dryers, disposals and so forth. Even Hilton can't beat that—Conrad, not William.

NAME: Hilton Head Inn
INNKEEPER: Tom Scott
ADDRESS: Hilton Head Island, S.C. 29928
TELEPHONE: 803-785-3333
DIRECTIONS: The inn is 31 miles from Savannah, 95 from Charleston. By car, take U.S. 17 to the intersections with Ga.

170 or U.S. 278, then go east and follow the Hilton Head signs (once you cross the toll bridge to the island you still have another 10 miles to go); by air, to Savannah or Charleston, then by regular air taxi to Hilton Head, or direct to Hilton Head by Air South from Atlanta; by Amtrak, to Savannah (limousine service from Savannah).

RATES: MAP or EP, but because of the dining room problem take the European Plan; a complex rate structure depending on building and view—December and January, $19 to $40; March and April, $29 to $50; February and May 1 through November 30, $27 to $48; apartment and villa rates (with maid service) run from $32 to $48 in fall, winter and spring, and from $42 to $58 in summer.

MEALS: Breakfast, lunch, coffee shops, dinner (to 10 p.m.); room service (inn only); jacket and tie in the evening, except in Harbour Town.

SEASONS: Open all year; crowded seasons are Easter, July and August (when there may be as many as 10,000 tourists on the island); you can play golf and tennis any time of the year, and spring usually comes in February; check for conventions in winter.

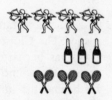

THE CLOISTER
Sea Island, Georgia

You should really arrive at The Cloister in a shiny surrey topped by a tasseled fringe and pulled by a pair of frisky white horses. This is the quintessential, plantation South, a dreamy otherworldly Eden where the Spanish moss dangling from the live oaks sets the pace for the whole island. The relaxed atmosphere begins at the main lodge, with its patios and plashing fountains, and wafts across manicured lawns to the five miles of superb private beach and 12,000 acres of unspoiled dunes, forests and marshes. If you're on your first visit you'll be welcomed

154

as someone they'd like to see back again; and the thousands who do come back year after year are welcomed with an enthusiasm that goes beyond fine old Southern hospitality. There's a very special ambiance about The Cloister, closer to a country club than a hotel, closer to a country home than a club; credit the old-fashioned ideas of the owners.

Keeping behind with the Joneses

A remarkable family with an unremarkable name, Jones, has owned The Cloister since 1928, and for much of that time the hotel has been run by Irving Harned, "one of the best resort men in the country," according to his peers. The Joneses are a bit behind the times: they plow all their profits back into the hotel. They've expanded slowly because they never build an additional room until they have the cash in the kitty, and until Irving Harned has had a chance to train extra staff and inculcate them with the special Cloister brand of service; and while other resorts point merrily to their new rooms and condominiums, the Joneses haven't cluttered their plantation with subdivisions. It may sound like a funny way to run a hotel these days, but what the Joneses and Harned have created is one of the three or four finest resorts along the Atlantic Coast. Maybe *the* finest.

In many ways The Cloister is a perfect resort: it's detached

from the everyday world, yet it's accessible; it basks in a delightful climate the year round; it's immaculate (the staff takes tre-
mendous pride in the place—like old family retainers rather
than employees); it's well-groomed outside (the hotel employs
fifteen gardeners and a hundred groundsmen, and even the
lamps that light the trees at night are disguised as lily pads);
because of its unspoiled acres you have a marvelous sense of
freedom, of quiet spaces where you can wander off and do your
own thing; it's restrained and soft-spoken, but far from stuffy
(when New Year's Eve in 1972 fell on a Sunday, a day on which
Georgia law forbids the sale of liquor, The Cloister celebrated
the Hong Kong New Year, twenty-four hours early, and then
topped off the shindig with a pantry raid in the wee dry hours
of Sunday morning).

Sports galore

Whatever you want The Cloister to be, it is. For some people,
it's folksy, friendly and relaxed; for others, it's a playground
where they can flit from sport to sport. A quick tally of the
facilities: fourteen tennis courts (you can play at any time of
the year, $4 an hour); bikes ($2.50 a half day); riding stables
and virtually unlimited trails along mossy lanes, even along miles
of beach; private pool with saunas; boat docking; fishing; pitch
and putt and croquet. Its thirty-six-hole Sea Island Golf Course
is on an antebellum plantation; the clubhouse was once a barn,
and the second floor that used to store corn and fodder is now
a plush ladies' dressing room; out on the fairways, you'll spot
turtles dozing on wooden bridges, and African grass-eating fish
in the ponds.

Dining in, out, on the beach

The Cloister mollycoddles you when it comes to dining. Where
would you like to have breakfast? In your room, in the dining
room, at the beach club—or a late breakfast in the Solarium

with its two huge cages of parakeets and finches. Lunch? Dining room, beach club, golf club—or a picnic in a quiet grove screened by Spanish moss. Afternoon tea? In the Solarium. For dinner you can choose the dining room and the serenading of a string orchestra (it's a huge Y-shaped dining room so the music won't overwhelm the meal), or you can join an oyster roast on the beach. Best of all, call room service and have the waiter bring your dinner over by bicycle; then, if you're staying in a beachfront villa, you can finish your bottle of Pouilly-Fuisse on the balcony, the air soft and balmy, the palms riffling in the breeze and a full moon shimmering on the surf. The beachfront villas are the first rooms to be filled (the other seventy-two rooms are in cottages or the main building), but spend a few days at The Cloister even if you have to take a chauffeur's room. And even if you have to arrive in a newfangled horseless carriage.

NAME: The Cloister

INNKEEPER: Irving A. Harned

ADDRESS: Sea Island, Ga. 31561

TELEPHONE: 912-638-3611

DIRECTIONS: By car, from north or south via Interstate 95 and U.S. 17, from the west via U.S. 25/84/341, and enter causeway off U.S. 17 at Brunswick (10 miles from Sea Island); by air, to Brunswick or Jacksonville (75 miles); by Amtrak to Thalmann (30 miles); limousine service from airports or station.

RATES: AP, complicated tariff because of the range of rooms— $49 to $77 from June 1 through August 31; $51 to $79 from September 1 through January 31; $59 to $87 from February 1 through May 31.

MEALS: Breakfast (to 11 a.m.), lunch (indoor or poolside), afternoon tea, dinner, oyster roasts; room service; in the dining room, jacket for men at lunchtime, jacket and tie in the evening.

SEASONS: Open all year; peak season in spring, quietest in the fall and winter; sports all year round, and a few conventions in the winter.

KING & PRINCE HOTEL
St. Simons Island, Georgia

For the benefit of the K&P fan club, the imperturbable Anna Curr is still ruling the kitchen, still concocting her famed deviled crab a la Anna; Geneva Walker is still stuffing the stuffed shrimp a la Geneva; Charlotte Ward is still in charge of the ham and red-eye gravy. And you can still enjoy these delicacies in the Delagal Room with its stained glass windows.

For the benefit of non-Southerners, the King & Prince is a Spanish *palacio* by the edge of a superb beach, on the largest of Georgia's Golden Isles. It opened its doors, in a classic feat of bad timing, on July 4, 1941 and didn't really get into its stride until after the war; lately it seemed to have fallen on, if not bad, then mediocre times. Now it's under new owners (the Messrs. Clay and Ashmore of Atlanta) and a new manager (Baxter Webb, who came up from the Caribbean to take charge).

Most of the former gracious atmosphere has been retained— in some cases by public demand: when the new owners installed central heating and air conditioning, the old clientele insisted that they leave the old blade fans in the ceiling. They did. The former elegance survives in the Sidney Lanier Room, a sunny lounge with Queen Anne and Chinese Chippendale furniture, and the patios have been replanted with oleanders and azaleas. A covered walkway has been converted into eight cabana suites with sunken living rooms and entrances directly onto the beach. The remaining eighty-odd rooms are spread over three floors, all with private bathrooms, air conditioning, room phones, color TV and those lazy ceiling fans. There's an unusual Bridal Tower (room #300), a pink-and-green circular room at the top of a spiral stairway, with a semi-private entrance to the beach and an almost-360-degree panoramic view of the ocean.

K&P facilities include a freshwater pool (also circular), a private beach (floodlit in the evening), and three new tennis courts; elsewhere on the island guests have a choice of forty-five holes of golf, stables and a gun club. Many of these facilities are shared with guests from The Cloister. If you don't want to fork out The Cloister's Modified American Plan rates, the King & Prince is a happy alternative—especially if you plan to spend most of your time on the beach.

NAME: King & Prince Hotel

INNKEEPER: Ryburn G. Clay
   (Baxter Webb, resident manager)

ADDRESS: St. Simons Island, Ga. 31522

TELEPHONE: 912-638-3631

DIRECTIONS: By car, take U.S. 17 or U.S. 341 to Brunswick, then follow the signs to St. Simons and continue around the waterfront to the K&P; by air, to Brunswick or the island's McKinnon Field; by Amtrak, to Thalmann (30 miles away).

RATES: EP—from post-Labor Day through February, $20 to $33 Court View, $28 to $33 Ocean View, $33 to $48 Ocean Front, $43 to $48 Cabana Suites; March through August $22 to $35, $30 to $35, $35 to $50 and $45 to $50.

MEALS: Breakfast, lunch, dinner; room service; informal and/or jacket and tie in the evening.

SEASONS: A summer resort, but open all year, and wonderfully relaxing in winter, if there are no conventions in the house.

GREYFIELD
Cumberland Island, Georgia

Cumberland Island is not of this world. It exists somewhere between Atlantis, Bali Hai and the Garden of Eden, eighteen miles of wilderness, of sea oats, marsh grass, forests of wizened live oaks, and beaches a couple of hundred yards wide. Alligators wallow in the marshes, wild boars snuffle around among the trees and wild horses canter through the fields, their manes flowing in the wind, like pent-up poodles let off the leash in the park. The island's human population is twelve; you can walk a hundred yards here, pick out a sheltered dune and slip out of your swimsuits without having to crane your necks every five minutes. This is pure escapism. You can reach Cumberland only by private boat or chartered plane. Fly over and you'll get a bird's-eye view of the gray-green, gray-white island as you come in to land. Your pilot circles the inn to alert the innkeeper that a guest is arriving; you approach the vague landing strip, and hope the boars will get out of the way before you land. A few minutes later, Jim Nesbit comes jouncing along in his beat-up jeep, and jounces you back along overgrown lanes, and across the dunes to the inn.

If Greyfield didn't exist, Tennessee Williams or Somerset Maugham would have invented it: a slightly decaying, peeling, three-story plantation mansion in a grove of live oaks, with a flight of stairs rising from the hitching posts up to the veranda. There's a spooky quality to the garden, and inside, the inn is creaky and ancestral.

Tea from a silver pot

Every guest is welcomed with a cup of tea served from a silver teapot, in a parlor brimming with family clutter—ivory-inlaid chairs, rolltop desks, a shell collection, silver candlesticks, bulky scrapbooks with yellowed curling pages. But these are no ordinary family heirlooms: it's a Carnegie silver pot your tea is poured from, and it's a Carnegie sofa you're sitting on.

Greyfield was built in 1901 as a summer home for the family of Thomas Carnegie, brother and partner of Andrew, and it's been in the family ever since. In 1966, Lucy Ferguson, the current head of the clan and granddaughter of Thomas, decided to invite paying guests from their wide circle of friends. It's still pretty much a family affair, but they now take in a few guests from beyond their immediate circle. In fact, you may be asked to send references with your reservation. Send them; Greyfield is worth a ten-page résumé. There's nothing like this anywhere else along the entire coast.

To their undying credit, Carnegie's descendants haven't tried to jazz up the old home. The rooms are still those of a well-to-do family's beach home, and the rooms still have the names the family gave them—"Statesman's Choice," "Mr. Buzzer," "The Artist's Room" (some evening, over a sherry, Jim Nesbit will tell you the story about the people behind the names). Some of the rooms have private baths, most of them don't. There's no television, no pool, no tennis court, no golf. Not even a bartender; when you want a drink you go and mix it yourself, and pay for it on the honor system.

Roast suckling pig and quail

You dine family style off the Carnegie mahogany table. The meals don't try to be gourmet; the kitchen makes do with what's around the island—oysters, clams, mullet, flounder, shrimp, occasionally roast lamb or roast beef. One evening you may have roast suckling pig, another the island's unique quail. Before dinner, retire to the snug library and skim through a volume from the collected works of Abraham Lincoln; after dinner, sip a nightcap out on the veranda beneath the moon.

Breakfast in bed, fun on the beach

Cumberland days begin with breakfast in bed, and while you're waiting for the bathroom to become free you have time to decide what you'll do for the rest of the day. It's strictly a back-to-nature existence on Cumberland Island. Digging for clams. Building sand castles. Kicking the surf at each other. Swimming, sunning, shelling, surfing. Riding a one-horse shay. But on an island as serene as this, lovers don't need prompting; they know what to do, and they have all the time in the world to do it.

Maybe.

"Cumberland Island is the nation's foremost example of an unspoiled wilderness island," said Georgia's governor, with the best of intentions. All the property on the island is owned by only a few families, and when one landowner tried to sell off some lots, the State stepped in and had the island declared a National Seashore. Now 70 percent of Cumberland Island is owned by the National Parks Service, which plans to preserve the nation's foremost example of an unspoiled wilderness island by introducing ferry services for an anticipated 10,000 beer-can-tossing trippers *a day*. The only people allowed to stay overnight on the island will be campers, and Greyfield, as an inn, may join the other Carnegies as a pleasant memory. Hurry.

NAME: Greyfield

INNKEEPER: Jim Nesbit

ADDRESS: P.O. Drawer B, Fernandina Beach, Fla. 32034

TELEPHONE: 912-496-7503

DIRECTIONS: By "R.W. Ferguson" from Fernandina Beach, or by charter flight from Sea Island ($20 by Golden Isles Airways—ask for Lee Kerr).

RATES: MAP—$35, year round.

MEALS: Breakfast (to 9 a.m.), lunch, dinner (to 7:30 or 8 p.m.); no room service (except breakfast); jacket and tie at dinner.

SEASONS: Open all year round; busiest in summer, but Cumberland can be balmy and blissful in winter.

THE BREAKERS
Palm Beach, Florida

Walking into The Breakers' lobby you get something of the soul-soaring lift opera buffs get when they walk into the Met. All that marble. All those frescoes. All that gilt. All those glistening, glittering, scintillant chandeliers. It's enough to make you launch into a duet from *Tosca*.

Oddly enough, Tosca and Cavaradossi and other lovers from the realm of opera might feel at home here, because the archi-

tect commissioned to design The Breakers way back in the Twenties got so carried away with its oceanside location that he decided that the only thing to do it justice would be an Italian palazzo. But what he finally put together was a pastiche of Italian palazzi: the twin towers and arches of the exterior were inspired by the Villa Medici in Rome (which is rather like saying the Washington Monument was inspired by the Campanile in the Piazza San Marco); the ornate ceiling in the Gold Room was copied from the Palazzo Ducale in Venice; the frescoes in the lobby are based on those in the Palazzo Carega in Genoa; and so on, marble column after marble, gilt column and frescoed ceiling after frescoed, gilt ceiling. It may not add up to a true palazzo but it certainly is quite a place to show off your latest Puccis.

From manse to mansion

The Breakers is, in fact, a memorial, built by the trustees of the Flagler estate and dedicated to the creator of the Flagler millions. Henry Morrison Flagler was a poor boy who figured there had to be a better way of life than his minister father could offer in Hopewell, New York; so at 14 he left the family manse, went into business, and after a series of ups and downs joined forces with a man called John D. Rockefeller; together they formed a company that went on to prosper as the Standard Oil Company of New Jersey. Many years and many, many millions later, Flagler built railroads to the South that ultimately brought him to Palm Beach, and with remarkable vision was able to foresee that that expanse of swampland could become America's answer to Europe's Riviera. Everywhere his railway went, Flagler built a hotel; in Palm Beach he built two, both of which disappeared, but to commemorate the great man, the Flaglers built The Breakers in 1926. It's still owned and operated by the family.

How do you pass the charmed hours in surroundings of such opulence? Slip into your beach Pucci and shuffle down to the private beach. Or sample the hotel's new beach club, said to be the most modern in the world: carpeted dressing rooms, sauna, massage, and your choice of pools—outdoor saltwater, indoor freshwater. The outdoor pool is surrounded by an outdoor restaurant with sky-blue patio furniture, the indoor pool by a restaurant with yellow patio furniture beneath a tent of tinted glass and hanging plants (a beautiful room—the Medicis would have loved it).

For something less languorous, try tennis or golf, water skiing, snorkeling, sailing or fishing; or take a bike and go riding through gardens filled to tropical excess and looking like nature's answer to all the gilt and marble indoors.

In the evening, dress up and treat yourselves to a slap-up dinner in the Rotunda—a great circular dining room reaching for the heavens in a dome of glass above a gigantic Venetian chandelier, and surrounded by mirrors, crystal and frescoes that make most other dining rooms look like pizza parlors. Then, if you've had the foresight to reserve a room in the new oceanside wing, you can top the evening off with brandy on the balcony looking down on the real breakers—the kind that lull you to sleep.

And you certainly won't lose any sleep thinking about the bill *if you come to The Breakers in summer: this palatial splendor, which will set you back at least $75, Modified American Plan, in winter, will cost you only $24 (without meals) in summer or early fall.*

Ah, but what's the weather like in Palm Beach in summer? Average maximum temperatures between June and October range from 85 to 91 degrees. Perfect temperature for a Pucci (and don't worry if it's not an original—the palazzo isn't an original either).

NAME: The Breakers
INNKEEPER: Thomas S. Kenan III
ADDRESS: P.O. Box 910, Palm Beach, Fla. 33480
TELEPHONE: 305-655-3355
DIRECTIONS: From Interstate 95 or U.S. 1 go east on Palm Beach Lakes Boulevard or Okeechobee Road; by air or Amtrak to West Palm Beach (limousine service).
RATES: EP in summer only (June 1 through October 1)—$24 to $40; MAP the remainder of the year—$55 to $85 in the pre-season (October 15 through December 15) and post-season (April 1 through June 1); $65 to $95 in the mid-season (January 2 through February 1); $75 to $105 in the winter season (February 1 through April 1); special rates for Christmas and New Year's.
MEALS: Everything—breakfast, lunch (indoor or outdoor), dinner; room service; dressy, definitely jacket and tie in the evening.
SEASONS: Open all year, a beehive of millionaires in winter, an uncrowded bargain in summer.

BOCA RATON HOTEL AND CLUB
Boca Raton, Florida

The Saturday Evening Post once called this "Florida's flossiest hotel," and Frank Lloyd Wright called its architect "little more than a scenic designer." Both critics have gone, but the Boca Raton keeps getting bigger and bigger.

The original 1926 hotel had a hundred guest rooms built in the style of a cloister around formal gardens; in 1928 the inn was bought by a tycoon named Clarence H. Geist, who had a penchant for wandering through the lobby in his bathrobe, and who added 300 more rooms; more recently another 257 rooms have been tacked on, in a twenty-six-story tower just east of the original cloister, on the edge of Lake Boca Raton, overlooking the Intracoastal Waterway. The hotel is no longer a quiet little hideaway, flossy or otherwise, but it's still true to the original affluent concept.

Many of the original antiques are still there—priceless then, more priceless than ever now: the wooden beams and carved wall brackets from the University of Seville, a splendid refectory table, a massive 17th-century credenza and gold embossed mirror from Spain, countless artifacts from country churches in Guatemala. You'll dine here in a salon whose columns are covered with fourteen-carat gold leaf.

Pleasure domes

If its architect was little more than a scenic designer, the story of its creation was downright horse opera. Addison Mizner had come to Palm Beach in 1918 in failing health, planning to spend his few remaining weeks or months on earth in one of earth's balmier corners; there he encountered another invalid ready to breathe his last, Paris Singer, the son of the Singer who invented sewing machines. Singer was not only prepared to breathe his last but also to spend his last, and together they concocted plans for the ultimate pleasure domes. Since neither of them died as soon as expected, they went on to build some of their dream palaces and Mizner became the most demanded architect in Florida. The Boca Raton is one of the offshoots of this strange partnership. It was originally called the Cloister Inn, and when it opened on February 6, 1926, there was such a dazzling array of tycoons, movie stars and royalty on the doorstep that the hotel still keeps the guest register of that auspicious evening under glass in the main lobby.

But never in their wildest dying dreams did Singer and Mizner conceive something like the present-day Boca Raton Hotel. When you come here to please yourselves in this pleasure dome, you'll find a thousand acres of semi-tropical paradise with secret places among the angel trumpet, creeping gif, gumbo limbo trees, monkey apple, golden dewdrop, Spanish bayonet, screw pine and shaving brush trees. This being a millionaires' resort, you have everything at your fingertips. Tennis? Thirteen courts. Golf? Four courses. Sunning? A mile of beach and a cabana club. Bikes? Bikes. Fishing? Boats and tackle and bait. Polo? Every Sunday afternoon from January through April.

But at $65 a day minimum you may prefer to spend most of your time in your own room, and that's not such a bad idea either: love nests don't come much plusher than this. Rooms #220, #221 and #222 in the original inn are probably still the most romantic in the hotel, but if it's grand gesture time, the celebration of a year-old affair or consummation of a day-old affair, rent one of the executive suites in the new tower ($400 a night), or take over the entire Presidential Suite, with its private elevator, grand piano, step-down bath of Italian marble, and a leopard-skin chaise positioned to give you a dramatic view of the ocean and the feeling that you're king and queen of the castle.

If you want to be away from the mainstream, rent a villa alongside the golf courses—a bedroom, a parlor, kitchen and balcony, within walking distance of the hotel (from $115, or from $65 without the parlor).

NAME: Boca Raton Hotel & Club

INNKEEPER: L. Bert Stephens

TELEPHONE: 305-395-3000

DIRECTIONS: 45 miles north of Miami, between Ocean Highway (A1A) and U.S. 1, and between Palmetto Park Road and Camino Real; by scheduled air service to Fort Lauderdale or by private or charter flight to Boca Raton Airport; by Amtrak to Deerfield Beach.

RATES: Very complicated rate structure based on building, floor, exposure, but basically from $60 to $130 between October 1 and December and between May 1 and June 1; and from $70 to $155 the remaining months—all full AP.

MEALS: Breakfast (to 10:30 a.m.), lunch, dinner (to 8:30 p.m.); room service; jacket and tie in the evening (but turtle-necks in the main dining room only when part of formal attire).

SEASONS: October 1 through May 30, peaking from January 3 through Memorial Day; lots of conventions.

PIER HOUSE
Key West, Florida

"Long, boozy breakfasts," promises David Williams Wolkowsky, the Pier House's owner. Fresh tropical fruits, eggs benedict, maybe a soufflé, served from seven in the morning to three in the afternoon, beneath the lazy, long-bladed fan and palm frond roof of the new Tiki restaurant right on the beach.

This beach is more or less the spot where the old Havana ferry used to set sail for Cuba, which places the Pier House right at the end of the Overseas Highway, in the very heart of Old

Key West, a shuffle away from the shrimp boats, Sloppy Joe's and other haunts of Ernest Hemingway. To get to the Pier House, you have to cross a car park, but then to get to the beach, you almost have to push your way through a garden of hibiscus, oleander and coconut palms—none of which prepares you for what is, as Rene D'Harencourt of New York's Museum of Modern Art noted, "the most unusual motel design in America." It's a modern habitat-like structure of painted cinder blocks (not the most romantic material but useful to have around you in a tropical storm) that gives every room a patio or balcony, and almost all of them a view of a multi-hued sea at the very spot where the Atlantic caresses the Gulf.

The ninety rooms (no two are identical, but they all have color television and air conditioning) include a couple of duplex apartments and a penthouse built over the Gulf, where you feel like you're on a cruise ship, with the sea lapping the pilings below the balconies. The newest buildings are constructed around an indoor tropical garden, giving you the feeling of being outdoors even when you're in. Wolkowsky's own favorites are in the section known as the Old Navy Officers' Quarters, which he has had moved in as a part of his complex; there are six units here, including two on the second floor with two bedrooms each and a long porch running the length of the building and overlooking the pool, the gardens and the Gulf.

The Pier House's facilities include a private beach, freshwater swimming pool, rental boats, a lounge (the Chart Room). It has some motelly things like free coffee and doughnuts in the morning and coin machines for soft drinks, ice and snacks; but it's also filled with all manner of surprises—an original watercolor by Tennessee Williams in the lobby, a glass case with a huge collection of birds dating back to the Audubon period, and a huge figurehead handcarved in Switzerland in the 1800s and rescued by Wolkowsky from a ship about to be scuttled.

The figurehead is not the only thing David Williams Wolkowsky has saved from scuttling or decay; he restored Captain Tony's (Key West's oldest bar, which had been owned by his grandfather and frequented by Hemingway), and helped preserve and develop Pirate's Alley, a picturesque old street of boutiques, cigar factories, restaurants and craft shops. All interesting spots to visit—if you ever finish breakfast.

NAME: Pier House

INNKEEPER: David Williams Wolkowsky

ADDRESS: 5 Duval Street, Key West, Fla. 33040

TELEPHONE: 305-294-9541

DIRECTIONS: Keep driving until you run out of America; by air, scheduled flights several times a day direct from Miami.

RATES: EP—$14 to $20 from April 16 to December 15, $24 and $28 from December 15 to April 16.

MEALS: Breakfast (to 3 in the afternoon), lunch (see breakfast), dinner (to 10 p.m.); no room service; informal—if you wear a jacket here, people may think you're from the CIA.

SEASON: Open all year, busiest in winter, unique at any time.

THE HEARTLANDS
AND
THE DEEP SOUTH

And when Love speaks, the voice of all the gods
Makes heaven drowsy with the harmony . . .
SHAKESPEARE

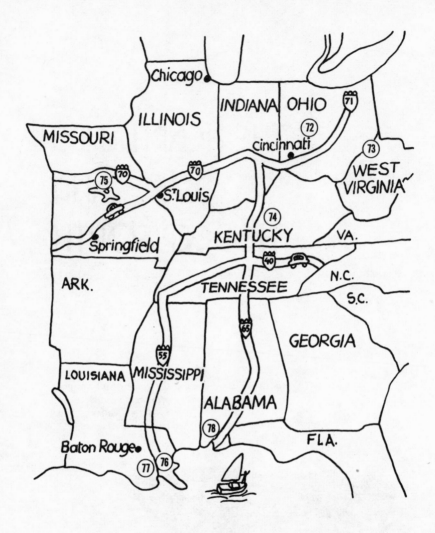

72. The Golden Lamb
73. Wells Inn
74. The Inn at Pleasant Hill
75. Lodge of the Four Seasons

76. Hotel Maison De Ville
77. The Saint Louis Hotel
78. Grand Hotel

THE GOLDEN LAMB
Lebanon, Ohio

¢

This is Ohio's oldest. Since it opened its doors in 1815, The Golden Lamb has hosted ten Presidents (including U. S. Grant and John Quincy Adams), several writers (Charles Dickens for one), and statesmen (De Witt Clinton and Henry Clay, among others). But when *they* stayed here they didn't have great trucks growling past the window at three o'clock in the morning. If the Lamb were out in the fields, it would be an ideal nook for lovers; as it is it's right smack in the middle of town, so it can only be recommended as a pleasant place to spend a night on the way to somewhere else. The rooms are charmers—all done in period furniture, many of them with private bathrooms, some with big fourposter beds and rag rugs, most of them with TV and air conditioning. Beware: people who drop in for dinner are invited to take a look at the guest rooms when the doors are open, so remember to keep yours closed (and to be on the safe side, keep it *locked* when you're using it). All the rooms are named for notables who've visited the inn, and even if you've never heard of Ormsby Mitchell ask for his room; it's pink and pretty with a pencil post bed, and it's on the quiet side away from the main street.

Diners at the Golden Lamb seem to outnumber staying guests by a thousand to one, and dining can be a hassle (no priority for overnight guests, tut-tut). However, the dining rooms are attractive in a ye-olde-tavern sort of way (apart from the intrusive piped music that does nothing to enhance the 19th-century atmosphere); the food is hearty and tasty, and the menus feature curiosities like Shaker sugar pie and prune and butternut fudge pie.

Right inn, wrong place.

174

NAME: The Golden Lamb
INNKEEPER: Jackson Reynolds
ADDRESS: 27 S. Broadway, Lebanon, Ohio 45036
TELEPHONE: 513-932-5065
DIRECTIONS: Halfway between Cincinnati and Dayton, 7 miles east of Interstate 75, 3 miles west of Interstate 71, and right in the heart of a 6,000-population town.
RATES: EP—from $12 to $15 with private bath, from $6.50 without private bath, year round.
MEALS: No breakfast. Lunch and dinner. No room service; jacket and tie in the evening.
SEASONS: Open all year.

WELLS INN
Sisterville, West Virginia

I can't think of any reason in the world for you to take a lover to Sisterville, but if by some disaster of navigation you find yourself driving along the eastern banks of the Ohio River, past the power plants and charcoal factories south of Wheeling, take heart. Before long you'll come to the Wells Inn, an oasis of tasteful Victoriana, where you can drink a grateful toast to Ephraim Wells who built the inn in 1894, and to John Wells Kinkaid, who restored it a few years ago.

Sisterville is an old oil town, which once boasted 2,500 wells, an opera house and a great deal of vice. That's what *was;* what *is* is a dreary little backwater of a town that happens to have a delightful little hotel filled with antique brass cuspidors, grandfather clocks, mahogany woodwork, flocked wallpaper and chandeliers. The thirty-six bedrooms have all been restored in period style—and there's nothing at all in town to keep you from tumbling into bed at seven o'clock in the evening.

On second thought, if you're slipping off for a secret tryst,

Sisterville is probably a good place to go—no one would dream of looking for you here.

NAME: Wells Inn
INNKEEPER: John Wells Kinkaid, Jr.
ADDRESS: 316 Charles Street, Sisterville, W. Va. 26175
TELEPHONE: 304-652-3111
DIRECTIONS: On West Virginia 2, in the center of town.
RATES: EP—$11 to $23.
MEALS: Breakfast, lunch, dinner (to 9 p.m.); no room service.
SEASONS: Open all year.

THE INN AT PLEASANT HILL
Shakertown, Harrodsburg, Kentucky

This is probably an ironic choice for a lovers' hideaway—the restored village of a religious sect that banned sex, where boys and girls were never allowed to be alone together, and where the houses had not only separate dormitories for each sex but separate doors and stairs. Not surprisingly, the sect is all but extinct ("celibacy contributed to their undoing," as one commentator put it) but their village remains as a placid anachronism, a freeze-frame in the movie of history.

First, the location. Pleasant Hill is about twenty miles southeast of Lexington, which puts it right on the edge of Bluegrass Country, along a winding fence-lined lane. This, they say, is the only historical village in the country where you can spend a night in the original houses (not inns, but houses). Spooky? Only if total silence punctured by rattling windows and creaky floorboards turn you to Jello; if they do, just make a grab for each other.

The twenty-odd clapboard or birch houses in Shakertown are neatly lined up on either side of an unpaved street which in turn is lined by picket-and-plank fences and mulberry trees.

Rag rugs, trundle beds

The main lodge, Trustees' House, has been putting up guests since Shaker times, but you can also spend the night in, say, the Ministry's Workshop, or the East Family Sisters' Shop (above the spinning and weaving room), or the East Family Brethrens' Shop (above the carpenters' tools and farm equipment). All the guest rooms feature the ascetic, precise, well-proportioned Shaker decor (it's like living inside a painting by Mondrian); plain walls trimmed with wood in brown or blue, plank floors with hand-woven or rag rugs, curtains in the Shakers' traditional "dogwood" pattern, stout twin beds (some of them trundles). The Shakers draped everything over wall pegs—sconces, clothes, mirrors, even chairs—and that's the way it is at Shakertown. (Note, by the way, that this creates a resonant acoustic, so take it easy or you may keep the neighbors awake, wondering if they're hearing the spirits of the former inhabitants at one of the "shaking" parties from which they got their name.) Conces-

sions to the 20th century include tiled bathrooms, air conditioning, fire sprinklers, and television sets (which are as jarring in
this setting as a naked body must have been to a Shaker).

Marshmallows in your apple sauce

The Trustees' House has four dining rooms, including a "conservatory" with tall windows overlooking the garden, bare brick
walls and scrubbed wooden tables. The waitresses are dressed in
authentic Shaker checked dresses, and Mrs. Kramer's menu is
a combination of Shaker and Kaintuck cooking. Village hot
breads and the relish tray come automatically. Thereafter you
have a choice of four appetizers (including eggs in aspic or
anchovy toast), five entrees (say, pork tenderloin which comes
accompanied by piles of fresh vegetables from the village garden,
and apple sauce with marshmallows). The five choices of dessert
include chess pie and Shaker lemon pie—which leave you feeling that at least the Shakers got *some* pleasure out of life.

There are no frivolities here like swimming pools and saunas.
Instead you can go for long walks through the fields, or long
drives through the Bluegrass Country; but spend at least one
morning or afternoon visiting the village exhibits, buying Shaker-
inspired gewgaws, and getting to learn something about these
remarkable people. In some ways they were ahead of their time.
They were pioneers in organic foods and the medicinal use of
herbs; they invented several of the labor-saving devices we take
for granted—the washing machine, for one; they were pacifists,
women's libbers (they believed Christ would appear the second
time as a woman), and in a sense they were doing something
about the population explosion long before everyone else
awakened to its threats. They themselves expected to survive by
conversions and adoptions; but since they also had the work
ethic with a vengeance, in the end they didn't have much to offer
the younger generation. But they left quite a legacy here at
Shakertown.

178

NAME: The Inn at Pleasant Hill
INNKEEPER: Betty Morris
ADDRESS: Route 4, Harrodsburg, Ky. 40330
TELEPHONE: 606-734-9111
DIRECTIONS: Pleasant Hill is just a couple of miles from U.S. 68, about 20 miles southwest of Lexington, about 8 miles from Harrodsburg.
RATES: EP—$12 and $16, year round; *no tipping.*
MEALS: Breakfast (to 9:30 a.m.), lunch and dinner (to 7:15 p.m.); no liquor license; no room service; informal, but jacket and tie preferred in the evening.
SEASONS: Open all year; cluttered with day visitors in the summer months, but relatively uncrowded in the evenings; seminars and things in the winter, but they usually take place in their own compound.

LODGE OF THE FOUR SEASONS
Lake of the Ozarks, Missouri

There's only one place to stay in these parts and this is it. (The Lake of the Ozarks, for the record, is a man-made body of water surrounded by man-made honky-tonk.) Everything you could ask for on vacation is a five-minute walk from your bed—an outdoor pool in a Japanese garden, and an indoor pool; a spa with saunas, whirlpool baths, massage, exercise rooms; sightseeing boat trips on the lake, boats for rent; golf, including a brand new eighteen-hole Robert Trent Jones course; tennis, fishing, riding, hiking, water skiing, archery, games room; a private 680-acre shooting preserve; a Jerry Lewis movie theater. There are ample dining facilities—a lakeside coffee shop and a lavish circular restaurant called the Toledo Room, hosted by a maitre d' who'd be a credit to most restaurants in New York. After dinner you can whoop it up in the discotheque or nightclub with live entertainment.

Lanais and casas

The lodge's 250 rooms are spacious, comfortable and equipped with telephones, television and individually controlled heating and air conditioning. They're spread out through a four-story lodge, two four-story motel wings known as the Casadero, lanai rooms facing the pool and Japanese garden, and lakeside casas. The quietest rooms are the casas (except during the boating season, because they're right above the marina), or the Casadero rooms (which also have good views, and balconies for enjoying them).

This is a much better hotel than most people would expect to find out there in the Ozarks among all those hillbillies; in fact, you'd expect a colorful resort like this in Miami or San Juan rather than Missouri, and you may find yourself wishing that there was just a touch more of the hillbilly about the place. Even that the persistent piped music could be coaxed into playing Bluegrass now and again.

NAME: Lodge of the Four Seasons
INNKEEPER: R. Scott Morrison, Jr. (V.P. and general manager)
    T. Steele Edwards (resident manager)
ADDRESS: Lake Ozark, Mo. 65049
TELEPHONE: 314-365-2381
DIRECTIONS: Southwest of St. Louis 170 miles, and southeast of Kansas City; from Interstate 70, take U.S. 63 or U.S. 65 south (following the signs for Lake of the Ozarks, and Bagnell Dam), then drive west 2½ miles from Business 54 to County HH; by air, to Lake of the Ozarks' Lee C. Fine Airport from Kansas City and St. Louis, and by limousine to the hotel.
RATES: EP—$28 to $45 for rooms, $55 to $110 for suites from April 15 through October; lower the rest of the year; also special inclusive Summer Safari rates of $113.90 weekdays, $127.90 weekends.
MEALS: Breakfast (to 10 a.m.), lunch, pool snack bar, dinner

(to 10 p.m.); room service to midnight; jacket and tie, or informal, in the evening.

SEASONS: Open all year; quietest in winter, unless there happens to be a convention on board; however, the lodge might be one exception to the "avoid-convention" rule when it holds its annual Bluegrass jamboree in February and the corridors are filled with plucking fingers.

HOTEL MAISON DE VILLE
New Orleans, Louisiana

Even if you've never been there, you probably know from photographs what the typical *Vieux Carre* townhouse looks like—two-story facade with wrought-iron balconies, and a courtyard with slave quarters at the rear. The slave quarters at 727 Rue du Toulouse date from 1783 and may be among the oldest buildings from the days of the Spanish grandees; the elegant main house was rebuilt in the early 18th century, and was at one time the home of M. A. A. Peychaud, the ingenious apothecary who is said to have invented the cocktail. You could almost be persuaded that M. Peychaud still lived behind this grandly carved door and cut-glass window if it weren't for the gleaming brass nameplate announcing Hotel Maison de Ville.

Inside you step back a century or two to the days of the Spanish and French beau monde, into a miniature palace filled with antiques—a Biedermeier love seat in crushed velvet, an 18th-century bombe commode, a carved Louis XV trumeau. You may while away your nights of bliss in a Chippendale bed draped with French silk, or a double bed covered with a Belgian sable spread trimmed in black velvet, or twin beds with brass headboards for curling your toes around.

Three of the double rooms are in the slave quarters, connected by a careworn wooden staircase to the courtyard—a leafy, sun-dappled pocket park with a three-tiered cast-iron fountain trickling into a fish pond. This is pure Vieux Carre, and to crown it all you can enjoy several felicities of service: you get your shoes polished when you put them outside your door; you have a concierge to attend to details—like reserving a table for two at Brennan's; ice, mixers, soft drinks and newspapers are on the *maison;* breakfast arrives in your room on a silver tray—freshly squeezed orange juice, freshly brewed New Orleans coffee, freshly baked brioche from the Four Seasons Pastry Shoppe. The Maison de Ville doesn't have its own dining room but you can order room service from the restaurant behind the courtyard wall—the Court of Two Sisters (and hopefully the service will be more attentive than the pell-mell assembly line you find in the touristy court itself). There are only fourteen rooms here. It's no place to be if you like spacious lobbies and roomy rooms; but if you like gems, here's one.

NAME: Hotel Maison de Ville

INNKEEPER: Virginia W. Karmgard

ADDRESS: 727 Toulouse Street, New Orleans, La. 70130

TELEPHONE: 504-523-1189

DIRECTIONS: Smack dab in the heart of the French Quarter, a slow saunter from everything (but for all that, quiet).

RATES: EP, but with Continental breakfast—twins and doubles $25 to $35 from June 1 through October 31, $35 to $45 from November 1 through May 31; suites $45 and $55; all prices higher during Mardi Gras, assuming you can get a reservation.

MEALS: Complimentary breakfast anytime; otherwise, room service from the Court of Two Sisters.

SEASONS: Open all year, quietest in summer.

THE SAINT LOUIS HOTEL
New Orleans, Louisiana

A count might have lived here a century ago, greeting lovely crinolined ladies in the courtyard by the fountain. The fact is, there was a bottling plant here until a few years ago when William H. Henderson, a local entrepreneur who had always wanted a hotel like the Ritz in Paris, pulled the plant down and built this hotel. He spared few expenses—least of all in "aging" the facade to make it look like the sort of place a count might have entertained in a hundred years ago. The predominant color is cantaloupe (or "a melon smoked salmon shade" as one of the designers calls it), which is the color theme used in bed linen and table linen. The lobby looks like the salon of a Parisian townhouse, dominated by a century-old gilt mirror; beyond it French doors lead through to the inner courtyard (which, by a directive of the New Orleans Vieux Carre Commission, must represent 30 percent of any property).

Begin your stay at the Saint Louis in this delightful spot. Find a table beneath a slowly turning blade fan, order a cool drink, hold hands and admire the banana palms, the golden rain tree and the baby weeping willow. Then trot upstairs and ease into the cuddly terry towel bathrobes hanging in the dressing room. The eighty bedchambers are luxurious—furnished in the style of Louis XV or XVI, Empire or Directoire (reproductions, alas, but then people in cuddly terry towel bathrobes shouldn't expect everything). All the rooms have air conditioning, color TV, electric shoe polisher and bidet. If you want to fork out $150 a night you can have the Presidential Suite—all the above plus log fire, spacious patio, kitchen, dining room, two baths, and a bedroom with mirrored closets.

Candlelight and profiterolles

One problem with New Orleans is that it has so many fine restaurants, and you feel you *must* eat in the legendary Gala-

toire's, Antoine's or Brennan's; which is a shame because Le Petit Restaurant in the Saint Louis is a cozy nook with brick walls, blade fans, candlelight and that lovely cantaloupe table linen. Specialties include pompano de chef, noisettes d'agneau, paupiettes de veau, and freshly baked *profiterolles* and *tarte aux pommes* (dinner here will cost you about $8 a head without wine—which is also reasonable, like $6 for a bottle of Mouton Cadet).

NAME: The Saint Louis Hotel

INNKEEPER: Cesar F. Martino

ADDRESS: 720 Rue Bienville, New Orleans, La. 70130

TELEPHONE: 504-581-7300

DIRECTIONS: In the French Quarter, or Vieux Carre, 2 blocks from Canal Street, and 3.5 minutes from Preservation Hall and its Dixieland Jazz.

RATES: EP, but with Continental breakfast at Le Petit Restaurant—$40 for a twin room, $45 double-double, $50 king-size, $55 studio; from $65 to $85 for a suite, $150 for the Presidential Suite, year round.

MEALS: Breakfast (to 10:30 a.m.), lunch, dinner (to 11 p.m.); room service; jacket and tie in the evening.

SEASONS: Open all year; June through early September are the slow months, October through May the busy months, although even then it's not too crowded on weekends; there may well be small groups in residence during the October–May period, and you'd better book at least a year in advance for Mardi Gras.

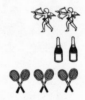

GRAND HOTEL
Point Clear, Alabama

The Point is a giant V formed by two long strips of white sand beach surrounded by turquoise sea. Within the V you have 500 acres of pines, live oaks and gardens, and, somewhere among it all, the Grand Hotel. There's an air of quiet elegance about the place, luxury without ostentation. The buildings are a muted gray, with brick-and-timber interiors; the fifty bed-sitting rooms have wall-to-wall carpeting, color television, and terraces or balconies facing the gulf or the gardens.

What do you do on a sunny day in Alabama? Just about everything. You can plunge into the freshwater swimming pool (it's enormous—140 feet in diameter); suntan on the white sands; water ski; sail on the bay (there are Rhodes 19 daysailers for rent); play tennis; or ride a horse or tandem through the 500 acres of pines and live oaks. In the evenings you can stroll over to Julep Point and enjoy the view, or a julep, or a seafood luau. If you have any energy left after the day's activities you can even do a spot of dancing under the stars. Take an after-dinner stroll on the white sands, sniff the soft air and you could be in the Caribbean.

NAME: Grand Hotel Point Clear
INNKEEPER: Jim Pope
ADDRESS: Point Clear, Ala. 36564
TELEPHONE: 205-928-9201
DIRECTIONS: Point Clear is 23 miles south of Mobile via Battle-ship Parkway and U.S. 98, and 49 miles west of Pensacola, Fla.; limousines will meet your plane at Mobile Airport on request, and private planes can land at Fairhope Airport, 4 miles away.
RATES: MAP—from March 1 to May 31, and October 15 to November 15, $54 to $64; remainder of the year, $49 to $59; 15% service charge added to bill; EP available June 15 through Labor Day.
MEALS: Breakfast (to 10 a.m.), lunch, dinner (to 10 p.m.) including seafood luaus, steak fries; sports clothes by day, jacket and tie in the evening.
SEASONS: Open all year, most popular in spring and fall, but not too warm in summer and not too chilly in winter; small groups in winter.

THE ROCKIES
AND THE MESAS

Trip no further, pretty sweeting,
Journeys end in lovers meeting,
Every wise man's son doth know . . .
SHAKESPEARE

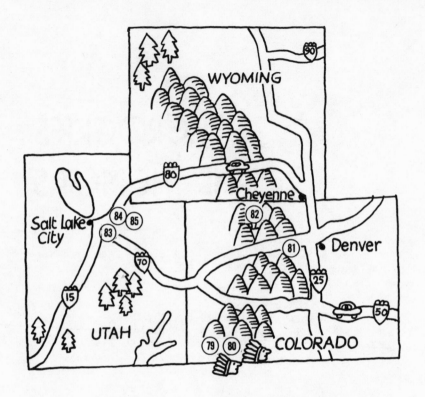

79. Far View Lodge

80. Strater Hotel

81. C Lazy U Ranch

82. The Timbers

83. Sundance

84. The Lodge at Snowbird

85. Alta Lodge

FAR VIEW LODGE
Mesa Verde National Park, Colorado

You can scout high and low but you'll be hard pressed to find a love nest in a more *dramatic* location: on top of the mesa, a tortuous forty-five-minute drive from the park entrance, on an elevation looking across 125 miles of wilderness to Shiprock, the Carrizo Mountains and most of the thirty-two canyons that slice the mesa. It is Nature at its most shuddery spectacular. By day it's mellowed by gardens of serviceberry, gambel oak and rabbit brush, by the flash of green-tailed towhee, piñon jay and the northern pileolated warbler, by the reminders of a modern world in the steady stream of cars. But in the evening, when the day-trippers have wiggled their way back to the highway and the towhees and warblers have turned in for the night, you're alone on top of the world, alone with the stars and the coyotes that holler at each other across the canyons, and you'd better be in love with each other.

Bill Winkler, who put the project together (it opened its doors in the spring of 1973) has been dreaming of this resort for years. He has a deep respect for the weird heritage of this particular plot of earth, and has tried to blend as much Indian tradition as possible into the demands of a modern resort. The main lodge is inspired by an Indian *kiva,* or ceremonial chamber, and decorated with Navajo sand paintings and rugs and Pueblo pottery. The Sipapu Lounge, or Den of Firewater, is dominated by a hanging Navajo rug of blazing desert red. The tri-level dining room has acres of windows so that you don't have to forgo the view when you settle down to dine. Again, the menu tries to reflect the Indian heritage—but with the Food and Drug Admin-

189

istration and the Department of Health breathing down their necks, this is more of a token gesture.

Hopi taco and chokecherry syrup

Still, the menus feature "the Indian's Holy Trinity—corn, squash and beans." You'll be able to sample Hopi taco (fried Indian bread, cheese, chili and onions, served with pintos), carne asado, fried corn meal mush with chokecherry syrup, old-fashioned Indian corn soup with chip beef; potatoes yield to yams, beans and squash, and your meal is accompanied by heaps of fresh-baked Indian bread and wild blackberry jam. Even the Sipapu Lounge has its specialty firewater, like a Teresa Maria (which hopefully tastes better than it reads—cranberry juice, tequila and lime).

The lodge's hundred rooms have walls of Douglas fir decorated with Indian paintings, but otherwise they're simply attractive, comfortable, modern guest rooms; all rooms have balconies or terraces with panoramic views and, in many cases, with benches wide enough for alfresco love making—your turn to give the coyotes something to shout about.

NAME: Far View Lodge
INNKEEPER: Bill Winkler
ADDRESS: Mesa Verde National Park, Colo. 81330
TELEPHONE: 303-529-4421
DIRECTIONS: Far inside Colorado's Mesa Verde National Park —a 15-mile, 25-hairpin drive up the side of the Mesa from U.S. 160, and worth every bend of the way.
RATES: EP—$15.50 for rooms, $18.50 for suites with small refrigerators.
MEALS: Breakfast, lunch, dinner; no room service (but there are facilities for self-service take-out if you want to eat on your balcony); informal.
SEASONS: May through September (but check precise dates in advance); small groups and seminars (of conservationists and the like) in spring and summer.

STRATER HOTEL
Durango, Colorado

Here's another pleasant Victorian Revival in a town that's no-where near as romantic as its name or history. Still, there's a lot to explore in the surrounding countryside, where four states (Colorado, New Mexico, Arizona, Utah) meet, so keep the Strater in mind as a refuge if you happen to be in this part of the world.

This red-brick-with-white-trim hotel recently celebrated its 90th birthday but it's a spruce and spry nonagenarian, refurbished to re-create the elegance of its early years when miners and merchants fought in the saloon, and some fabled poker games took place in a back room that's now the accountant's office. Through the years its guest list has included luminaries such as Will Rogers, Lowell Thomas and JFK.

Of the hotel's hundred TV-and-phone-equipped rooms, forty-five are Victorianized (the others are basic motel/hotel, because that's the way businessmen like them, and businessmen are a major part of the clientele). The pinnacles of opulence are suites #333 (king-size bed, writing desk, modern bathroom, TV nook with elegant Victorian sofa) and #322 (where you can play Victoria and Albert in an enormous hand-carved, half-tester bed or in a real old-time, freestanding, four-legged bathtub).

Melodrama and olio

The Strater has its own Diamond Circle Theater, a 300-seater establishment where $6 will buy you a pair of tickets for a three-act show of melodrama, olio and vaudeville. *Time* magazine called it one of the three best shows of its kind in the country—and you'll have to take *Time*'s word for it unless you make a reservation for the theater (open from Memorial Day to Labor Day only) when you reserve your room. Likewise if you want a ride on the other attraction that brings 5,000 visitors per summer day to Durango—the hair-raising, breathtaking, mountain-clinging ride on the narrow-gauge Denver and Rio Grande Railway. Don't say you weren't warned—5,000 visitors a day. That's a good crowd if you're a Will Rogers looking for an audience, or a JFK looking for votes, but if what you have in mind is a quiet, romantic little nook you'd better reschedule your trip.

NAME: Strater Hotel
INNKEEPER: Earl Barker Jr.
ADDRESS: 699 Main Avenue, Durango, Colo. 81301
TELEPHONE: 303-247-4431
DIRECTIONS: The town is on U.S. 160, the so-called Navajo Trail, and the hotel is on the main street, a couple of blocks from the railroad station; by scheduled air service to La Plata County Airport.
RATES: EP—in summer (mid-May to mid-October) $16 to $26 for rooms, $22 to $30 for suites (like #333 and #322); in winter, $14 to $20 and $18 to $22.
MEALS: Breakfast, lunch, dinner (to 10 p.m., except on Sundays in winter); room service; informal.
SEASONS: Open all year, mobbed in summer, sometimes taken over by conventions in winter.

C LAZY U RANCH
Granby, Colorado

What this ranch has going for it is its lazy-making setting—a sheltered valley of meadows and pines and streams, 8,000 feet up in the Continental Divide.

It's a real-life working ranch, and in June you can watch the roundups; at other times you can attend nearby rodeos and county fairs. Most people come here, however, for the riding, since it's free. There's a horse for every guest, and once you pick a mount to suit your skills, it's your personal horse all the time you're there. Between breakfast and dinner you can ride all the way up to Rabbit Ears Pass, or along the famous Trail Ridge Road through the Rocky Mountain National Park, or as far as the old mining town of Central City. If you can afford to ignore the fact that you're paying for horses but still don't want to ride, you'll find plenty of other pastimes to keep you occupied —a heated pool, ping-pong, fishing, a skeet range, horseshoe pitching, a jogging track and a couple of new tennis courts. There are miles of walking trails to lonely groves, and unlimited spectacular sightseeing if you want to go for a drive. If you're here in the snowy months you'll find winter horseback riding, ice skating, snowshoeing, sleigh rides, and hot buttered rum before the big fire in the main lodge.

The ranch consists of a big, red-roofed lodge facing a lake and flanked by smaller guest cottages. The six rooms in the lodge are the originals, and the most charming. The other rooms are spacious and decked out with "custom-built functional furniture," but they have little personality. (The Mobil Guide consistently gives C Lazy U a five-star rating and calls it luxurious; the Ritz in Paris is luxurious, the Santa Barbara Biltmore is luxurious, but the C Lazy U Ranch is comfortable and pleasant—which is really all you ask of a working guest ranch.)

What happens in the evenings? You seem to spend most of the time eating wrangler-sized meals; but the ranch prides itself on its friendly, first-name atmosphere, and if you feel like mixing you'll find conviviality, cocktails, a Baldwin grand piano and (horrors!) a jukebox for dancing. Forget the jukebox, get to bed early, and get up early to enjoy the mountains and the meadows. Or just B lazy old U.

NAME: C Lazy U Ranch
INNKEEPER: Katie Schoenberger
ADDRESS: Box M518, Granby, Colo. 80446
TELEPHONE: 303-887-3344
DIRECTIONS: From Denver, take Interstate 70 and U.S. 40 to
    Granby, continue a couple of miles to Colo. 125, then go

north for 8 miles; from Rocky Mountain National Park, take U.S. 34 to Granby, then go west to Colo. 125; $50 charge per car if you're picked up in Denver.

RATES: AP (*including unlimited horseback riding and tennis*)— June 1 through 10 and Labor Day through October 1, $70 a day, $380 to $760 a week; June 10 through Labor Day and December 15 through January 5, $90 a day, $500 to $960 a week.

MEALS: Breakfast, lunch, dinner, snack bar, cookouts, buffets— the works; no room service; informal.

SEASONS: Closed January 6 through May 31 and October 1 through December 14; book well in advance for July and August.

THE TIMBERS
Steamboat Springs, Colorado

Something unusual—a full-scale tennis resort 7,200 feet up in the Rockies. And so new it won't be completed until sometime in 1974. However, already half of the dozen championship courts are in action. Cliff Buchholz is the champion behind this tennis clinic, and he'll be backed up by a team of ten instructors, video-tape playbacks, ball-throwing machines, an indoor training center with mirrors, classrooms and special tennis alleys, and an exercise room. (Note: In summer, there are special clinics for teenagers, who'll be fed and housed in a separate part of the hotel; and six courts will be reserved at all times for guests.) There will also be an indoor-outdoor mineral spring pool, sauna, therapy pool and a new Robert Trent Jones golf course. If you're slightly adventurous you can float down the Yampa River in an inner tube. In winter, there's cross-country skiing from the lodge, and a free shuttle bus to the ski slopes.

This unusual new resort is a condominium development (a

tasteful one) clamped to the side of a mountain, with stunning views over the Yampa Valley and the Flattop Mountains. The buildings are striking structures of rugged, rough-hewn timber, glass and moss rock. The rooms are modern-rustic, with private bath-showers and spacious patios. For the rest, you'll have to sample The Timbers for yourself when it's fully under way. The setting alone should improve your game.

NAME: The Timbers
INNKEEPER: Dennis Grady
ADDRESS: Box 1033, Steamboat Springs, Colo. 80477
TELEPHONE: 303-879-1584
DIRECTIONS: On U.S. 40, 154 miles from Denver, 199 miles from Grand Junction, 5 miles from Steamboat Ski Area.
RATES: EP (including Continental breakfast)—February 1 through April 15 and June 1 through Labor Day, $24; Labor Day through December 12 and January 2 through 31, $21; December 23 through January 1, $26.
MEALS: Breakfast, lunch, dinner, steak fries, wine and cheese parties; room service; informal.
SEASONS: Open all year.

SUNDANCE
near Provo, Utah

Shangri-la is Chinatown at the rush hour compared to this: a grove of quaking aspen and pines serenaded by a babbling brook, watched over by the Wasatch National Forest and towering Timpanogos Mountain. You wander along pathways lined with kinnikinnick, drink fresh spring water, and share 4,300 acres of wilderness with inquisitive deer and pot guts (Rocky Mountain ground squirrels). Since there are only nine houses on the estate, you can go from breakfast to dinner without seeing another human.

If you want to know precisely how ravishing Sundance is before you go barreling out to Utah, see *Jeremiah Johnson*. It was filmed there. (And just for the record, the resort was known as Sundance long before Robert Redford made *Butch Cassidy and the Sundance Kid,* and he and his buddies bought up the place.)

The place is a marvel of unspoiled tranquility, partly because of the setting, partly because when Redford and his posse rode in they laid down firm laws: chop one tree, plant two; hide all buildings among the trees; no hunting, ever.

Until six years ago, there wasn't much here except a short ski tow, thousands of trees and the pot guts; there still isn't much. So what is Sundance? Hard to say. It's sort of a ski resort, but it certainly isn't a hotel—to stay there, you rent one of the nine private vacation homes (cabins, they modestly call them) dotted among the trees. There are no hotel services, except daily maid service.

Bosky love nests

All nine "cabins" are different, and there's no way of knowing which one will be available when you get there. When you arrive, ask Brent Beck to take you on a tour to show you which homes are free. With luck he'll offer you the Magelby Home. This one is named for a local artist who traded his artistic skills for a plot of land, and then built himself a Hansel-and-Gretel cabin of rough-hewn timbers and filled it with stone fireplaces, wood paneling from an old barn, a couple of cuddly bedrooms (one with a fireplace), and antiquey things like old ice skates, a retired bear trap, and an antiquated pedal organ. It's positively the most romantic spot in Utah, and if you hurry you may be able to rent it for $35 a night.

A slightly larger house higher up the hill belongs to an anonymous Hollywood person, who designed it and even did a lot of the chopping and sawing himself. A labor of love for love's labors: all pine and glass, with wrap-around veranda, a kitchen the size of the Magelby Home, two bedrooms, bathrooms and sauna. As if that weren't enough, he then erected a crow's-nest balcony halfway up the living room, padded it with carpet, and installed a hi-fi and a sofa where you can lounge yourself into euphoria just looking at the trees and listening to the music, but chances are you'll think of lots of other things to do at that idyllic elevation. Being larger, this nest costs $50 a night.

Although Sundance is basically a ski resort, there's plenty to do here in summer and fall. For a start, those 4,300 acres are great for walking and picnicking. There's a stable with thirty-five horses ($3.50 an hour), and you can go trotting off on your own without taking a wrangler along—or with a wrangler, on an overnight pack trip into the backwoods. There's no pool (but you can drive to one of the lakes in the neighborhood for swimming and water skiing), and no tennis (although sixteen courts are promised).

Fresh-baked bread and honey

Otherwise, Sundance has a main lodge that includes a village store, snack bar and restaurant. The snack bar's most gobbled lunch is a giant hunk of freshly baked bread smothered with melted butter and honey. It costs twenty-five cents a piece, and has enough calories for an entire meal, and if you're not careful you may end up looking like a pot gut. Dinner is served in the Tree Room, which has a Douglas fir growing through the roof, Navajo rugs and stills of *Jeremiah Johnson* on the wall. The steaks and seafood are so good here, people drive over from Salt Lake City for dinner—and the Sundance outdoor theater.

"Bordello Bandito"

The irrepressible people who run Sundance have built themselves an unusual open-air theater, where they put on plays and musicals which they compose, write, design and produce themselves. A recent hit was called "Bordello Bandito," but you might also be there for an afternoon of rock or a moonlight recital of chamber music. Sundance is nothing if not surprising.

It will soon have a complete Ghost Town, assembled from the remains of several old mining towns around Utah. They're installing a new ski lift to the top of the mountains, so that Robert Redford can enjoy championship skiing without having to drive over to Snowbird. (It's enough to make you want to be a movie star.) They also plan to hide Sundance. The parking lot, now the first thing to greet you, is being shunted off to a tree-screened location behind the lodge, and the forecourt will be landscaped with more trees. *More* trees? Shangri-la never had it so good.

NAME: Sundance

INNKEEPER: Brent Beck

ADDRESS: P.O. Box 837, Provo, Utah 84601

TELEPHONE: 801-374-8444

DIRECTIONS: Take Interstate 15 to the Provo or Orem exits (don't be dismayed by the belching steel plant), then follow U.S. 189 about 10 miles into the canyon to Utah 80, where you go left (for its seclusion, it's surprisingly accessible); by air to Salt Lake City; by Amtrak to Ogden.

RATES: EP—$35 to $50 a night, and weekly terms are usually less than 7 times that amount.

MEALS: Breakfast (any time), lunch, dinner (to 10 p.m. or thereabouts); no room service; informal (but not sloppy).

SEASONS: Open all year; basically a ski resort at this point, but busy on summer evenings when the open-air theater is filling the valley with un-Shangri-la-like thoughts; since there are only nine cabins, make your reservations well in advance.

THE LODGE AT SNOWBIRD
Snowbird, Utah

Utah has some of the most good-God-will-you-look-at-that scenery on the face of the earth, but until recently the only places to stay were run-of-the-mill motels. New ski resorts are changing all that. The most spectacular of these resorts is Snowbird, three years old and created from scratch eight miles inside Cottonwood Canyon, which is so narrow you can almost throw snowballs from one side to the other. From the skier's point of view the Snowbird statistics are as thrilling as a slalom: 3,000 feet of vertical rise, 450 inches of snow a year (more than Aspen and Vail *together*), and an aerial tram that hoists 1,200 hopefuls an hour to the top of the runs.

Your first view of the Lodge at Snowbird is a two-story structure of rough-cast concrete and cedar trim, snug with the side of the canyon, and so diffident about its majestic surroundings that you have to peer twice to see the name plate. In the lobby you're confronted with duplex floor-to-ceiling windows framing a stunning view of the slopes, and when you step out onto the terrace you realize you've seen only two of the lodge's seven stories. The other five go *down* the hillside. Seven stories of concrete and a mammoth aerial tram may not sound like the best thing that could happen to a lovely, virgin canyon, but in fact Ted Johnson and Dick Bass, the founder and funder respectively of Snowbird, seem to have been at great pains to preserve and protect the environment. Item: of the total of 860 acres owned by the duo, only twenty acres will actually have buildings (hooray for the high-rise); item: no private land is being offered for sale, so they keep control of all the architecture; item: the 150,000 square feet (the equivalent of three and one-half acres) of the Lodge at Snowbird were sited in such a way that only four evergreens had to be removed; item: in the master plan, all buildings will have natural sod-covered roofs so that skiers who have the nerve to look up on the way down will have a better view. On the other

hand, there's something scary in a master plan that still calls for a nineteen-story condominium, a new 162-room lodge, and a new forty-court tennis center. But give the place a chance.

Granite fireplaces, fluffy flokati

Now for the lodge itself. It has 160 condominium rooms, in three types of accommodations—bedroom, studio and suite. The suites are Playboy Seductive, with granite fireplaces, enough logs for a protracted seduction, fluffy flokati rugs, stylish leather-and-teak Scandinavian sofas and chairs; a kitchen for mixing wicked drinks; and a loft with queen-size beds and bentwood rockers. Each suite's two floors of window open onto that spectacular mountain view, but since the terrace outside the window runs the full length of the lodge and people can pass to and fro, keep the lights low when you're admiring the view if you're admiring each other at the same time. The studios are similar to the suites, but without the loft bedroom; the bedrooms are spacious, motel-type rooms with two double beds. All the rooms have modern bath/showers, television, room telephones. (Note: the adjoining sixty-eight-room Turramurra Lodge has identical accommodations, same rates.) The only problem at Snowbird is the one you have in most ski resorts: the staff is full of enthusiasm—for skiing. So things like ashtrays can go unemptied for days, and the fluff in the flokati is often the previous guests'. Otherwise, a nice place to be, especially in summer when the last skier has gone clomping and stomping off with his zombie boots, and tranquility reigns once more (except maybe for the construction crews, who're under strict instructions to get on with it without interfering with the guests' pleasures).

Summer idylls

All of Snowbird Village's facilities are operating in summer— four restaurants, shops, delicatessen, an unusual bar built around the exposed workings of the giant aerial tram. The tram itself is slowed down from its regular six-minute ride for impatient skiers to a twenty-four-minute ride for leisurely sightseers ($3.50 up, $3.50 down per person), from 8,100 feet at the plaza to 11,000 at Hidden Peak.

There are heated pools, saunas, four tennis courts, and backpacking trips to study the region's archaeology, and others to study the flora and fauna. A big tent is set up on the plaza, where a theatrical troupe from Salt Lake City puts on plays by, say, Shakespeare, Thurber and Woody Allen. But best of all are the tram trips up the mountain, especially at sunset; and even if it hauls up a full load of 125 people there are still plenty of out-of-this-world spots among the trees and the peaks.

NAME: The Lodge at Snowbird
INNKEEPER: Sal Raio
ADDRESS: Snowbird, Utah 84070
TELEPHONE: 801-742-2222
DIRECTIONS: Take Interstate 15 to the Sandy exit, about 20 miles
    south of Salt Lake City, then go east another 12 miles or so

on Utah 210; by air to Salt Lake International Airport; by Amtrak to Ogden.

RATES: EP—December 22 through January 5 and from February 1 through April 22, $38 (bedroom), $42 (studio) and $66 (suite); from November 1 through December 21 and from January 6 through January 31, $32, $36 and $54; and from April 23 through May 14, $24, $28 and $42; from May through November 1, $24, $26 and $40. (Note: Same rates for Turramurra Lodge.)

MEALS: Breakfast (to 11 a.m.), lunch, snack bars, dinner (to 10 p.m.); no room service; informal.

SEASONS: Open all year; skiers in winter, mud in May, peace and quiet (except for occasional groups) in summer and fall.

ALTA LODGE
Alta, Utah

Alta is one of the granddaddies of ski resorts, one of the first in the U.S. to hoist skiers up the mountain with a chair lift. But it was originally discovered by people who were more interested in getting *into* rather than up the mountain—budding miners with the same gleam in their eyes that you see in skiers after the first snowfalls of the season. Some people made fortunes in silver up here, and in the last part of the 19th century Alta had a population of 5,000. When you go walking in the woods you can still stub your toes on the remains of their homes and mines. Its population is now reduced to a few quiet dozens in summer, nature-lovers and the like.

Several of Alta's ski lodges remain open through the year. The most popular of them is also one of the oldest, the Alta Lodge. Its fifty-six rooms include a few dormitories and some luxurious bed-sitting suites. Most of the rooms are in a new chrome-and-glass wing tacked on to the side, with wall-to-wall carpeting, king-size beds and picture windows with views of the mountains; the most popular rooms are the handful of old-style pine-paneled nooks in the chalet-like main lodge. It's nothing very special, but a great spot for a relaxed summer or fall vacation in heady air, 8,600 feet above sea level.

NAME: Alta Lodge
INNKEEPER: Frank Menendez
ADDRESS: Alta, Utah 84070
TELEPHONE: 801-742-3500
DIRECTIONS: Same as for Snowbird, then add on a couple of miles.
RATES: EP—June 21 through October 1, $15 (standard room), to $22 for the corner rooms in the new wing.
MEALS: Breakfast, lunch on request, dinner; no room service; informal.
SEASONS: Open all year; best time for non-skiers is summer and fall.

THE DESERTS AND
RESORTS OF THE
GREAT SOUTHWEST

What men call gallantry, and gods adultery,
  Is much more common where the climate's sultry . . .
                                                    BYRON

86. The Bishop's Lodge

87. Rancho Encantado

88. Tom Young's Tres Lagunas Guest Ranch

89. Sagebrush Inn

90. Thunderbird Lodge & Chalets

91. Saint Bernard Hotel & Chalets

92. Hotel Edelweiss

93. Hacienda de San Roberto

94. Arizona Inn

95. Hacienda del Sol

96. Tanque Verde Ranch

97. Wild Horse Racquet and Riding Club

98. Saddle and Surrey Ranch

99. John Gardiner's Tennis Ranch

100. Marriott's Camelback Inn

101. Casa Blanca Inn

102. Hermosa Inn

103. Arizona Biltmore Hotel

104. Carefree Inn

105. The Wigwam Resort

THE BISHOP'S LODGE
Santa Fe, New Mexico

Here's a resort that owes its existence to an apricot tree. About a century ago, Archbishop Lamy (he's the one featured in Willa Cather's novel, *Death Comes to the Archbishop*) was wandering through the Little Valley of the Tesuque when he discovered an old apricot tree with particularly succulent fruit. He liked the fruit, and the valley, so he built himself a small hilltop retreat and an adobe chapel with belfry steeple and handpainted "stained glass" windows. The chapel is still there, and the apricot tree, now a gnarled 350 years old, still welcomes you to the lodge.

At the turn of the century the archbishop's estate was bought by newspaper tycoon, Joseph Pulitzer, who built a couple of villas for his daughters; Jim Thorpe's family, in turn, bought it fifty-five years ago and converted it into a resort in 1920—which probably makes it the oldest resort in the Southwest.

Ideal location

The location is ideal: a five-minute drive from the bustle of downtown Santa Fe, yet sheltered from the rest of the world, a valley in the foothills of the Sangre de Cristo Mountains, a private estate of 800 acres with five miles of frontage on the Santa Fe National Forest, 7,300 feet above sea level, almost in the desert but shaded by cottonwoods, mountain poplars, crepe myrtle, lilac, Castilian roses—and fruit trees planted by the archbishop. Days are warm and sunny up here most of the year, but even in midsummer the nights are cool and you'll want to snuggle under a blanket.

The resort consists of the main lodge, with lounge, dining room and cocktail lounge, all with Southwest decor, the two Pulitzer villas, and a couple of new wings put up in the past ten years: sixty-one guest rooms in all, and most of them are in authentic Southwest/New Mexico/Mexico decor, or something very close to it. For the record: the dreamiest is room #8, all adobe, with chunky beams, flagstone floor, Navajo rugs, fireplace and Mexican handcarved bed ($34); suite #1 is a corner room with patios facing Colorado, plus a small lawn out front, cozy bedroom, fluffy carpets, fireplace and viga (or rough-hewn beam) ceiling ($48); suites #21 and #22, in the old Pulitzer House, have fireplaces, huge bathrooms with Mexican dressers, parlors (they're both $50, but #22 is probably the better buy because it has *two* fireplaces and a small garden). But all the Bishop's rooms are comfortable and/or charming, and a dozen of them have fireplaces.

Old woodcutters' trails

Riding is the big thing at the Bishop's. The half dozen wranglers handle sixty to sixty-five horses in summer (and they're all the lodge's own horses, $6 a half day), and if you can prove to the wrangler you know your way about he might let you go off on your own. There are miles of trails in and around the estate, but you can also follow old woodcutters' trails through the forest all the way to Colorado. Better take a picnic lunch along.

But you don't have to be an equestrian to enjoy the lodge. There are three new Laykold tennis courts (soon to be five or six) with a tennis pro, a big heated pool with saunas and a Jacuzzi, fishing and trap shooting. You can lie back and do a spot of bird watching (forty-four species at last count), or you can drive off and visit some of the Indian pueblos around Santa Fe. This is one of the most fascinating corners of America—and the Bishop's Lodge is perfectly located for local excursions.

Evenings at the lodge usually begin with a drink in El Charro, a manly sort of place with saddles, sombreros and spurs to remind you of *el charro*—the legendary cowboy of Mexico. The food is a mixture of Continental and American—mignonettes of beef, Rocky Mountain trout, boeuf a la Deutsch, Pacific red snapper (in the $6 range, if you're not on American Plan). The main dining room has a Mexican feel to it, with notched off-white beams, copper chandeliers, murals of Indian ceremonies, "cantina" furniture and hand-beaten tin doors. For some reason, when the dining room is not full the staff will seat you in a rather dull extension to the dining room. Don't let them; have them set up a table in the Mexican part—it's so much nicer (except for the piped music). On warm evenings you can dine on the terrace and sniff the perfumed air that lured the archbishop here in the first place.

NAME: The Bishop's Lodge
INNKEEPER: Jim Thorpe
ADDRESS: Box 2367, Santa Fe, N. M. 87501
TELEPHONE: 505-983-6378
DIRECTIONS: Three miles north of Santa Fe Plaza on Bishop's Lodge Road (via Washington Avenue from Plaza, via Camino Encantado from U.S. 285/64/84); by air to Albuquerque (an hour and $32 away by Lodge limousine); by rail via Amtrak to Lamy ($9.50 by Lodge limousine).
RATES: AP only—$48 to $92 in June; $52 to $100 in July; $56 to $108 from August 1 through Labor Day; $44 to $112 in March, April, May, September and October (European Plan also available during these months); no tipping—12% added to bill.
MEALS: Breakfast (to 9:30 a.m.), lunch, dinner (to 8:30 p.m.); room service; jacket and tie in the evening.
SEASONS: Closed mid-October through mid-March (when the chef, bartender, maitre d' and Jim Thorpe become bricklayers, carpenters and plumbers, and build new additions); the "Texas invasion" and lots of children (they eat and play separately) in summer; probably most beautiful in spring and fall; groups to 150 in the off-season months.

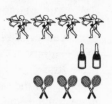

RANCHO ENCANTADO
Santa Fe (more or less), New Mexico

Beautiful. No, enchanting, like it says. By day there's desert as far as the eye can see; by night, there are stars as high as the eye can see; and there are interiors filled with art, artifacts and antiques.

The ranch's 168 acres are surrounded on three sides by the Nambe Indian Reservation and on the fourth by the Santa Fe National Forest; to the east are the Sangre de Cristo Mountains, to the west (away to the west) the Jemez Mountains. The grandeur of the setting and the charm of the ranch have corraled the likes of Nelson Rockefeller, Henry Fonda, Kirk Douglas, Maria Callas, Gregory Peck, Robert Culp and the Duchess of Argyll. Some posse.

The ranch got its start back in the early Thirties when a young lady who learned her innkeeping at The Bishop's Lodge decided to branch out on her own; she chose this spot and had her brother-in-law put up the buildings (he also made a lot of the furniture, some of it still there in the lobby). But the ranch's present name and personality are the creation of its present owner, Betty Egan, a widow from Cleveland, who started a new life here six years ago with her four teenagers. Among them, and with the imagination and taste of their interior designer, Donald Murphy, they've created the sort of guest ranch you always hope a desert ranch will look like.

The lobby's flagstone floors and raftered ceiling set the tone; the lounge is a casually elegant room with a huge adobe fireplace, cowbells, a skylight above the fire, rawhide tables and lamps, decorative tiles and hand-woven cushions. The dining room is three tiers of white adobe, decorative tiles and flagstone floors, with most of the tables commanding a view through tall windows and across the terrace to unending, unspoiled desert. There are lots of neat little touches about the place—like a wall plaque with nineteen (*19*) types of barbed wire, and a hand-carved armoire concealing a cigarette machine.

Rafters, tiles, retablos

The twenty-two guest rooms are equally enchanting—all in Southwestern style, with Franklin stoves, antique lamps, raftered ceilings, tiled floors, Indian rugs and wall hangings, *retablos* and so forth. The quietest rooms are in the cottages (they also have fireplaces), but the prettiest is probably #8, up a beautiful tiled stairway to the second floor of the main lodge. All the rooms have private bathrooms with tub/showers, but no television (you can have one installed if you're gauche enough to ask for it).

Despite all this luxury, Rancho Encantado is an outdoorsy sort of place. One of its earliest horseriding guests, a Mrs. Sage Underwood, used to turn up with her own cowboy; today she'd probably be happy to rely on Phil Kniffer, probably the most dapper wrangler in all the Southwest. His stable has ten frisky horses and a somnolent buffalo named Gertrude. (Horses rent for $4 an hour, and you'll probably have to be accompanied by a wrangler.) There's also an elevated swimming pool with sun terraces and a stunning view across the desert. Sharpshooters will find the skeet and trap range across the road. Tennis buffs have to share a solitary court, but they can while away the time between sets playing pool or having a beer in the Cantina Lounge, next to the courts.

Sopaipillas and 14-ounce steaks

It would be a shame if the ranch's meals were a letdown for its lovely dining room. They're not. At lunchtime try a snack called The Bread Board, which is just that—a wooden bread board with slices of apple, Dutch cheese, and a glass of red wine ($2). For dinner you can go Mexican with a Tesuque Special (enchiladas, tamales, tacos, guacamole, tostadas and home-made sopaipillas with honey—$4.50) or carne asado (steak marinated with chili strips—$7.25); or go cowboy with steaks (8-, 10-, 12- and 14-ouncers) and butterfly porkchops cooked in beer ($6.50). Top that off with something that's neither Mexican nor cowboy, just sinful—a concoction called a Flower Pot ($2.50 worth of ice cream and goodies). Wines? Everything from Paul Masson's Cabernet Sauvignon at $4.50 to Chateau d'Yquem at a Rockefellerish $20. If it means the difference between staying here and not staying here, settle for the Paul Masson. Or a glass of beer. Or even a glass of water.

NAME: Rancho Encantado
INNKEEPER: Betty Egan
ADDRESS: Rt. 4, Box 57C, Santa Fe, N. M. 87501
TELEPHONE: 505-982-3537
DIRECTIONS: Follow U.S. 285/84/64 to the intersection with N.M. 22 (just south of the Santa Fe Opera); a few miles past a village called Tesuque, turn right at the Rancho Encantado sign and follow that road another mile or so.
RATES: EP—$40 to $45, from one week before Easter through September 30; 25% less the remainder of the year.
MEALS: Breakfast (to noon), lunch, dinner (to 9 p.m. in winter, 10 in summer), snacks and sandwiches throughout the after-

noon; room service; informal or jacket and tie (depending
on whether you ask the room clerk or the rather formal
maitre d').

SEASONS: Open all year, busy from June through September and
on holidays the rest of the year; make your reservations well
in advance at any time of the year.

TOM YOUNG'S TRES LAGUNAS GUEST RANCH
Pecos, New Mexico

Another side to New Mexico—a Maine-like setting of log cabins
dwarfed by pines and firs, with a bubbly mountain stream, between Willow Creek and Holy Ghost Creek. Tres Lagunas is
billed as a family resort, but this doesn't mean it's overrun by
kids in summer; rather, it means that the resort is *run,* mop, pot
and barrel, by the Tom Youngs and their ten Youngsters. In fact,
the children are the reason why the resort added the words Tom
Young to its name a couple of years ago: he came up here for a
vacation and liked the place so much he bought the resort "just
for the kids." Lucky kids.

Besides the natural glories of the Pecos Wilderness area, Tres
Lagunas has a stable with fifteen horses ($3 an hour, and you
can go riding off by yourselves); a heated pool; three trout-
stocked lakes and a private mile-long stretch of the Pecos for
fishing; and mile after mile of walking tracks, along the stream
and up the road (it goes nowhere so it's never crowded).

The cabins look just rustic and right in this all-embracing
greenery, but you don't have to rough it. They have stone fireplaces, bathtubs in wood-walled bathrooms, Navajo rugs and
porches. Socializing takes place in the main lodge, an oversized
log cabin with a comfy lounge and library; and meals are served
in the wonderfully woodsy Waterfall Room overlooking the Pecos
River and the Ponderosa pines. A great place for kids—to spend
their summers pampering you.

NAME: Tom Young's Tres Lagunas Guest Ranch
INNKEEPERS: The Young family
ADDRESS: Rt. 2, Box 100, Pecos, N. M. 87552
TELEPHONE: 505-757-6194
DIRECTIONS: Leave Interstate 25 at the N.M. 63 Pecos/Glorieta exit (16 miles east of Santa Fe); the ranch is 12 miles north of Pecos, still on N.M. 63; by air or Amtrak, the Youngs will pick you up by limousine ($12 for two from Santa Fe or Lamy).
RATES: AP—$56.
MEALS: Breakfast, lunch, dinner; no room service; informal.
SEASONS: Open from May 1 through October 20; busiest (but never crowded) in June, July and August.

SAGEBRUSH INN
Taos, New Mexico

This is the sort of inn you hope to find in a place like Taos, with its clusters of terra-cotta adobe buildings, its cherished Southwestern ambiance, and its love affair with Indian, Mexican and Western art. The Sagebrush is shaded by cottonwoods and filled with the works of local artists. It's slightly ramshackle—but even that's part of the Taos charm. The main lounge is an authentic hacienda room—viga ceilings and a massive adobe piñon-burning fireplace, Navajo rugs, handcarved *santos* and handpainted *bultos,* rare pottery, and paintings by some of the old masters and some of the not so old and not so masterly artists who live in and around Taos. Las Maracas, the cocktail lounge, is as snug as a pub, with an open fire and rawhide and wicker furniture, and a folk singer strumming through a repertory of Spanish, Mexican and flamenco songs; the dining room is colorful Mexican—wicker chairs and wooden tables, candles and paintings—and a popular spot with the poets, artists, musicians and assorted dilettantes who've been here long enough to call themselves *taosenas.*

The guest rooms are grouped around a courtyard at the rear and linked by a shady ramada—except for a few rooms in the second story of the main building, and one rather drafty room in the penthouse of the mission-style tower. They're also in Southwestern style, and some of them have adobe fireplaces in the corner (they're the most popular buys, because you may think you're out in a blazing desert in Taos but in fact you're 7,000 feet up and it can get chilly there, even in midsummer). Unfortunately, there's nothing very Taosy or romantic in the inn's setting—plunk by the side of the highway like any common or garden motel; and the South Santa Fe Road only proves that the main drag into a cultured, historic spot like Taos can be as dreary as any other main drag. So use the Sagebrush Inn as a base for exploring the art galleries, boutiques, restaurants, old churches, that marvelous, multi-story Indian pueblo just north of town, and the other sights of this extraordinary corner of the United States. Otherwise don't leave your cozy little Sagebrush room except to lounge in the lounge, drink in Las Maracas or replenish your energy in the dining room.

NAME: Sagebrush Inn
INNKEEPER: M. D. Vallier
ADDRESS: P.O. Box 835, Taos, N. M. 87571
TELEPHONE: 505-758-2254
DIRECTIONS: Two miles south of Taos and just north of Rancho de Taos, on the South Santa Fe Road (U.S. 64).
RATES: EP—$9.50 to $19.50, year round.
MEALS: Breakfast (to 10 a.m.), no lunch, dinner (to 9 p.m.); no room service; informal.
SEASONS: Open year round; busiest July and August, and on weekends during the skiing season.

THUNDERBIRD LODGE & CHALETS, SAINT BERNARD HOTEL & CHALETS and HOTEL EDELWEISS
Taos Ski Valley, New Mexico

Taos Ski Valley is the brainchild of a champion called Ernie Blake, and it's reputed to have some of the toughest ski runs in the world. That may be; right now we're considering the valley as a nice place to go in summer and fall. Taos Valley is tucked away, nineteen miles deep within a steep-sided canyon, a place of pines and peaks and peace. The valley floor is speckled with half a dozen hotels and lodges, but the trio above is enough to keep you contented in summer. They follow the usual pattern of ski lodges—simple but comfortable rooms with private baths or showers; both the Thunderbird and the Saint Bernard also have chalets, which have more personality than the main lodges. Between them, the lodges offer pools, sauna, tennis courts, horseback riding, jeep rides and a choice of hearty restaurants. They're bases for walking through forests or hikes up mountains, but they're also escape from the hordes of summer visitors in Taos itself. In July and August you get an extra bonus when the Saint Bernard hosts a mini music festival of chamber concerts and recitals.

NAMES: Thunderbird Lodge & Chalets
    Saint Bernard Hotel & Chalets
    Hotel Edelweiss
ADDRESS: Taos Ski Valley, N. M. 87571
TELEPHONE: 505-776-2266 (reservations for all lodges in the valley)
DIRECTIONS: Nineteen miles north of Taos on N.M. 3 and N.M. 150; by private or charter air flights to Taos Municipal Airport; by Amtrak to Lamy.
RATES: EP—$12 to $18 in non-ski season.
MEALS: Breakfast, lunch, dinner; no room service; informal.
SEASONS: Open all year, but avoid ski season and muddy May.

HACIENDA DE SAN ROBERTO
El Prado (near Taos), New Mexico

This is the alternative to the Sagebrush if you want lots of local charm, but don't want to be next to the highway.

The Hacienda has seven suites, and that's it. Seven rooms. All suites. It was built in 1966 by a wealthy Ohian for other wealthy Ohians, or at least for well-to-do types who wanted to get away from it all without having to sacrifice any of their comforts—other than radios, telephones, television and air conditioning. All the suites have two rooms, adobe fireplaces, heating lamps in the bathrooms, and porches at the front door with views across the valley to stands of gambel oaks, piñon and junipers.

The Hacienda is on the sunny side of a forgotten canyon at the entrance to Taos Ski Valley, a few feet above the trout-filled Rio Hondo, and about 8,000 feet above the sea. You're greeted in the lobby by *pianissimo* Bach, so you won't be surprised to learn that Lan and Elizabeth Farley discovered the Ohian's hideaway when they came this way for the music festival up at Taos Ski Valley; they loved the location and the inn, and since they were bored with their jobs as school teachers in California, they bought the place in November 1972. A bold move for a young couple—but they have the enthusiasm to be successful innkeepers. What they have to offer besides enthusiasm are a heated pool (sauna and Jacuzzi are on the way), horses (included in the rate—but check that the stable is open before you go), and all those gentle gestures of nature, like deer browsing on the lawn, stellar jays fluttering among the bushes, and porches and a dining room facing dazzling desert sunsets.

The Farleys will serve your dinner in your room, but the dining room is a lovely spot—just half a dozen tables and a big fire crackling in the adobe fireplace.

Potentially, a perfect spot for lovers.

NAME: Hacienda de San Roberto
INNKEEPERS: Lan and Elizabeth Farley
ADDRESS: P.O. Box 449, El Prado, N. M. 87529
TELEPHONE: 505-776-2630
DIRECTIONS: Follow U.S. 64 5 miles north from Taos, then go right on N.M. 150 through Valdez; the Hacienda is a few miles beyond that, just before you go into the canyon that takes you to Taos Ski Valley; or by air from Albuquerque for $40 per plane.
RATES: AP—$68; lower in winter.
MEALS: Breakfast (to 9 a.m.), lunch, dinner (to 8:30 p.m.); closed Wednesday; room service; informal; no liquor license, but bring your own and the Farleys will supply the set-ups.
SEASONS: Open all year, busiest in July and August (but even when full it's never crowded); spring and fall (fall especially) are the most beautiful seasons.

ARIZONA INN
Tucson, Arizona

Let them know when you're arriving and they'll have the fire burning for you. When you settle in, call room service for dinner, then curl up for the evening before the crackling mesquite. Next morning when you wake up, you'll find yourself in an oasis—pink stucco cottages blushing among fourteen acres of greenery. Lawns everywhere. Beds of violets and poppies. Anchor doves flitting among the palo verde, poplars, bottlebrush and longneedle pine. Eight gardeners silently trimming, weeding, watering. You could easily fool yourself into thinking you're out in the country. In fact, you're smack in the middle of suburbia, and the Arizona Inn is merely a cocoon coddling you from the real world.

It wasn't always that way.

When it first opened forty-odd years ago, the Arizona was

indeed away out in the middle of the desert, but then the almost-perfect climate of Tucson lured more and more vacationers to the area, and then more and more residents, and slowly the city besieged the inn. You'd never guess that from inside the inn, and there's no reason to leave. You have everything you need for unwinding right there within the pink stucco walls.

You have a private patio for sunbathing; an uncrowded swimming pool with a sun terrace on one side and a leafy arbor on the other; a couple of Har-Tru tennis courts (floodlit for evening play) and a pro shop; a croquet lawn and a putting green; and a pampering staff.

Strawberries, figs and baked winesap apples

Goodness, how you'll be pampered. Morning paper waiting at your door. Breakfast on your patio (anything from muffins, strawberries, apricots and figs to hot clear bouillon, kippered herring and baked winesap apple). Lunch by the pool. Dinner by the fire. "We don't try to be 'gourmet,' " says Ash Purse, "we just serve good, plain, wholesome food." Which means that your roast leg of lamb comes with real mint sauce and not the usual paper cup with a glob of green gelatin.

This is the sort of place where personal service still means *personal* service. The poolside waiter gets quite upset if he can't remember your name when you order your second round—and the fact that he's been remembering names correctly for over thirty-seven years doesn't console him. More than half the staff has been at the Arizona Inn for twenty years or more (not too many hotels can make a claim like that), which is probably one reason why so many of the guests have been coming back year after year since the inn was surrounded by desert. They're not only loyal, they're a pretty distinguished group, too—from Winston Churchill and assorted English lords to Salvador Dali and Cary Grant. John D. Rockefeller liked it so much here, he kept a cottage for his permanent use. And apparently the inn still gets the patricians, because the registration card includes space at the bottom for the names of your chauffeur and maid.

Miss Greenway and the WWI veterans

This special place came about in a rather unusual way. Shortly after World War I, a local lady by the name of Miss Greenway started a plan to help veterans adapt to postwar conditions: they made furniture by hand, their wives decorated it, Miss Greenway bought it. They must have been eager beavers because after a short time Miss Greenway had more furniture than she could use. So she built an inn out in the desert.

But don't get the idea that the Arizona Inn is a rickety place filled with old hand-made furniture. It isn't. Miss Greenway added some of her own family heirlooms, and regional decorations made from copper and cactus. It's a luxurious place, with a full-time decorator on the staff to make sure everything stays immaculate. The lounge is fit for a Spanish grandee—dark wooden ceiling and rafters, stately furniture grouped around a huge fireplace, and custom-designed carpets hand-woven in Morocco. The rooms are equally comfortable, with armchairs, desks, coffee tables, private patios or sun parlors, tiled bathrooms—but no TV in the interests of peace and quiet. Air conditioning has just been installed for the first time (1973 was the first time the inn stayed open all year). In winter, of course, you don't need air conditioning, because the days are like spring and the evenings like fall—and you're glad you asked for a room with a fire.

NAME: Arizona Inn
INNKEEPER: Ashley A. Purse
ADDRESS: 2200 East Elm Street, Tucson, Ariz. 85719
TELEPHONE: 602-325-1541
DIRECTIONS: Get off Interstate 10 at the Speedway Boulevard exit, go east on Speedway to the University of Arizona, turn left on Campbell, drive 5 blocks, turn right and you're on E. Elm, almost at the inn; regular air and Amtrak service.
RATES: AP only—$48 to $72 between November 1 and January 14; $64 to $92 between January 15 and April 30; summer rates much lower, with EP rates also available; tennis free.

MEALS: Breakfast (to 9:30 a.m.), lunch (indoor or poolside), dinner (to 8:15 p.m.); jacket and tie in the evening; room service.

SEASONS: Open all year; peak months (mostly old folks) January through April; small (up to 155 only) groups during the summer.

HACIENDA DEL SOL
Tucson, Arizona

The well-to-do of Tucson are taking to the hills, most of them to the foothills of the Catalinas.

The Home of the Sun beat them to it. And its knolltop perch will probably stay inviolate for years to come, because the owner of this swatch of desert lives on the neighboring knoll and he likes the view the way it is. When you drive up past the saguaro and palm trees you're welcomed to the hacienda by a mission gateway; a gently splashing blue-tiled fountain and a pathway shaded by orange and grapefruit trees lead you inside. The hacienda is a cloister-like cluster of adobe casitas, with arches and red-tiled roofs. Very Mexican, very Spanish.

It was built originally as a girls' school, back in 1929, and was transformed into a guest ranch in 1946. The Hartmans took it over three years ago, and moved in their personal collection of Mexican and Indian art—Aztec suns, gods' eyes, handpainted chairs and coffee tables, hand-beaten and hand-carved tin-and-timber screens and chandeliers. The dining room is roofed by heavy carved beams and highlighted by silver lamps and sconces, and a big hutch with antique tin and silver; the lounge has a blue-adobe fireplace, Navajo rugs and Kachina dolls. The Southwest with style and taste.

It's a wonderfully detached, restful place, up there above the city. You can lounge in the courtyard beneath the orange

and grapefruit trees, sun yourself around the heated pool, soothe yourself in a therapy pool. At tequila time you can pull up a chair by the windows of the *Casa Feliz* and look down on Tucson's sprawling lights and pretend they're moonlight shimmering on a lake. Then a leisurely dinner in that beautiful dining room, and a stroll around the garden before turning in for the night. The rooms are, well, snug. They were, after all, girls' dormitories. If you need more space, ask for a room or a suite in one of the cottages at the rear. All thirty-five rooms have private bathrooms, Mexican/Spanish/Southwest decor, and some of them even have air conditioning (although you'll hardly need it up here at 2,750 feet).

Despite all this charm and style, the hacienda is really a ranch, and its wranglers will take you riding up and down that inviolate hillside.

But maybe you can't bear the thought of all those hoofs and you'd rather just lounge around and enjoy silence. How often do you have a chance to do that?

NAME: La Hacienda del Sol

INNKEEPER: Robert E. Hartman

ADDRESS: Rt. #5, N. Hacienda del Sol Road, Tucson, Ariz. 85718

TELEPHONE: 602-299-1501

DIRECTIONS: Follow Campbell Drive from the University of Arizona to River Road; halfway up the hill, turn right until you come to Hacienda del Sol Road, which you stick with all the way; the Hacienda is 8 miles from downtown Tucson.

RATES: AP only—$40 to $60 from November 1 through December 15; $48 to $70 from December 15 to May 1; riding extra ($5 a day).

MEALS: Breakfast (to 10:00 a.m.), lunch (poolside), dinner (international with a dash of Norwegian, served from 6:30 to 7:30 p.m.); room service; informal, but you'll probably need a jacket in the evening anyway.

SEASONS: Open winter months only; quietest times are first 2 weeks in November, first 3 weeks in January; but relaxing at any time.

TANQUE VERDE RANCH
Tucson, Arizona

Many desert moons ago, the Tanque Verde's owner was strung up by the neck over the rafters of what is now the Reading and Card Room. Not by irate guests, but by outlaws out for his petty cash. That was back in the days when the ranch was a stagecoach stop on the San Pedro run, and it had its fair share of Injun raids and cattle rustling. Nowadays, the posses heading out of the corral are harmless and wobbly tourists, and the ranch is one of the most peaceful spots in Arizona.

It could hardly be anything else, given its location. It's 2,800 feet up in the foothills of the Tanque Verde Mountains; its eastern border is 1,385,307 rugged acres of the Federal Coronado Forest Preserve, and its southern border is the 63,000-acre Saguaro National Monument. Tucson is eight miles and twenty-nine dips away along the Speedway Boulevard. All that wilderness shuts out the rumbles of civilization and you're left with the cry of the coyote and the assorted chirps, warbles, cries and whistles of the red-shafted flicker, LeConte's thrasher, the bridled titmouse, Williamson's sapsucker and the lesser scaup. There's a birdbath in sight of every room, so you can sit on your porch and watch the cavortings of the common bushtit, black phoebe, boat-tailed grackle and Inca dove. Look farther and you may spot a bald eagle. More than 124 species have been spotted here. (There's a bird-banding every Thursday, and guests are invited to join in.)

Most people don't come here, though, to watch the birds. They come to ride over desert trails, past giant saguaro, and up into the mountains to *Campos Americanos* and the *Puerto de Cabeza de la Vaca* (the Cow-headed Saddle). This is very much a horse-and-wrangler type of ranch—and you can take your

pick from a string of eighty palominos, appaloosas, sorrels and buckskins. Unlimited riding (but only with escort) is included in the rate, so most people ride. But if you get saddle sore, don't despair. You can take a dip in the heated outdoor pool, in the indoor pool or the Jacuzzi whirlpool, work out in the exercise room, or dry out in the sauna (male and female separately, but if you talk to the right people you can arrange to sauna together). When your muscles have recovered, get out on the court for a fast set of tennis before dinner.

The oldest part of the ranch, dating from 1862, is now the office/lounge, alongside a low-ceilinged wing of adobe rooms sheltered by an authentic ramada of rough-hewn timbers topped by a roof of ghost saguaro. Hammocks dangle between the timber pillars. Antique Mexican pottery dots the garden, among the eucalyptus, pepper and wild orange tree (if you're lucky you may even sample a wild orange pie some evening at dinner).

Across the garden is the old adobe bunkhouse which has gone through a few transformations and become the Dog House Bar—a bottle club with flagstone floor, adobe fireplace, rawhide chairs, and pictures of Wild Bill Hickok, Wyatt Earp, Luther Patton and that notorious Wild West dog-kicker, W.C. Fields. This is the gathering place after a day riding the range. Here, or up on the sun-deck above the Sonora Health Spa and Recreation Center. The spa is where you'll find Tanque Verde's indoor pool, sauna and exercise rooms. Unlikely items on a dude ranch? But this is no ordinary dude ranch.

The Ph.D. and the stewardess

How could it be with a manager who speaks fluent French, Chinese and Japanese, and earned his Ph.D. with a thesis entitled, "A Russian Agronomist's Influence on Japanese Agriculture"? DeeDee Cote was a stewardess who used to come here between flights to ride her favorite horse, Champ, before she realized she was really coming because she was in love with the manager. So they got married.

And where else will you find a dude ranch with one German and one French chef, and a pastry chef from Berlin ("Red" Kronschnabel, a name that translates like the name of one of the neighborhood birds—Red Crown Beak). So you won't have to settle for chuckwagon food. Some evenings you'll find German dishes, other evenings Polynesian. And on Mexican nights, you can taste tacos and tamales made as authentically as if Kronschnabel from Berlin was really Coronapico from Nogales.

Comfy cottages

Tanque Verde's sixty patio lodges and cottages all have private baths, individual thermostat heat controls and room phones. No room service or TV (there's a set in the lounge). Many of the rooms have log burning fireplaces, many have private patios. No two rooms are alike, so take a peek and pick the one that suits you before you move in. Room #7, for example, is a suite with adobe fireplace, fitted carpet, wood walls ($74 in season); suite #22 has corner windows facing the sunset, a garden patio and fireplace ($90 in season); and if you're more interested in riding than in comfort, you can have a small "ramada" room (only $55—but remember that includes all meals *and* riding).

NAME: Tanque Verde Guest Ranch
INNKEEPERS: Bob and DeeDee Cote
ADDRESS: Box 515, Route 8, Tucson, Ariz. 85710
TELEPHONE: 602-296-6275
DIRECTIONS: Follow East Speedway east until it goes no farther —15 miles from the center of town; by air or Amtrak to Tucson.
RATES: AP only *including* rental of horses and all other facilities —$39 to $72 from May 1 through December 15; $50 to $90 from December 16 through April 30; summer and fall lower still.
MEALS: Breakfast (to 9:30 a.m.), lunch, dinner (6:30–7:30 p.m.), cookouts—the works; informal; no room service.

SEASONS: Open all year, but the biggest posses ride off from December through April.

WILD HORSE RACQUET & RIDING CLUB
Tucson, Arizona

They say you can still find Indian relics within walking distance of this ranch (Cochise and his braves used to scout these parts); and don't be surprised if deer, wild pigs or coyotes cross your path because the land around here is part of a wildlife preserve.

Some of the riding trails may even look familiar because nearby Box Canyon pops up frequently on TV shows like *High Chaparral* and *Bonanza;* and if you can remember all the way back to Hollywood's epic *Arizona,* you may recognize the covered wagon that welcomes you to the ranch.

The Wild Horse Racquet and Riding Club is located twelve miles northwest of Tucson, in the foothills of the Tucson Mountains. It's been a guest ranch since the Twenties, and has been owned by Howard and Marion Miller for more than thirty years. Since it's also their home, you'll find that everything is spic-and-span, with just the right modern touches to make it comfortable, without stifling the Old West atmosphere.

Kachina dolls and kumquats

The public rooms, particularly, put you right in the mood. Throughout the ranch, you'll see a fine selection of early paintings of the Old West by artists like Ray Strang, Dale Nichols and Carolus Verhaeren. The Branding Iron Room, the bar, was inspired by the Old Trading Post at Ganado (now a national monument). The unstuffy library is decorated with Navajo rugs and Kachina dolls—a pleasant spot to rest up between rides, and bring yourself up to date on the lore of the pioneers. The dining room is brightly Mexican, with an indoor-outdoor garden that makes you less reluctant to come in out of the greenery outside—a stampede of joshua trees, date palms, ironwood, sweet-scented jasmine and bougainvillea, pomegranates, olives, kumquats and over a hundred types of cactus. Every few yards you come across bird feeders that lure whitewing doves and orioles and quail. Somewhere in the midst of all this nature are the cottages. With a build-up like that garden, they turn out to be a bit disappointing. Spic-and-span, *sí;* Southwestern, Mexican, ranch-like, *no.*

If you want to spend most of your time in bed, this isn't the place for you; but if you want to spend some time by a pool, ride horses, stroll along nature trails, play tennis, or look for the head of a tomahawk—then consider the Wild Horse.

NAME: Wild Horse Racquet & Riding Club

INNKEEPERS: Marion and Howard Miller

ADDRESS: P.O. Box 5505, Tucson, Ariz. 85703

TELEPHONE: 602-297-2266

DIRECTIONS: Leave Interstate 10 at the Cortaro exit, north of Tucson; turn left under Freeman, then follow the Wild Horse ranch signs.

RATES: AP—$40 to $56 from October 1 to December 15, $44 to $70 from December 15 to April 30; closed rest of year; tennis and riding are included.

MEALS: Breakfast, lunch, dinner, cookouts; at dinner "you will wear about the same type of clothes you would wear going to a buffet supper at your Country Club"; no room service.

SEASONS: Quietest months are early fall and early spring, but since there are only 44 rooms, make your reservations well in advance.

SADDLE AND SURREY RANCH
Tucson, Arizona

A smaller version of Tanque Verde and Wild Horse, this ranch accommodates thirty guests only. And since horse riding is included in the room rates, most of these thirty people spend as much time on horseback as their flesh will allow. Their enthusiasm makes for a clubby atmosphere. So does the rawhide-and-blue-tiled cantina, a bottle club where the riders gather after their day among the sagebrush.

The Saddle and Surrey is up in the foothills of the Tucson Mountain, a short gallop from the Wild Horse Ranch. It's part of the same 100,000-acre wildlife refuge, so the ranch wranglers have plenty of open spaces to herd their string of seventeen horses. They also organize desert cookouts and breakfast rides, and barbecues in the garden. The Saddle and Surrey is an informal, easy-going sort of place, casual as a cowpoke. No jacket and tie for dinner here, but you are expected to be in the lovely Mexican-styled dining room at seven on the dot. The only facilities on the ranch besides horses are a heated pool and a TV lounge.

NAME: Saddle and Surrey Ranch Resort
INNKEEPERS: Jack and Colette Jackson
ADDRESS: Box 941, 4110 Sweetwater Drive, Tucson, Ariz.
   85705
TELEPHONE: 602-622-7133
DIRECTIONS: Get off Interstate 10 at Corsaro Road exit, about
   5 miles north of town; go west to Silverbell Road, then
   south to Sweetwater.
RATES: AP only—$50 to $62 from October 1 to December 15;
   $56 to $68 from December 15 to May; all horseback riding
   included.
MEALS: Breakfast (to 9. a.m. only), lunch, dinner (at 7 p.m.),

breakfast rides, desert cookouts, barbecues; informal; no room service.

SEASONS: October 1 through May 1 only; with only 14 rooms the ranch is usually busy, so make your reservation well in advance.

JOHN GARDINER'S TENNIS RANCH
Scottsdale, Arizona

Put forty modern casitas on the side of a desert hill. Add three heated swimming pools. Fourteen Plexi-Pave tennis courts. Closed-circuit TV. One of the greatest players who ever whipped a backhand. That's a tennis ranch. Now people it with Beautiful, Bronzed, Athletic People. That's John Gardiner's Tennis Ranch at Camelback. This is one of the most unusual resorts in the Southwest. The forty-one casitas are actually private play homes owned by well-heeled sporty types who rent them out when they're off making the money to pay for their play homes. These cozy little nests are just about everybody's idea of a dream house in the desert—beamed ceilings, open fireplaces, spacious patios, air conditioning, big windows looking across the valley, pullman kitchens in the suites (but oddly enough, square tub/ showers, not the stretch-out-in kind of bathtub you'd probably welcome after what you've been through down there on the courts).

3,000 strokes an hour

If you join one of the special clinics, you'll be on the courts from nine to twelve-thirty every morning for five days, or from two to five-thirty, and struggle through sessions with an automatic ball machine that pops out 3,000 balls an hour.

So you'll spend your days here walking from the luxury of your casita to the tennis courts; then to one of the three pools for a breather and suntan, maybe a sauna and massage; then lunch (an extravagant buffet); then a siesta; then more tennis. Everybody takes his or her tennis seriously here, but there are enough duffers and fluffers to keep Ken Rosewall and his pros wincing.

Unfortunately, or fortunately, depending on your muscles, the courts are not floodlit, so you can get dressed for dinner in the ranch's restaurant, or take advantage of your luxurious surroundings, call room service and have your meal in front of your juniper-burning fire. That way you get to bed sooner. To rest up for tomorrow's tennis, of course.

NAME: John Gardiner's Tennis Ranch at Camelback

INNKEEPER: Ray Farrow

ADDRESS: 57000 E. McDonald Drive, Scottsdale, Ariz. 85252

TELEPHONE: 602-947-2461

DIRECTIONS: From Sky Harbor Airport, or the interstate, go north on 24th Street to Camelback, then go east to 44th Street, then left and stay on 44th until it makes a right turn and becomes McDonald Drive; by air or Amtrak to Phoenix.

RATES: MAP (breakfast and *lunch,* not dinner)—$60 and $82 from October 1 to January 15 and from April 16 to May 31; $70 and $98 from January 16 to April 15; tennis free; special 4-day clinic rate of $350 per person (which includes all meals and tennis lessons).

MEALS: Breakfast and buffet lunch, dinner optional; tennis gear by day ("white is right" is the rule), jacket and tie at night; room service.

SEASONS: October through May.

MARRIOTT'S CAMELBACK INN
Scottsdale, Arizona

"Where time stands still" is one of their slogans. Unfortunately, it doesn't. Neither does progress, and the Camelback is getting bigger and bigger (they've just discovered condominiums). There are 326 rooms now, and before long there will be 410. However, the Camelback Inn is one of the few resorts in this area that stays open all year—and in summer it's a whopping bargain. And 60 percent less crowded.

The inn is spread over a 120-acre estate on the lower slopes of Mummy Mountain, across the valley from its more famous twin—Camelback Mountain. The original building, the lobby and lounge, was built in 1935 in true adobe style—from the mud dug up for the foundation. The newest buildings' guest rooms are inspired by Indian kiwas, or five-sided ceremonial chambers. Each room has a private patio (some with views of the mountains, others with views of other patios), individual temperature controls, refrigerator, color TV—and is decorated in the colors and fabrics of the Southwest and Mexico. The most luxurious rooms are bilevel suites (which you can rent for only $75 in summer, half the winter rate), living room with bar on the ground floor, bedroom, bathroom and carpeted patio upstairs; the most charming rooms are at the rear of the hotel, in the colorful garden surrounding the pool, but unfortunately there are plans to rebuild them and they may not be so peaceful and charming after that.

Other new plans include a health spa, with exercise room and masseur, and a few more tennis courts to add to the present six, all floodlit. You won't be at a loss for things to do since there are already two swimming pools, two therapy pools, billiard room, putting green, table tennis, shuffleboard, bikes ($3 a day), an eighteen-hole pitch-and-putt course, and a 6,687-yard championship golf course with a new clubhouse (green fee $8). You can go riding on an Indian reservation a few miles down the road, or take a breakfast ride and watch the sun rise over Camelback Mountain while you're munching sausages, eggs and hotcakes cooked over an open fire up in the foothills of Mummy Mountain.

Remember, you'll be sharing all those facilities with fewer people in summer and even if the temperatures are up in the nineties at least it's a *dry* heat.

NAME: Marriott's Camelback Inn
INNKEEPER: Adam Byrd
ADDRESS: P.O. Box 70 Scottsdale Ariz. 85252
TELEPHONE: 602-947-3561 (or 800-228-9290 toll free)
DIRECTIONS: On East Lincoln Drive, the main east-west road on the north side of Camelback Mountain; about 10 minutes from Scottsdale, 20 minutes from downtown Phoenix, Sky Harbor Airport and the Amtrak depot.
RATES: EP—$18 to $75 (bilevel suite) between June 1 and September 14; $35 to $120 from September 15 through January 14 and May 1 through May 31; $52 to $150 from January 15 through April 30.
MEALS: Breakfast (to 11 a.m.), lunch, dinner (to 11 p.m.), snacks, cookouts; jacket and tie in the evening; room service to 10 p.m.
SEASONS: For economy, go in the summer (but beware of conventions); for weather and small crowds, spring and fall.

CASA BLANCA INN
Scottsdale, Arizona

If you can't make it to Morocco, enjoy a touch of Arabia in Arizona. Your first sight of the Inn is a white minaret jutting incongruously up from the surrounding suburbia. What's a minaret doing in the middle of Scottsdale? Answer—a fantastically wealthy tycoon was living out his fantasy. This tycoon created a twenty-acre estate with symmetrical gardens radiating from a fountain and one white meditation bench; at one end he built a low, white casa in Spanish-Moroccan style and filled it with antique flagstone floors, wall-filling tapestries, antique chests and chairs, and carved wooden doors from an old mission in Spain. In 1947, the mansion was enlarged and encircled by casitas spotted among the acacias, jacarandas and ocotillas. The Casa Blanca has 115 rooms, and all have patios, TV, individually controlled refrigerated air conditioning, and enough closet space for a harem. Some of the twenty-three even have patios private enough to do some of the things people do in a harem.

Otherwise, there are two tennis courts, a swimming pool, and golf at the nearby Scottsdale Country Club. And you can always wander through the gardens reciting from *A Thousand and One Nights* and plucking lantanas and oxellas for your beloved.

(Note: In 1972, the inn was bought up by Ramada Inns, which made its reputation operating medium-priced motels, and they still have to prove themselves in this kind of operation; and when the new management refers you back to head office for answers, that can be a bad sign. So keep your fingers crossed that your visit doesn't turn out to be a thousand and one night-mares.)

NAME: Casa Blanca Inn
INNKEEPER: Jim Daly
ADDRESS: 5001 N. Casa Blanca Drive, Scottsdale, Ariz. 85252
TELEPHONE: 602-945-6391
DIRECTIONS: Keep your eyes open for a white minaret.
RATES: EP—$32 to $90 from January 20 to April 23; $26 to $75 from October 15 to January 19 and April 23 to June 1.
MEALS: Breakfast (to 9:30 a.m.), lunch, dinner, indoors or out (to 9 p.m.); jacket and tie in the evening; room service to 11 p.m.
SEASONS: Closed in summer.

HERMOSA INN
Paradise Valley, Arizona

Here it is—the desert equivalent of a small country inn in New England. Just twenty-eight rooms, hidden away somewhere between the Arizona Biltmore's estate and Camelback Mountain, across a canal, near a small white church with a big black cross, surrounded by cactus—and silence.

The Hermosa is a low white hacienda—a paella of Spanish, Mexican and Indian. The tiny lobby has a pair of open fires that fill the cool desert evenings with the smell of burning mesquite. An archway leads through a quiet courtyard to a colorful dining room, all beams and gleaming table linen. The guest rooms are brick pueblos, nestled among seven acres of trees and cactus, decorated in what's usually called "Mediterranean style," with bare brick walls, soft light, wooden furniture, boldly patterned spreads and carpets. All rooms have radio, TV and individual controls for heat and air conditioning. The inn's seven acres of grounds include a small heated pool, tennis court and shuffleboard. *Hermosa:* beautiful, handsome. Hermosa it is.

NAME: Hermosa Inn

INNKEEPERS: Bob and Jackie Louis

ADDRESS: 5532 N. Palo Cristi Road, Paradise Valley, Ariz. 85253

TELEPHONE: 602-955-8660

DIRECTIONS: Drive along Camelback Road to 32nd Street, then go north; at Stanford Drive turn right, then left at the white church.

RATES: EP—$20 to $28.50 from October 15 to January 14 and April 15 to June 15; $28.50 to $36 from January 15 to April 14; special summer rates.

MEALS: Breakfast (to 10:30 a.m.), lunch (poolside service), dinner (to 8:30 p.m.); informal day and night; room service for breakfast.

SEASONS: Fall and spring are your best bets.

ARIZONA BILTMORE HOTEL
Phoenix, Arizona

The lobby, lounge and dining room have ceilings of pure gold leaf. Frank Lloyd Wright designed the texture of the facade (not the building, not even the facade, just the *texture*). And, this being desert country, the hotel has its own 3½-million gallon reservoir just to make sure your shower doesn't dry up. No run-of-the-mill resort here.

You notice this the minute you arrive at the entrance to the estate, drive past the gatehouse and up a sweeping half-mile driveway lined with wild orange trees and a dozen hideaways owned by shy tycoons who occasionally shuffle over to the hotel to check the Dow-Jones ticker in the lobby.

1,164-acre playground

That driveway sweeps you into a completely different world. The Great Gatsby wouldn't feel out of place here. The city of Phoenix is encroaching, but it's still held at cactus length by the estate, stretching from the foothills of Squaw Peak and the edge of town to the foothills of Camelback Mountain. Away off in one corner of the 1,164-acre estate there's the Biltmore Equestrian Center, with eighty box stalls, eight turn-out paddocks, a railed quarter-mile track, an arena with bleachers, exercise ring, club house, and *twenty-six miles* of desert and mountain trails all within the estate. Horses rent for $3.50 an hour, and if you can prove you're experienced riders you can go galloping off by yourselves to some secluded grove of saguaro.

Weeping bottlebrush, snapdragons and calendula

And then there are gardens. Ralph Hall and his crew have filled the grounds with thousands of plants and the air with a hundred perfumes. You can walk for miles among snapdragons, calendula, Iceland poppies and delphinium, Ponderosa pines, fan palms and weeping bottlebrush trees. You can reach up and help yourself to an orange or grapefruit. No apples, but Eden enough.

Tea in the afternoon, Cole Porter at midnight

The Arizona Biltmore seems to be one of the few hotels that retains the nice old custom of tea and dainty English-style sandwiches in the afternoon. (But get there early; some of those little old ladies gobble sandwiches at an alarming rate.)

Room service here comes with all the trimmings—including white-gloved waiters. But since this is resort living in the grand, almost forgotten manner, put on some clothes one evening and dine beneath the gold leaf in the great dining room. Executive chef Frank R. Nikodemus has a reputation far beyond the estate, and people come from all over the valley for delicacies like petit marmite Henri IV en cocotte and rack of lamb. (The five-course table d'hote dinner costs $9.75, but there's a less expensive a la carte menu after 9 o'clock, which you may have to ask for.) The impressive wine list takes about five minutes to read—everything from half bottles of Californias at $2.50 to a Romanee Conti ('67 and '69) for $53.

The orchestra plays for dancing (quietly, never louder than mezzoforte) in the dining room, and there is a trio in the lounge for more dancing and Cole Porter until 1 a.m.

Villas and patios

The hotel's 224 rooms are, well, classical, from the heyday of the Great Gatsby, but all with air conditioning and TV. The snuggliest rooms are in the fourteen villas behind the main hotel, where you'll find fireplaces, windows overlooking the garden and hills, and patios surrounded by flowers and oleander hedges. If the hotel is full to overflowing when you arrive and they ask you if you'd mind staying in the "annex," consider yourself lucky, because they're talking about La Colina Solana, a majestic twenty-three-room mansion on top of a hill overlooking the hotel. It once belonged to a famous chewing-gum family who won't allow its name to be used, and it's furnished in magnificent style. (The only problem about staying there is that you can only get up and down the hill by the hotel's limousine, mainly because of all the priceless antiques strewn around the place; but with those surroundings they could wheel me up and down in a barrow.)

The Arizona Biltmore, in other words, is not the sort of place you want to drop into just for a night. Savor it. There aren't too many hotels like this left.

NAME: Arizona Biltmore Hotel

INNKEEPER: Laurence J. Boyle

ADDRESS: P.O. Box 2290, Phoenix, Ariz. 85002

TELEPHONE: 602-955-6600

DIRECTIONS: Just off 24th Street, between Camelback Road and Lincoln Drive, 15 minutes from the airport, highway and Amtrak.

RATES: EP—$36 to $48 September 22 through December 14, January 2 through January 31 and May 1 through May 25; $54 to $66 February 1 through March 15; $46 to $58 March 16 through April 30.

MEALS: Everything—even afternoon tea on the house; coffee shop to 6 p.m.; poolside buffet; chuckwagon breakfasts; room service to 10 p.m.; jacket and tie in the evening.

SEASONS: Closed from May to September, busiest during February and March and holidays; fall and spring best (but check first to make sure there are no large conventions, although they'll rarely get in the way).

(Note: Since these paragraphs were written, the Arizona Biltmore has been sold to Talley Industries, and has undergone a substantial refurbishing program; however, since Laurence J. Boyle is still president and general manager, chances are the atmosphere and style won't have altered much.)

CAREFREE INN
Carefree, Arizona

Take a bike ride in the desert. Chase a roadrunner through the cactus. Hunt for white-speckled quartz. Walk down to Cave Creek, push through the swing doors of a saloon and have a drink with real cowboys. Explore the neighborhood for ghost towns, old gold mines, Hohokan ruins and Indian petroglyphs. Up here in Carefree you're closer to the desert than in Phoenix or Scottsdale. But hurry. Carefree isn't exactly car-free, and it's getting more built-up every day.

Carefree is a new town, a planned community that has some respect for the desert. It's 1,400 feet higher and thirty-five miles northeast of Phoenix. Up here the sun shines smoglessly nine days out of ten; and some people will swear it's the most beautiful spot on earth when the palo verde blooms yellow in the spring, or when summer showers turn the ocotilla crimson.

The inn itself looks like a motel—a pair of two-story wings embracing a pool surrounded by rocks and cacti. There are also a few casitas with kitchens, wet bars and sunken tubs, and some new townhouse-style units across the parking lot. The rooms are oversize, the beds are oversize, the closets are oversize, and they all have balconies, refrigerators, electric blankets, electric alarms, TV and room phones. Nothing exceptional—just very roomy and very comfy.

But you're not going to be indoors much, especially with the lights on. Most of the time you'll be playing tennis (seven Laykold courts, five floodlit, all free), riding horses or playing golf on two of the most spectacular courses in the Southwest. If you really want to get into shape, trot over to the Health Spa and put yourself in the capable hands of the resident physician and masseur.

In the evenings you can dine formally or informally (some folks drive all the way up from Phoenix for dinner here); and if you want a change of cuisine, you can drive over to Carefree town and dine beneath the stars in the patio of a Spanish restaurant.

Note the summer rates. They're a steal. And don't let the heat put you off: temperatures average 84.5 degrees in July, 87.8 in August, but the average relative humidity is 10 percent to 20 percent. That shouldn't stop you taking a bike ride in the desert —especially if you go by tandem.

NAME: Carefree Inn
INNKEEPER: Bill Pullen
ADDRESS: Carefree, Ariz. 85331
TELEPHONE: 602-944-2673
DIRECTIONS: Keep going north on Scottsdale Road until you come to the signs, about 30 miles.
RATES: EP, doubles from $48 to $95 (January 1 through April 30); from $30 to $60 (May through May 31 and September 15 through December 31); *and from only $20 to $37 (June 1 through September 14)*.
MEALS: Coffee shop and dining room (to 11 p.m.), jacket-and-tie or casual; room service; cookouts, breakfast rides.
SEASONS: Open all year; busiest in winter, quietest in summer (but check for conventions).

THE WIGWAM RESORT
Litchfield Park, Arizona

Back in World War I the United States needed Sea Island cotton fast for revolutionary new tires. So the Goodyear Tire and Rubber Company rolled to the rescue and went into the cotton plantation business on a stretch of desert seventeen miles west of Phoenix. To keep its uprooted executives happy, the company built a guest house, known as the Organization House, which became so popular that it was converted into a resort in 1929. That may seem an unpromising beginning for a resort inn, but you just try to get a reservation here in February or March. The only signs of the ownership are occasional fly-overs by the Goodyear blimp, and the name of the resort's golf course— the Goodyear Golf and Country Club. Even a B. F. Goodrich stockholder couldn't be offended.

The Wigwam is surrounded by a garden suburb, Litchfield Park, which in turn is surrounded by a 14,000-acre operating ranch that branched out from the original cotton to alfalfa, grains and melons; but several of these 14,000 acres are still native desert where the inn's wranglers will lead you along cactus-lined riding trails.

Casitas and eucalyptus

The inn itself is a series of one- and two-story pink stucco casitas sheltered by palms, eucalyptus and bougainvillea, or flanked by the velvet fairways of Robert Trent Jones's masterly golf courses.

The 205 rooms are divided into five types of accommodations —something for everyone. Even the simplest rooms give you space to stretch out, and they all have TV and individually controlled heating; many of them also have dressing rooms and refrigerators.

The Wigwam probably has more lounges than any other hotel

anywhere, with all sorts of quiet nooks and crannies, fireplaces, potted plants and magazines. But with winter weather like Arizona's, you'll probably prefer to do your lounging around the pool, or on the rooftop solarium. The Goodyear Golf and Country Club, besides forming a lovely background for the inn, is also one of the most famous golf clubs in the Southwest, with two superb golf courses (but be careful, because ladies may be restricted to certain hours on Wednesdays, Saturdays, Sundays and holidays).

New tennis courts, practice alleys

Until recently it was golf that lured visitors to the Wigwam, but in 1973 the resort opened a new tennis club, with eight Plexipave courts, a pro shop, and four practice alleys with automatic ball pitching machines to give your strokes a workout. The Organization House has come a long way.

NAME: The Wigwam
INNKEEPER: Reade Whitwell
ADDRESS: Litchfield Park, Phoenix, Ariz. 85340
TELEPHONE: 602-935-3811
DIRECTIONS: From Phoenix, drive 15 miles west on West Indian School Road; from Los Angeles, take Interstate 10 and U.S. 60 to Litchfield Road, then turn right for 9 miles; from San Diego, take Interstate 8 and U.S. 80 to Litchfield Road, then turn left and drive 5 miles; if you come by air, the Wigwam limousine will pick you up at Phoenix Sky Harbor Airport or the Amtrak depot ($8 a couple).
RATES: AP only. October 7 through February 2 and April 7 through May 28 from $48 to $74; February 3 through April 6 from $58 to $86; golf $6 and $7; tennis $4 an hour per court, $2 per half hour for practice alleys; horseback riding $6 for two hours (with guide only); bicycles $5 a day.
MEALS: Breakfast in rooms and dining room to 9:30 a.m., then Continental breakfast in the lounge until 11; poolside lunches,

lavish dinners until 9 p.m. (American cooking most of the time, with occasional treats like Chicken a la Kiev); room service; jacket and tie in the evening.

SEASONS: The big push is during February, March and the first week of April, when the regulars move in for weeks at a time and you'll be lucky to get a reservation for less than a week; closed May through October 7.

THE SUNNY COAST
OF SOUTHERN
CALIFORNIA

The sweetest hours that e'er I spend,
Are spent amang the lassies, O!

BURNS

106. Inn at Rancho Bernardo

107. Rancho La Costa Resort Hotel & Spa

108. La Valencia Hotel

109. The Inn at Rancho Santa Fe

110. Beverly Hills Hotel

111. Bel-Air Hotel

112. Santa Barbara Biltmore Hotel

113. The Alisal

INN AT RANCHO BERNARDO
Rancho Bernardo (San Diego), California

The first owner of this Spanish land grant was an English sea captain, Joseph Seven Oaks, who retired from the sea to the life of a Spanish grandee—with the name Don Jose Francisco Snook. Snook's nook was all hills and vales with a smattering of trees; now it has 40,000 trees, 20,000 inhabitants, shopping centers, riding stables and a golf course. And right in the middle of it all—the inn.

Hardly the most *idyllic* spot for a hideaway, but if you plan to play golf or tennis together, or ride horses along hilly trails, you'll find the Inn at Rancho Bernardo one of the most convenient places in the Southwest.

The inn is girdled by forty-three holes of championship golf (including an Executive Course with no par fives), driving range, practice trap and putting green. (The green fee is only $5 a day for inn guests, and they get priority on starting times.)

The inn's Trails and Saddle Club is five minutes up the road, on the edge of the town, with mile after mile of unspoiled trail beginning right at the hitching posts. (Horses rent for $4 an hour.)

The inn also has two heated swimming pools, and you can rent bikes for $2 an hour or $7 a day; but its most famous sporting facility is probably Vic Braden's Tennis College. The college consists of four courts (two lighted), video-tape instruction, practice machines and Vic Braden, who has been called "the greatest tennis teacher in the world" by Jack Kramer, no less. Its two-day crash course keeps you thinking tennis, playing tennis and watching tennis from nine in the morning to nine at night. Exhausting. Better plan on following through with a two-day crash course in love.

Oversize rooms, oversize beds

The 150 rooms are said to have Spanish decor. They're as Spanish as Don Jose Francisco Snook. However, they *are* spacious, and they do have two oversize beds (plenty of space for post-tennis back-rubbing), private decks or patios, double washbasins and a few nice little touches, like color TV sets concealed in handsome armoires, and heat lamps in the bathroom. The rooms overlook the golf course, swimming pool, tennis courts or parking lot: ask for second-floor rooms in the 400 and 500 wings, with a view of the fairways.

Tutuava and ertwensoep

The man in command of the kitchen is another seafarer home from the sea, this time an ex-Holland-America Line chef who doesn't have to change his name to make it resound—Marinus B. van Leyden. His cosmopolitan menus range from local seafood specialties like tutuava amandine to Dover sole specially flown in from Holland and prepared in half a dozen ways; from American steaks to Indonesian dishes and *ertwensoep,* that wondrous, thick Dutch pea soup. Van Leyden's dishes range in price from $3 to $9. The dining room is cheek-by-jowl with the cocktail lounge, so if you want to avoid the music and dancing, dine downstairs in La Fondita, specializing in steaks; or enjoy a change of pace at Rancho Bernardo's Mercado, a chic huddle of boutiques, craft shops and small restaurants serving up still more cosmopolitan fare.

NAME: The Inn at Rancho Bernardo
INNKEEPER: Richard T. Adair
ADDRESS: 17550 Bernardo Oaks Drive, San Diego, Calif. 92128
TELEPHONE: 714-487-1611
DIRECTIONS: Take U.S. 395 from San Diego to the Rancho Bernardo exit (about 25 minutes from downtown San Diego, 30 minutes from San Diego airport); from Los Angeles (2

hours), by Interstate 5 south to Oceanside, then California 78 east to Escondido and from there south on U.S. 395.

RATES: EP—$27 and $34 double, $70 for a parlor and one-bedroom suite, year round; also special golf and tennis packages.

MEALS: Breakfast (any time), lunch, dinner (to 10 p.m., 11 weekends), coffee shop for breakfast and lunch; jacket and tie in the evening; room service (but with beer served in plastic cups).

SEASONS: Busiest in July and August, but the weather's perfect for golf, tennis, riding and love all year round.

RANCHO LA COSTA RESORT HOTEL & SPA
Rancho La Costa, California

This must be the Cecil B. DeMille of resorts. Four swimming pools. Thirteen tennis courts. Twenty-one miles of riding trails. Visiting palmist. Its own post office. Movie theater. Three restaurants and two snack bars. Four hundred rooms, suites or cottages. Eight hundred employees. And a health spa with rock steam baths, sitz baths, colonic baths, roman baths, salt glows, and a Swiss shower with seventeen shower heads that zap alternating hot and cold water on your tingling flesh. Overdone? Well it certainly isn't Longfellow's Wayside Inn. It's not the coziest place or the friendliest place, but you'd be surprised at the number of renowned anatomies that have suffered that fiendish Swiss shower. The Rancho La Costa is only sixty limousine miles from Los Angeles and thirty from San Diego, so it's a convenient place for the beautiful people to nip off to for a few days to tone up between movies, tournaments, big deals and Watergate coverups. It's ultra chic, and everyone seems to be dressed to the nines—which frequently end up looking like sixes and sevens despite the efforts of the Swiss shower to trim the waistlines.

Double drapes, electric beds

The rooms are equally plush. Pile carpeting. Double drapes.
Color TV (some concealed, some with bedside controls). Some
rooms have wet bars, others (in the 600 wing) have bookshelves
stacked with books, pullman kitchens and electric beds that
disappear into the wall. If you want to get a jump away from
the mainstream, ask for a room in one of the cottages facing the
fairways and the rising sun; for complete privacy, rent a complete villa (many couples do just that) and you have a choice
of two bedrooms every night; or hole up in the lavish accommodations attached to the health spa and you won't have to wear
yourself out before you get to the Swiss shower.

Costa Curves, Costa Capers

The ranch covers something like 5,000 acres, and the brochure
promises you riding along protected trails "where the mustard
blooms yellow and where the scent of eucalyptus mixes with the
ocean breeze . . ." Quite a ride, presumably, because most of
the rancho's 5,000 acres seem to be taken up with new or about-
to-be-built homes and condominiums. You really have to work
at solitude here, unless you do what most of the movie biggies
do: check into the health spa and stay there, surviving on special
calorie-conscious diets, enjoying group classes with intriguing
titles like Costa Curves and Costa Capers, shuddering in the
Swiss shower, glistening in the salt glow. Think what all this
will do for you in bed (you'll sleep like a baby).

NAME: Rancho La Costa Resort and Health Spa
INNKEEPER: Donaldo Soviero
ADDRESS: Costa del Mar Road, Rancho La Costa, Calif. 92008
TELEPHONE: 714-729-9111
DIRECTIONS: From Interstate 5, take La Costa Avenue exit, then
    along El Camino Real to the rancho (30 miles from San

Diego); 3 miles from Palomar Airport; airport limousine from San Diego, $6 a head.

RATES: EP—rooms $38 to $52, suites $69 to $121 from September 16 to June 30; and $43 to $57 and $79 to $136 between July 1 and September 15; tennis free, golf extra ($7); special Spa Plan includes all meals, golf, tennis, spa facilities for three nights at $130 a night.

MEALS: Everything available—breakfast to 11 a.m., lunch by the pool or tennis courts, dinner (to 10 or 11 p.m.) in one of three restaurants; jacket and tie at dinner (and the snazzier the better); room service.

SEASONS: Summer is busiest, but the weather fluctuates only 10 degrees over the year (averaging around 75 degrees); check for conventions, groups, and tennis tournaments at other times.

LA VALENCIA HOTEL
La Jolla, California

Groucho Marx used to skulk behind the pillars in the lobby and leer at startled ladies. Charles Laughton visited the bar every afternoon in summer to order "a pot of real hot tea, please." Evangelist Aimee Semple McPherson used to slip off here for weeks at a time with her current boy friend ("She was a grand woman," says a long-time member of the staff, "but oversexed"). Those were the days when everyone who was anyone in Hollywood went to La Valencia to get away from it all—Greta Garbo, John Gilbert, Ramon Navarro, Joan Crawford, David Niven, Gregory Peck, Audrey Hepburn—the whole gang.

La Jolla is no longer the unspoiled, secluded little seaside village it was in Hollywood's heyday, and the Valencia Hotel is now hemmed in by bulky condominiums, but they're by no means has-beens.

La Valencia is still, as it has been since it opened its doors in 1926, *the* place to go in La Jolla. Its Mediterranean entrance is still shaded by jungly podacarpus; little old ladies still have luncheon in the mosaic courtyard; and a jigsaw puzzle still waits on the table for someone to drop in the magic piece.

Terraces, tiles and potted plants

The hotel sits on a bluff above a bluff above La Jolla's famous rocky cove. Its gardens terrace down the hillside, then sweep around the swimming pool to the street and the park by the edge of the ocean. Pictorial tiles jostle with clumps of flowers for the chance to beguile your eye, and create petaled nooks if you want to be alone. The hotel itself is eleven stories of pink stucco, Spanish style, with a pink tower. Beyond its leafy patio you enter a cool lobby leading to the big-windowed lounge overlooking the ocean—an impressive room with Spanish tiles, potted plants, a golden piano, tiled fountain, and a hand-painted ceiling. This, you feel, is how a hotel in California should look.

The hotel's 110 guest rooms include some conventionally modern units in the new Valencia West wing, so be sure to ask for something in the original building. The higher the better. The decor is understated and graceful with richly-striped wallpapers, hand-woven Portuguese bedspreads, beamed ceilings and elegant sofas and armchairs from England, Italy, Spain and France. The corner rooms on the eleventh floor also have small sun-decks (yet cost only $30 a night). There are also a couple of unusual rooms in a bungalow in the garden, if you want extra privacy, but they're not quite "La Valencia": Room #3 has an attic ceiling, white walls and furnishings, and a king-size bed, and #2 downstairs is a suite with a fireplace.

Outdoor and tower-top dining

For a hotel its size, La Valencia presents you with plenty of options when it comes to dining. You may be tempted to stay a few days longer so that you can sample a different eating spot at each meal. Say, lunch on the patio and dinner in the elegant ocean-view Surf Room (steak au Poivre, rack of lamb Persillade for two, veal Oscar). Second day, lunch in the Skyroom on the tenth floor, with windows on three sides (and a grandstand view of migrating whales if your timing is right); then dinner on the patio beneath the moon. Third day, lunch on the patio and dinner in the Cafe la Rue, next to the Whaling Bar. Dining at La Valencia is neither as expensive nor as fuddy-duddy as you might expect. The filet mignon is only $6.50, sautéed filet of tutuava $4.95, and there's a supper menu with items from $3.50 to $4.95. The Whaling Bar itself is one of La Jolla's favorite watering spots—a shuttered, leather-boothed room with authentic harpoons, New Bedford lanterns, pewter candles, and paintings of whaling scenes. And, all the posh notwithstanding, you never have to wear a jacket and tie at La Jolla.

Sun, surf and snorkeling

The hotel's free-form swimming pool is one of the more placid spots in La Jolla for working up a tan. A few steps from the garden entrance, though, and you can be taking a dip in the surf, or floating off with a snorkel to discover some of the region's unusually prolific underwater life. You never know what's going to pop out from behind a rock and leer at you.

NAME: La Valencia Hotel
INNKEEPER: Richard P. Irwin
ADDRESS: 1132 Prospect Road, La Jolla, Calif. 92037
TELEPHONE: 714-454-0771
DIRECTIONS: Fourteen miles north of San Diego; get off Interstate 5 at the San Clemente Canyon Road cloverleaf, and follow Ardath Road to and around the waterfront.
RATES: EP—from $21 to $30 between April 11 and July 20, and Labor Day to January 10; $23 to $30 January 11 through April 10; $26 to $32 from July 21 to Labor Day; suites to $60 in season.
MEALS: Breakfast (to 10:30 a.m.), lunch and dinner (to 9 p.m.), indoor or outdoor, throughout the year; informal (but not sloppy); room service.
SEASONS: Busiest in summer, but beautiful any time of the year (average temperatures vary only about 10 degrees between winter and summer).

THE INN AT RANCHO SANTA FE
Rancho Santa Fe, California

It was raining outside and mystery-writer Helen MacInnes was standing in the lobby armed with a golf umbrella. We discussed the weather, traded accents, and discovered we came from the same rain-haunted part of Scotland. Then, this being California rather than Scotland, the rain stopped, and she went striding off through the garden, no doubt concocting some intricate new plot for her next best-seller.

When you think of it, the Inn at Rancho Santa Fe is the perfect setting for a thriller—secluded, unhurried, slightly mysterious. This Santa Fe is only twenty-seven miles north of San Diego, but it's a cousin of its New Mexico namesake through the Atcheson, Topeka and Santa Fe Railroad. Apparently, at the turn of the century, an ATSFRR bigwig went off to the antipodes, brought back eucalyptus trees from Australia and New Zealand and planted them on this old Mexican land grant. His intention was to create an endless supply of railroad ties for his company, but the plan didn't take root. The trees, however, did. They grew and grew and grew into a languid grove. In the Twenties the ranch was transformed into one of the country's first planned communities (although it doesn't *look* regimented) and the inn was built in 1924.

It's an enclave of adobe cottages adding up to seventy-five rooms, but if you didn't know it was there you'd drive past it. The inn's eight gardeners (eight gardeners to only seventy-five rooms—remarkable) seem to feel it's their duty to disguise the inn, to hide it behind a proliferation of eucalyptus, Brazilian peppers, acacia, strawberry trees, avocado trees and bougainvillea. They've certainly created one of the most fragrant hideaways in the West.

Multilevel garden, multilevel menus

The gardens and cottages are on several levels, and as you weave among the foliage to your room it's easy to forget that you're in an inn. All the rooms have views of the gardens, the trees or the mountains beyond. Some have showers, some have baths; and a third of them have fireplaces and kitchens. The decor is as varied as the flora and fauna. My own favorite is #221, with period decor and wallpaper, and a large sundeck overlooking the dell at the rear; room #38 has a window alcove, armchairs, French doors on to a terrace, a concealed wet bar; and #35 has hideaway beds and huge windows overlooking the terrace and lawn, a pullman kitchen, and a eucalyptus-burning fireplace.

Even the menu is remarkably varied for an inn this size, serving everything from snacks to Continental dishes. It's surprisingly inexpensive, too—say, Bayshore combination seafood plate (tutuava, shrimp, scallops, bluepoint oysters) for $4.50, stuffed crepes with Bay shrimp for $4, steaks and roast beef from $5, with a wine list to match. You can enjoy your meal in the sunny Garden Room overlooking the pool, the leather-and-wood-paneled Vintage Room, the Patio Courtyard and, in summertime, by the pool.

Baronial lounge, quiet library

The Inn at Rancho Santa Fe is essentially a place for relaxing, for lounging by the pool, with maybe an occasional game of tennis on the inn's three courts (free), or a round of golf over one of the three courses nearby (green fees around $8). In summer you can drive four miles to Del Mar where the inn has a beach bungalow (they'll also make up picnic lunches for you). Between swims and games, you can retire to the peace and quiet of the inn's baronial lounge, with its raftered ceiling, big open fire, voluminous sofas, Chinese screens and models of sailing boats. A comfy, clubby place for a pre-dinner sherry or after-dinner brandy. You can also browse for an hour or two in the inn's 4,000-book library. Maybe you'll pick up a thriller you won't be able to put down—which is as good a way as any of spending a rainy afternoon, next to writing one.

NAME: The Inn at Rancho Santa Fe
INNKEEPER: D. Royce
ADDRESS: Rancho Santa Fe, Calif. 92067
TELEPHONE: 714-756-1131
DIRECTIONS: From Interstate 5 take the Encinitas Boulevard or
    Lomas Santa Fe exits (from the north), the Via De La Valle

exit (from the south); the inn's limousine will pick you up at the airport in San Diego for $2.75 per person; or from the Amtrack depot in Del Mar.

RATES: EP—from $16 to $36, suites to $50, year round, depending on location (main building, cottage upper garden, upper terrace, garden cottage, etc.).

MEALS: Breakfast (to 10 a.m.), lunch (poolside in season), dinner (to 9:30 p.m.); jacket and tie requested in the evening; room service.

SEASONS: Summer is the busy season, but the difference between summer and winter averages is only 17 degrees; the inn accepts small management groups and seminars in the spring, fall and winter months.

BEVERLY HILLS HOTEL
Beverly Hills, California

"Daddy, this is such a beautiful hotel, and we love it so, I wish you'd buy it for us." So Daddy did, Daddy being New York lawyer and financier Ben Silverstein. Daughter Muriel was 18 at the time she dropped the hint, and the Beverly Hills Hotel was a trifling $5¼ million. Today, it's worth $15 million. Maybe more.

Bean fields and W. C. Fields

Long before there was a Beverly Hills there was a Beverly Hills Hotel. When it opened in 1912, Sunset Boulevard was a bridle path, and the new pink-and-green stucco structure was surrounded by bean fields. Its original function was to attract people to the area so that they'd buy land and build homes. And buy and build they did—the Pickfords, Tom Mix, Harold Lloyd, W. C. Fields.

Today the Beverly Hills Hotel sits among broad avenues lined by royal palms and million-dollar homes, screened from the world by sixteen acres of lawns and jungly gardens of banana trees, ginger plants, oleander and jacarandas, a haven for celebrities and nonentities.

The haven consists of 312 rooms, all individually designed, most of them in the main building. The remainder are in bungalows tucked away among the jacarandas and date palms and bougainvillea—perfect spots for trysting lovers and bashful movie stars because you can get to them through the foliage, without ever showing your face in the lobby. Renting a bungalow is like having your own home in posh Beverly Hills; each one has one to four bedrooms (you can rent them separately), plus parlors, wood-burning fireplaces, dining alcoves, kitchens, wet bars and garden patios. They're all luxuriously decorated—even the single rooms come with a small refrigerator.

The bungalows are expensive ($50 a bedroom, $200 or more for the lot), but they're still the most popular accommodations in the hotel. Except, perhaps, for suite #486 on the top floor of the main building—a sumptuous, peach-colored, $175-a-night suite with gold faucets, marble tubs, and a wet bar with a hundred glasses in case you're planning a little get-together. In recent years, this suite has hosted Prince Philip, Johnny Carson, Princess Grace and her prince, and other folks who can't afford the $200 for a bungalow. Big names, but then the history of the Beverly Hills Hotel is an anthology of anecdotes about the great and famous. Like the time Katharine Hepburn walked from the tennis courts to the pool, climbed the diving board and performed a perfect backflip—still in her tennis togs and shoes. Or the time Errol Flynn, lunching in the patio with his bride, Lili Damita, called for a telephone and organized an impromptu fashion show for Mrs. Flynn right there in the patio. Or the day cartoonist George McManus unscrewed a button marked "Press" from a urinal in the men's room, stuck it in his lapel and gate-crashed a party as a newspaperman. Or the time Frank Sinatra and Dean Martin got embroiled in a hell-for-leather, saloon-type fistfight in the Polo Lounge.

Bear steak for dinner, champagne for breakfast

To keep its 560 guests happy, the Beverly Hills has an army of 500 reception clerks, bellhops, waiters, chambermaids and chefs waiting to show you a thing or two about personal service. If you've been here before and made it known that you prefer a room at the rear, you'll get a room at the rear without asking; if you're the oil tycoon who has a penchant for bear steaks, a special order has already gone through to Alaska and your bear steak is waiting for you in the freezer; and if you're Brigitte Bardot you'll find the customary bottle of champagne on your breakfast tray. The hotel keeps track of these facts with a huge revolving card index system that records the basic facts plus the whims, foibles and preferences of every guest who has signed in during the past five years; and special briefing cards are issued to key personnel, who are also expected to add to the list of foibles. The first test of Beverly Hills service is to pick up your telephone the minute you enter your room, and one of the hotel's forty operators will address you by name. (Or should. Last time I stayed there, she didn't, but maybe she didn't know how to pronounce it, and was too polite to guess.)

Hamburgers with roses

If you want an excuse to telephone, call room service. This is another of the hotel's fortes. Obviously, if a big oil tycoon wants bear steak, he gets it. And when Howard Hughes calls over for chocolate layer cake at two in the morning, it's a case of one chocolate layer cake coming right over Mr. Hughes. How about ordinary mortals? Try ordering a hamburger. It will arrive within twenty minutes on a silver tray, with your beer in an ice bucket and one perfect red rose in a bud vase. (There are roses everywhere; the hotel goes through a hundred dozen roses a week.)

You can also look forward to a rose with breakfast in bed,

but here's another suggestion. Enjoy a whole gardenful of flowers with your muffins and coffee—in the Italian Garden, just beyond the fabled Polo Lounge, a patio built around an aging Brazilian pepper tree with pink azaleas dripping from its branches. The edge of the patio is scalloped with little alcoves of white brick, surrounded by hibiscus, camellias, birds of paradise, pituporum and night blooming jasmine, where you can linger over your fresh strawberries and cream and listen to the birdsongs. It's a lyrical way to begin a day. There are, to be sure, some people who find the Beverly Hills Hotel less than lyrical. Some people think it's overpriced (and cubic foot for cubic foot it probably is, if you're interested in cubic feet). Some find the plumbing intrusive. Some people get fidgety waiting for the valet to bring their car round from the parking lot (a rather noisy production number in the evening, so demand a room at the rear), and others think that a $3 cab ride from downtown Hollywood is $3 too far. But for its loyal fan club, it's a matter of "Daddy, this is such a beautiful hotel, and we love it so, we hope you won't sell it." Even for $15 million.

NAME: Beverly Hills Hotel

INNKEEPER: Edward Springer

ADDRESS: 9641 Sunset Boulevard, Beverly Hills, Calif. 90210

TELEPHONE: 213-276-2251

DIRECTIONS: Oh dear, in Los Angeles? The simplest way is probably to get on to the San Diego Freeway (Interstate 405), get off at the Sunset Boulevard ramp and drive east until you come to a big pink-and-green building sticking above the palm trees; it's only ten minutes from the Pacific.

RATES: EP—$33 to $60 for rooms, $68 to $200 and up for suites and bungalows.

MEALS: Breakfast (any time), lunch, coffee shop, poolside buffet, dinner (to 10:30 p.m.), supper club; jacket and tie in the evening; room service (to 2 a.m.).

SEASONS: Busy all year round—but probably the only hotel in this guide that's less crowded on *weekends;* no need to worry about conventions ever (they don't even allow name tags), but forget about staying there on Emmy Awards night and so on—unless you want to book now for 1984.

BEL-AIR HOTEL
Westwood Village, Los Angeles, California

Truman Capote calls it "the greatest hotel in the world." Hotel? It's a magic bird cage in an enchanted garden. The first sights you see are an arched stone bridge, a white wrought-iron chair at one end, and masses of flowers everywhere. Walk across the bridge and you look down through the foliage to a lake with swans, and pathways winding to nowhere. Al Pelier and his team of gardeners have created a wonderland with pampas grass, jade plants, candytuft, tree ferns, tulip trees, red azaleas, ginger plants, coral trees, rose vines climbing stucco walls to tiled roofs, two

sturdy oaks and a rare silk floss tree, or *chorisia speciosa,* which is famous in horticultural circles. Opossum and deer often come down from the canyon to feed on the lawn.

Exercise ring, horse hospital

Actually the hotel's beginnings were more earthy—it was once a stable. The estate known as Bel-Air, hideaway of the upper echelon of show business, was founded by Alphonse E. Bell, a man of the cloth who happened to strike oil on his dairy farm and put his blessing into real estate. To attract the right type of resident he built a stable, with exercise ring, milk shed and horse hospital. A stable it remained from the 1920s to 1944, when it was converted into a hotel. Very skillfully, too—you'd never suspect that room #109 was once a horse hospital. The hotel is now owned by financier Joseph Drown, who wanted a hotel that is "relatively small, typically Californian in looks, built among gardens, around patios . . ." He wanted, he got.

Bel-Air's shangri-la has a cloister-like look, with Spanish arches, courtyards, patios, fountains, white and pink corridors linking white stucco bungalows with clay-tiled roofs—sandwiched between the garden and the sheer green wall of the canyon.

Wood-burning fireplaces, garden patios

All the guest rooms are different (except for an unexpected paper wrapper round the toilet seat announcing "Sanitized for your protection"). Each room in its individual way is a classic of refined elegance. Or elegant refinement. Most of them have woodburning fireplaces and garden patios. Some, like suite #160, have a marble fireplace, a small refrigerator and a patio the size of most people's homes (the Lunts and Rockefellers have paid $100 a night to stay here); suite #122 has a carved *wooden* fireplace, and harmonized wallpapers, drapes, upholstery, bedspreads, that change hue discreetly from parlor to bedroom. The most fairytale of the rooms is #240, halfway up a moss-topped tower, with a bay window and love seat overlooking Swan Lake. It's a tiny world all its own. It even has a small patio where you can have breakfast or sunbathe.

The Bel-Air is the ideal little hideaway. You don't even have to go through the lobby, which doesn't look like a lobby anyway, more like a mansion lounge, with a large log-burning fireplace; in one corner is a tiny office, where assistant manager Phil Landon sits with a jar of jelly beans on his desk, and quietly caters to the erratic tastes of the rich and the distinguished—princesses (Margrethe, Grace, Margarethe, Astrid), movie stars (Rex Harrison, Bette Davis), society (Fords, honeymooning Rockefellers, Marjorie Merriweather Post—who used to arrive with her own bed linen and toilet tissue), performers (Dietrich, Fischer-Dieskau, Renata Tebaldi, Tom Jones, Maria Callas), and people so famous they need only one name, like Twiggy and Pucci. Some stable.

Ironically, you have to leave the stable if you want to go horseback riding. Likewise if you want to play golf or tennis (Phil Landon will arrange guest privileges at one of the nearby country clubs). The Bel-Air has an egg-shaped pool and sun terrace, but that's it. Definitely a place for dalliance. Enjoy the garden. Enjoy the pool. Enjoy each other. Linger over dinner in the Bougainvillea Room. The romantic atmosphere is kindled here by soft candlelight, cozy booths, and a wall with a fireplace carved into the canyon rock and surrounded by Hawaiian-style greenery. Chef Heinz Rotzer has been regaling the famous here for almost fifteen years, serving up the sort of meal you want to spend an evening with—local fare with a Continental flavor, like Catalina sanddabs sauté Belle Meuniere, broiled Chinook salmon Mirabeau, roast rack of lamb Boulangerie or medaillons de veau Veronese. Even when you've added on vegetables and wine and trimmings you can still come out for under $30 for two.

The problem is—even if it means going over $30, in an atmosphere like this it's almost blasphemy not to order champagne.

NAME: Bel-Air Hotel

INNKEEPER: James H. Checkman

ADDRESS: 701 Stone Canyon Road, Los Angeles, Calif. 90024

TELEPHONE: 213-472-1211

DIRECTIONS: Drive along Sunset Boulevard until you come to Westwood Village and the entrance to Bel-Air estates (it's a mile and a half from the San Diego Freeway), then follow the signs, but look carefully because they're very, very discreet.

RATES: EP doubles $32 (bedrooms), $38 to $48 (bed-sitting rooms with private patios), $52 to $100 (one-bedroom suites).

MEALS: Breakfast, lunch, dinner (to 11 p.m.); jacket and tie in the evening; room service.

SEASONS: Busy at any time of the year, so just try your luck (but you never have to worry about conventions—they're not allowed over the bridge).

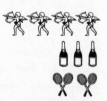

SANTA BARBARA BILTMORE HOTEL
Montecito, Santa Barbara, California

Ask the manager of a resort hotel which is the best resort hotel in the country and he'll say his own. Ask him which is second best and nine times out of ten he'll reply "The Santa Barbara Biltmore."

You'll find the first clue to the Biltmore's success when you walk through the arched door into the great lobby with its arched windows, flagstone floor, beamed ceiling and panels of antique Mexican tiles. The manager is sitting at a desk right at the door. Not the assistant manager. The manager. He's not some remote personage in a back room. He's right there, keeping an eye on everyone, and you sense immediately that you're in an establishment that purrs along like a Rolls-Royce.

From cowboy to superhost

This impressive hostelry is the creation of a cowboy—well, someone who was born on a ranch on the Great Plains but turned out
to be as successful at breeding companies as he was at breeding
cattle—Robert S. Odell. His dream hotel sits among lawns and
gardens by the edge of the Pacific in a bay just to the south of
Santa Barbara, sheltered from the landward side by the Santa
Ynez Mountains and from the seaward by the Channel Islands.
Its twenty-one acres are crowded with eucalyptus, ancient oaks,
yews, decorative bamboo, twisted junipers, natal plum, and
monkey trees. The hotel itself is a rambling group of Spanish-
mission style buildings and one-story cottages connected by
ramadas and patios.

Bob Odell's obsession with perfection follows you all the way
into the luxurious guest rooms. Every one of the 175 rooms is
different, but they all have air conditioning, television sets, refrigerators concealed in custom-designed armoires, and extra-
long extra-wide beds with Serta Perfect Sleeper or Beautyrest
mattresses. Now how does one find out a fact like that? Because
Bob Odell is so proud of his hotel that his brochures catalog some
of the features you don't find in the average hotel—three Wam-
sutta supercale sheets on each bed, scientifically-softened water,
large-sized adjustable Speakman and Moen showerheads, Fieldcrest Royal Velvet bath towels (extra large twenty-seven by fifty
inches), drinking glasses sanitized and individually wrapped.
(Sadly, the fireplaces have *gas* logs—urgh.)

Odell's finicky tastes show up in the dining room also: he
went to the old Stork Club in New York and lured away Chef
Jacques Le Borgne, and his wines are personally selected by
Alexis Lichine.

Only a perfectionist would care about these things, and for
that he should be applauded. Alas, a perfectionist is entitled
to his foibles—even if they don't coincide with your tastes. Former cowboys apparently like tidy people, so you'll find a note
accompanying your reservation confirmation pointing out that
". . . service will be refused to anyone in extreme or unconven-

tional dress and to gentlemen with long hair below the collar line." He means it, too; his other hotel in San Francisco, the Clift, recently turned away the conductor of the symphony orchestra —but then his hair is *very* long. This regulation would probably rule out half the clientele of the Beverly Hills Hotel, so obviously this is not what you might call a swinging hotel. What it is is a wonderfully serene, luxurious, efficient hideaway for a few days of peace and quiet and wholesome fun. Like swimming. You can swim in the heated pool in the garden, in the Pacific (at one of its safest points), or in the olympic-sized pool of the Coral Casino Beach and Cabana Club, across the street from the hotel. You become a guest member automatically, which also allows you access to the quarter-mile-long private beach where you can borrow a lazyback and wait for the Pacific to put on one of its scarlet, startling sunsets. They're the most ostentatious touch tolerated around here.

NAME: Santa Barbara Biltmore Hotel & Cottages
INNKEEPERS: Robert S. Odell (owner), Charles W. Saul (general manager)
ADDRESS: Montecito, Santa Barbara, Calif. 93102
TELEPHONE: 805-969-2261
DIRECTIONS: Take California 101 to the Olive Mill Road exit, a few miles south of Santa Barbara, then follow the road to the shore and Channel Drive; 1½ hours from Los Angeles, 6½ from San Francisco; or have the limousine pick you up at Santa Barbara airport.
RATES: EP exclusively, but a complicated rate structure because all the rooms are different—rooms from $26 to $40, suites from $44 to $112, year round.
MEALS: Breakfast (to 10 a.m.), lunch, dinner (to 9 p.m., 10 in summer), snack bar in the beach club; room service; jacket and tie in the evening (and no unconventional garb or long hair either).
SEASENS: Basically a summer resort, but since the climate is so equable here you can come at any time (average daytime temperature is 71 degrees); no conventions, but small semi-

nars and so forth are usually confined to private rooms—and positively no identification tags. Reservations are virtually impossible at Easter, Thanksgiving, Christmas (Mexican style) and New Year's.

THE ALISAL
Solvang, California

Solvang, of course, is that Danish-type village with windmills and tourists, bakeries and tourists, cheese shops and tourists, but if you come to The Alisal you won't be stampeded, because the ranch is three miles farther along the valley—one of the greenest, serenest valleys in these parts.

The ranch itself is part of a real working cattle ranch, lying in the bottom of the valley surrounded by sycamores, giant oaks, a river, a golf course and stables. It's first and foremost a place for horseback riding, but even if you just want someplace placid, and an occasional game of tennis or golf, you'll find it worth the shuffle through Solvang.

Its undulating golf course is less forbidding than, say, Pebble Beach, but it's still a challenging 6,434 yards. (For guests only, green fee $6.) The three tennis courts are in tiptop condition (and free). There's a free-form heated swimming pool surrounded by a sun terrace, loungers and beds of flowers; and if you want a dip in the surf, the Pacific is just fifteen minutes by car from the ranch.

But it's really the riding that corrals the guests, and ten thousand acres sprawling over the Santa Ynes Mountains, with sixty beautiful trails winding through the mountains (but you can ride only in the company of the wrangler).

The guest rooms are in small cottages scattered among the flower beds and lawns; they're not luxurious, but much more comfortable than you might expect on a ranch. No roughing it here. And when the sun goes down and the cattle come home, the ranch has two handsome restaurants serving Western food to take care of ranch-size appetites.

A real escape. A place to lie on the grass and look up at the sky until it's time to take a moonlight hayride and look up at the stars.

NAME: The Alisal Guest Ranch

INNKEEPER: Wilfred "Bill" White

ADDRESS: Box 26, Solvang, Calif. 93463

TELEPHONE: 805-688-6411

DIRECTIONS: The Alisal is 6 miles east of U.S. 101. If you're arriving from the south, watch for a sign saying Solvang-Nojoqui Falls, which is a short cut to the ranch; from the north, turn left at Buellton, drive 3 miles to Solvang and pick up the Alisal Road, then go right and drive 3 miles to the ranch.

RATES: MAP—$48 to $60 for rooms, $70 for suites; golf and horseback riding *not* included.

MEALS: Breakfast (to 9:45 a.m.), lunch (poolside buffet in summer), dinner (7 to 8 p.m.), breakfast rides, steak fries, cookouts; room service.

SEASONS: Open all year, busiest in summer, some groups at other times.

SAN FRANCISCO AND ITS NEIGHBORS

And when the west is red
With the sunset embers,
The lover lingers and sings
And the maid remembers . . .
ROBERT LOUIS STEVENSON

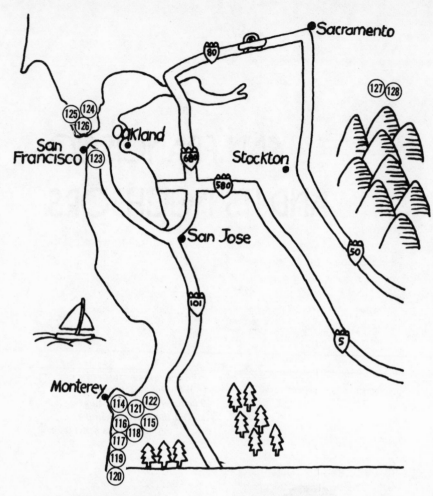

114. Del Monte Lodge
115. Highlands Inn
116. Pine Inn
117. Cypress West Inn
118. The Sandpiper Inn
119. Normandy Inn
120. Big Sur Inn
121. John Gardiner's Tennis
     Ranch

122. Quail Lodge
123. Miyako Hotel
124. Alta Mira
125. Sausalito Inn
126. Sutter Creek Inn
127. Hotel Leger
128. The Mine House

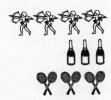

DEL MONTE LODGE
Pebble Beach, California

You wake up in the morning, step out onto the balcony and there spread out before you is a sight that will open wide the bleariest love-hooded eye: the eighteenth fairway of the Pebble Beach course running alongside the surfy Pacific, a flock of mudhens pecking the grass, the whole scene set in a curve of bay with rocks and pounding waves and pine and cypress trees. "A monument to the blessing nature can bestow on a golf course," as golf writer Pat Ward-Thomas called it. Even if you're not a golfer you'll probably still concede that a golf course is prettier to wake up to than a baseball diamond.

Golf made Pebble Beach famous, but you don't have to play the game to wallow in this *gloria* to the good life.

Private forest, seventeen-mile drive

In the beginning, the foursome who built the Southern Pacific Railroad built a hotel called the Del Monte over in Monterey, complete with the first eighteen-hole golf course in California, a race track, steeplechase course and polo fields (they really lived it up in those days). The original lodge at Pebble Beach was built in 1912 as an annex to the Monterey hotel, and then became the main hotel when the older one was demoted to an army camp.

The present-day Del Monte Lodge is a white, gleaming structure of slightly classical proportions, surrounded by two-story villas housing 142 rooms with views of the golf course or the ocean or both. It's on the famous Seventeen-Mile Drive around the Monterey Peninsula, which means it's part of the Del Monte

Forest, a private estate decked out with some of the loveliest mansions you've ever squinted at behind fences and hedge rows —a setting of almost unalloyed peace, even in August, when Carmel itself is awash in Bermuda shorts.

The guest rooms have big windows, big closets, big balconies, big beds; color TV, refrigerators and log-burning fireplaces; and they've all been gingered up from ceiling to underfelt in the past year, part of a rejuvenating program under the lodge's brisk new manager, Tom Oliver, a product of London's Ritz and Dorchester hotels. Since the rooms are all alike, more or less, the main difference is the view, and for my money the best views are from the rooms in the villas known as Colton, Alvarado and Portola —all $80 (but, remember, that includes all your meals).

Truffles and hand-flaked chocolate

Since the lodge operates on American Plan only, you'd better stroll over to the main lodge and have a look at the dining rooms. The main dining room, one floor above the fairway level, overlooks the ocean, and (nice touch) the tables that are not next to the window are turned to face the view. Up here, the table d'hote menu offers you a choice of six entrees—dishes like poached salmon Sauce Riche, chicken sautéed in champagne sauce, pork loin Grandmere; but downstairs in the Club XIX, you have a slightly fancier menu—poulardine Fine Champagne, cote d'agneau Vert-Pre and filet de boeuf en croute. The lodge comes closer to gourmet dining than most resort hotels, mainly because Executive Chef Marc Vedrine (a French graduate from the kitchens of the swank Connaught Hotel in London) heads up a team that includes no fewer than *ten* French chefs. Sticklers they are in the French tradition—real truffle slices on the eggs benedict, and the chocolate on the *Schwarzwalderkirchtorte* is melted and then flaked by hand by the pastry chef himself.

One problem with a dining room that serves good food is that it becomes popular with the locals, and on weekends you have to reserve a table—and sometimes you can't get a reservation. In this case, who needs it? Just call room service and have them set up your meal in front of the log fire, or out on the balcony where you can blend the surf sounds with the plashing of $15 Pommard in your glass.

A hundred miles of trails

Fortunately, you never have to wander far from the dining room or your balcony, because the lodge is a self-contained playground. Or rather, the lodge and the forest. You can rent horses and follow a hundred miles of trails through the trees and alongside the fairways. Or skip the horse and go for a walk. Down by the lodge, the beach club has a heated pool beside a curve of sandy beach, and the tennis club has eleven Laykold courts (none of them floodlit, unfortunately). Somewhere in the forest there's also a trap and skeet club. And then there's the golf.

But a blissful day here probably means simply wandering off along the Seventeen-Mile Drive to some quiet corner where you can hide under a knobby old Monterey cypress, or spread out on a swatch of sand and listen to the surf and the sea lions.

This is, as Robert Louis Stevenson once wrote, "the finest meeting place of land and water in existence." But then, he was in love, too.

NAME: Del Monte Lodge
INNKEEPER: Tom Oliver
ADDRESS: Pebble Beach, Calif. 93953
TELEPHONE: 408-624-3811
DIRECTIONS: Take California 101 to Carmel or Monterey then follow the signs to the 17-Mile Drive; the lodge's limousine can also pick you up at Monterey Peninsula Airport.
RATES: AP only—from $55 to $80 for rooms, from $95 to $108 for suites; tennis free, beach club free, golf green fees $10 and $12; tips added to bills automatically (10% of room charges, 15% of food and drink).
MEALS: Breakfast (to 11 a.m.), lunch (indoors and outdoors),

dinner (to midnight); jacket and tie in the evening; room
service (to 1 a.m.).

SEASONS: May, September and October are the big months, but
the climate is spring-like year round; avoid the weeks of Bing
Crosby's Pro-Am and other golf tournaments.

HIGHLANDS INN
Carmel Highlands, California

The bar is called the Sunset Room; the lounge looks toward the
Bird Rocks of Point Lobos (one of the most unspoiled, unusual
peninsulas along the entire California coast); the dining room
overlooks Yankee Point and its dramatic cedar-sided homes
(that's Kim Novak's right out on the point above the big rock
and the surf). Highlands Inn is a nest high on the granite cliffs
above a cove, and as if the natural setting weren't enough, Robert
Ramsey ("I'm a frustrated horticulturist") has transformed his
fourteen-acre hillside into a botanical garden with rare plants
from New Zealand, Japan, Australia, Peru, South Africa, Japan
and Ethiopia—2,000 types of flowers from California lilac and
Ponderosa lemons to heather and cypress.

Does the inn live up to the setting? Yes and no. With all this
sublime scenery you don't really need a piped-music rendering
of "Little Dutch boy and a little Dutch girl, sat dreaming on a
hill" at breakfast; or to watch bluejays kamikazing from the
pine trees to a jaunty rendition of "When the red, red robin
comes bob bob bobbin along . . ." Otherwise . . .

Credenzas and Chickerings

The inn's lobby is a depository of antiques, including a cherry-
wood credenza carpentered by Mormon Brigham Young for his

sixteen-year-old fourth wife, a cabinet belonging to the Emperor Franz Josef, and the first Chickering grand piano in California. The original guest rooms are Hansel and Gretel cottages secluded among the foliage; they all have ornate baths (and heat lamps), television with wobbly pictures, telephones, carpeting, log-burning fires and coffee makers. They're quiet, secluded, comfy, and strike possibly the right note between rustic and modern. But they don't have the views of the ocean and that's why the more functional lanai rooms are most popular.

Some of the lanais are quite luxurious. Room F4, for example, has a superb view, with big balconies overlooking Yankee Point and Kim Novak, a tiled balcony with wrought-iron furniture, white rough-hewn pine walls and king-size bed; and there are six rooms with balconies or patios to make the most of the sun—breakfast on the patio by the pool, dinner on the balcony overlooking the ocean. The Scott Wing, farther up the hillside, is the most modern, almost a motel, with brick fireplaces, patios, picture windows overlooking power cables, wall-mounted TV, king-size beds, big bathrooms. Lanai 24 is a suite with an enormous patio for sunning and dining, acres of window, a pink scatter rug in front of a fire, a red/white/blue bedroom with his and hers closets. In other words, among the inn's 105 rooms is something to suit every taste.

Six-course dinners, $65 wines

Your room rates include a six-course dinner that wallows from relish tray and strawberry freeze to a choice of four entrees—say, roast turkey, filet of sole, veal, roast prime ribs; and to match it there's an extraordinary wine list that ranges from humble Californians at $2.75 a bottle to an aristocratic Chateau Lafite Rothschild at $65. How's that for an elegant way to celebrate the sunset?

NAME: Highlands Inn
INNKEEPER: Robert J. Ramsey
ADDRESS: Box 17, Carmel, Calif. 93921
TELEPHONE: 408-624-3801
DIRECTIONS: On California 1, 4 miles south of Carmel, up a
  very steep hill.
RATES: MAP (lunch *or* dinner)—$50 to $64 for cottages, $70
  to $74 for lanai rooms, $80 to $90 for suites year round.
MEALS: Breakfast (to 10 a.m.), lunch (poolside or terrace in
  summer), dinner (to 9 p.m.), Sunday brunch to 3 p.m.; room
  service.
SEASONS: Busiest in summer, but because of its unique location
  and climate, you can come here comfortably any time of the
  year; small groups and seminars in non-summer months.

PINE INN

Carmel-by-the-Sea, California

This is not so much an inn as a village within a village. You can wander around its meandering courtyard and pick out something nice for each other in the boutiques, or just admire the awnings, street lamps (gas, no less), hedges and flowers. The inner courtyard is dominated by the Gazebo—a circular, flower-decked restaurant with glass walls and a sliding roof above a wrought-iron chandelier. Vivaciously Victorian—which is the theme of the entire inn.

Pine Inn was built at the turn of the century, when writers and artists had Carmel all to their Bohemian selves, so all the Victoriana is really a restoration. Bright red wallpapers brighten the lobby. A Tiffany glass canopy leads to the Red Parlor lounge. Glass insets in the windows, candle sconces on the walls, a brass screen in front of the lobby fire—you almost expect a palm court orchestra to play selections from Gilbert & Sullivan's latest hit.

All the inn's guest rooms have private bath or shower, television, telephone, carpeting, shutters, a mixed bag of antiques—marble-topped dressers, gilt mirrors, brass bedsteads, old prints. They've all been refurnished in recent months and look as fresh as if Victoria were still on the throne. The most stunning room is one of the penthouse suites (up a separate entrance at the rear of the hotel). It's #64, which you enter from an awning-covered, planted terrace; the room is dominated by a curlicued gilt bed with bronze-gold bedspread, bedside candelabra, a couple of sofas and an open fire. A bit precious maybe, but Victoria herself might have succumbed in this seductive setting.

There are six penthouse suites (around the $50 mark), but you can settle happily for a regular room at half the price; and if you're here in the busier weeks, ask for a room at the rear, because Ocean Avenue can be noisy.

A charming spot. Maybe not your idea of Carmel, but you'll

have to ask one of those turn-of-the-century Bohemians about that.

NAME: Pine Inn
INNKEEPER: Max McKee
ADDRESS: P.O. Box 250, Carmel-by-the-Sea, Calif. 93921
TELEPHONE: 408-624-3851
DIRECTIONS: Leave California 1 at Ocean Avenue and head for the beach; Pine Inn is on the right.
RATES: EP—rooms $15 to $38, patio suites and penthouses $38 to $150.
MEALS: Breakfast (to 11 a.m.), lunch, dinner (to 9 p.m.); Sunday champagne brunch (11:30 to 2:30); room service.
SEASONS: Open all year, but July and August mobbed.

CYPRESS WEST INN
Carmel-by-the-Sea, California

From the outside it looks like the townhouse of a wealthy Spanish philosopher: a glaring white facade broken by a tall, ornate brick door, a glimpse of red-tiled roof. A long lobby lined with potted plants takes you past a lounge and a patio with tables, chairs and an encroachment of camellias, cyclamen and fuschias. The inn was built in 1929 by Grace Deere Viering, of the tractor family, and for the past five years it's been operated by the friendly Fentons. It's very much a family affair: the three children help run the place, and Grandma did the paintings on the walls.

All the rooms are different. Room #215, for example, two floors up, has gold-white decor, a private terrace with table, chairs, a lounger, and a view of the coastline. Rate: $25. Room #217 is all red and white, with a small balcony. Most of the rooms have private bath and shower, but some have shower only;

they all have TV, phones, shutters rather than drapes, *and the bedspreads are washed every day.*

The inn has no restaurant or room service, but you can help yourself to coffee or tea (a choice of nine flavors) and fresh Danish pastries in a bright little room off the lobby. For other meals you can pop next door for crepes ($1.75 to $2.50), or round the corner to Aage Knudsen's Royal Copenhagen Bakery for scrumptious *macron snitter* or *kringlec.*

The inn has no liquor license, but the Fentons will supply set-ups and you can settle down with your drink in front of the big fire in the white-raftered, flower-fresh lounge, take a book from the library (if you don't finish it before you leave, take it with you and mail it back), and listen to Bach. There's always Bach or Beethoven or Brahms in the background; during the town's Bach Festival in July, it is often in the foreground and you may even hear some of the performers practicing. The Cypress Inn is a popular spot for them—singers like Evelyn Mandac, Leo Goeke and the voluptuous Carol Neblett, who created some kind of record by performing two scenes of Massenet's *Thais* nude in New Orleans. It's unlikely she'll rehearse *that* part at the Cypress.

NAME: Cypress West Inn
INNKEEPERS: Louis and Ruth Fenton
ADDRESS: P.O. Box Y, Carmel-by-the-Sea, Calif. 93921
TELEPHONE: 408-624-3871
DIRECTIONS: Take California 1 to Ocean Avenue, then drive about ¾ mile to Lincoln and turn left.
RATES: EP—rooms $16 and $18, suites $25; and no tipping.
MEALS: Complimentary breakfast only, until 10 a.m.
SEASONS: July and August are the busiest, Thanksgiving to Christmas are the quietest months.

THE SANDPIPER INN
Carmel-by-the-Sea, California

¢

It looks like a comfortable home. Inside, it *feels* like a comfortable home. And in a sense it is. Melvina and Clare Franklin came up from Bel-Air, where he was a financial consultant; they saw this guest house, loved it and decided to retire here. Since then, they've repainted, refurnished, brought in the family antiques (mostly from Indiana settler days) and created one of the coziest little inns in California.

There are only fifteen rooms, all with private baths. There's no dining room, but the Franklins serve a Continental breakfast (on the house and self-service) from eight to ten a.m. in the lounge, or outside on the patio. There's no liquor license, but most of the guests bring their own bottles; the Franklins supply set-ups and everyone sits around the fire in the lounge and chats. Some of them might even tune in the TV. You can borrow books from the Franklins' library and take them off to your room or the beach. The Sandpiper is half a block from the beach, and a few blocks from the shops and galleries. It's surrounded by quiet private houses, and the only reason it's there is that it happened to be a guest house before the zoning laws went into effect. Your luck—it's like living in a private house in a zealously private town.

NAME: The Sandpiper Inn
INNKEEPERS: Melvina and Clare Franklin
ADDRESS: 2408 Bayview at Martin Way, Carmel-by-the-Sea, Calif. 93921
TELEPHONE: 408-624-6433
DIRECTIONS: Follow the signs to Carmel Mission, then take Santa Lucia Avenue all the way to the beach; the last street on the left is Bayview.
RATES: EP only—$14 to $28.

MEALS: Complimentary Continental breakfast only.
SEASONS: Open all year, but avoid July and August.

NORMANDY INN
Carmel-by-the-Sea, California

¢

The facade looks incongruous in the resort bustle of Ocean Avenue—half-timbered like a country inn in France. Step through to the inner courtyard with its split-level beamed galleries, its oaks and pines and acacias, and you're in a sheltered world where squirrels sit on the fence and nibble nuts. Ocean Avenue could be miles away.

Most of the forty-four guest rooms are in this quiet inner courtyard, and each one is as charming as the next. Room #105, for example, has a corner fireplace, piney furniture, print drapes and valances, and beds set into the wall in country style; #303 is smaller, with shuttered windows overlooking a quiet residential street named for that legendary lover, Casanova; #316 has floor-to-ceiling windows with louvered shutters overlooking the treetops. All the rooms have private baths and king-size beds. Have a peek in the rooms before you decide which one you'll have; Sam Stanton will be happy to let you look around his inn.

His family has owned the Normandy since 1937, and its curious design is credited to his father (an architect), the decor to his mother (a former Party Editor of *House Beautiful*).

There's a terraced swimming pool at the rear, with sunbathing patios and patches of pink geraniums.

The inn has no dining room, apart from a charming small breakfast room facing the main street, decorated in a combination of French and Mexican, with Quimper wedding china on the wall and Mexican paper decorations on the tables. There's also a small TV lounge. From the breakfast room, you're a one-minute walk from the beach, and right among Carmel's stores and cafes and restaurants.

NAME: Normandy Inn
INNKEEPER: Samuel M. Stanton
ADDRESS: P.O. Box 1706, Carmel-by-the-Sea, Calif. 93921
TELEPHONE: 408-624-3825
DIRECTIONS: Leave California 1 at Ocean Avenue, then follow
    the avenue beachwards until you're almost at the beach; the
    Normandy is on the left between Monteverde and Casanova.
RATES: EP—$20 to $28, year round.
MEALS: Complimentary Continental breakfast only (to 11 a.m.).
SEASONS: Open year round; July and August are the busiest
    months.

BIG SUR INN
Big Sur, California

"The sun has set; light up the candles, put on the Mozart," and thus another evening at California's most tumbledown inn begins. The inn is high above the Pacific, squashed between Highway 1 and the Santa Lucia Mountains. In fact, it's practically *in* the mountains because Helmuth Deetjens, the Norwegian sea captain who built the place thirty years ago, blasted into the rock to make way for his inn. Then he gathered great piles of driftwood to build a clump of cabins that still look like driftwood, overgrown with trees and flowers and a general air of picturesque decay.

The rooms are rustic and spartan. A few of them have private baths; in most of them you have to share the toilets and baths with your next-door neighbors. Not the sort of place you want to bring a first date on a first night, unless she or he is into the Big Sur mystique. What the Inn has is personality, and a devoted following. Take a look anyway: you can always stop off for lunch or dinner (better make a reservation first). The low-ceilinged dining room looks like it's been modeled on a painting by Jan Steen, most of the items on the menu are around $4, and the Mozart and candlelight are on the house.

NAME: Big Sur Inn
INNKEEPER: Helen Deetjen
ADDRESS: Big Sur, Calif. 93920
TELEPHONE: 408-667-2377
DIRECTIONS: It's right on Highway 1, 25 miles south of Carmel.
RATES: EP—$7.50 to $15.
MEALS: Breakfast, lunch, dinner (to 8:30 p.m., family style, and
    by reservation only); no liquor license, but you can bring
    your own wine; no room service; informal.
SEASONS: Open all year, busiest in summer.

JOHN GARDINER'S TENNIS RANCH
Carmel Valley, California

If you're ever going to spend a few days nursing a tennis elbow, let it be in this idyllic glade.

Carmel Valley is a peaceful enough place, but the tennis ranch in turn is still more secluded, a valley in the valley, with the Rio Carmelo gurgling among its twenty acres of acacias, oaks and sycamores. The proportions of the ranch are encouraging—six pros, three chefs, three gardeners and two Gardiners. You know you're going to be well looked after. The accommodations are more luxurious than in most *hotels*—with open fires, rough-hewn pine walls, coffeemakers, fresh ice and set-ups every day, patios, carpeting, special closet hooks for your tennis rackets. The suites in Wimbledon House even have a second fireplace in the master bedroom.

They bring orange juice, coffee and a newspaper to your room at eight a.m., and then you have breakfast in a charming, plant-hung conservatory; lunch is served by the pool (or rather, by *one* of the two pools), cocktails on the terrace or in the white-hued lounge, and then dinner by the big fire in the dining room.

Tennis, health bar, tennis, sauna, more tennis

Between meals your day is filled with tennis instruction, a break for the Health Bar, more tennis, a swim, more tennis, then saunas and massage. The Gardiner System includes lessons with ball machines, instant television replays and a team of instructors, with the great Ken Rosewall as touring pro. If your elbow does act up, you can always lounge by the pool, either of them, and watch the others suffer the Gardiner grind.

NAME: John Gardiner's Tennis Ranch
INNKEEPER: John Gardiner
ADDRESS: P.O. Box 155, Carmel Valley, Calif. 93924
TELEPHONE: 408-659-2207
DIRECTIONS: On Carmel Valley Road, about 10 miles east of California 1; or by California G16 (a beautiful back road) from Soledad and U.S. 101.
RATES: Clinic Plan only—$450 to $500, including all meals, saunas, 2 massages and tennis instruction, from Sunday evening to Friday noon.
MEALS: Everything.
SEASONS: From April 1 to December 1; busiest in summer (when another part of the ranch is given over to a tennis camp for school children); limited to 20 guests at a time, so make your reservation in plenty of time—say 6 months in advance.

QUAIL LODGE
Carmel Valley, California

Someone went to a lot of trouble and expense here to create a perfect nest for lovers. A split of private-label champagne welcomes you to a room of muted colors, Ficks Reed furniture, Swedish string lamps, Fieldcrest towels, custom-made soap, rockstone tiles in the bathroom, electric percolator, *ground* coffee and ceramic mugs.

There are ninety-six of these rooms in beautifully designed board-on-board redwood cottages, some overlooking a lagoon with a Japanese bridge, others overlooking the golf course. They all have patios (but if you plan to spend much time on your patio, choose the rooms overlooking the golf course—they're farther from the highway).

Ducks on the fairways, doves in the lobby

Quail Lodge is part of the Carmel Valley Golf and Country Club, where the valley pushes aside the hills and spreads down to the sea. Most of the floor of the valley is the golf course, which golfers share with flocks of ducks, deer, opossum and raccoons. The clubhouse is a handsome white building surrounded by flowers and flowering plum trees, and with a big white wrought-iron cage of temple doves in the foyer. The club facilities are available to lodge's guests.

Guests of the lodge are automatically members of the club, which has one of the most comfortable lounges in any clubhouse and a big bright restaurant overlooking the fairways. Green fees are $10. There are also driving ranges, putting green, two heated pools, four tennis courts ($3 a day), a pro shop, and free bikes (it's a great spot for riding).

By the time you read this, the lodge will also have opened a second sixty-seater restaurant adjoining the guest rooms.

If you feel peckish during the day, you can stroll over to an unusual little collection of shops across the street from the lodge —a boutique, art gallery, hairdresser, liquor store and coffee shop.

But isn't it only fair that since someone took all that trouble with color schemes and fabrics, you should spend a lot of time in your room?

NAME: Quail Lodge
INNKEEPER: J. L. Huddleson
ADDRESS: 8205 Valley Greens Drive, Carmel, Calif. 93921
TELEPHONE: 408-624-1581
DIRECTIONS: Four miles along Carmel Valley Road, east of California 1—that is, 5 minutes from Carmel-by-the-Sea; or by lodge limousine from Monterey Airport.
RATES: EP—$28 to $42, including free Continental breakfast.
MEALS: Breakfast (to 11:30 a.m.), lunch (dining room, clubhouse or poolside), dinner (to 11 p.m.); room service.
SEASONS: Open all year; busiest in summer, but you can play golf or tennis any time.

MIYAKO HOTEL
San Francisco, California

What do you say to a sauna for two without leaving the privacy of your own room? Voluptuous? Then reserve one of the seven suites with sauna baths.

Or sample an oriental evening in one of the two Japanese *riyokan* rooms, with *tatami* mats and those voluminous quilts known as *futons,* which are spread on the floor to become beds. Have your dinner brought up, eat it crossed-leg on the floor, and then when you're finished simply roll over onto bed. Soft lights glow in an indoor bamboo garden to add a moonlight-over-Fujiyama touch to your frolics on the futon.

Even the ordinary rooms at the Miyako let you indulge in a delicious Japanese tradition—the sunken tub made for two, complete with low stool and bucket for sloshing each other with cold water between bouts in the hot tub. The hotel thoughtfully supplies a specially-imported perfumed powder that brings California's public utility water to the proper color and fragrance. In your subsequent state of euphoria, you may not notice the other features of the room—the delicate gold-brown-yellow decor of Japan, a *tokonoma* (the niche for flowers or Buddhas), *shoji* screens, brocade quilts and chairs covered with Japan's traditional chrysanthemum motif. There's also color TV—a Japanese make, of course.

Now why on earth would you want to stay in a Japanese hotel in San Francisco? Apart from saturnalian plumbing, none—except that Nihonmachi, the Japanese "Chinatown," is one of the oldest parts of the city the Japanese call Soho. Plus the fact that you have less chance in this 172-room hotel of being swamped by a convention, which is a possibility in all the other top hotels (except the remarkable Clift Hotel, which is under the same management as the Santa Barbara Biltmore, page 264).

Miso-shiru, sashimi and tempura

You can also enjoy Japanese food here—in the hotel or in the restaurants of Nihonmachi. The room service has a few Japanese dishes among the regular occidental delicacies like club sandwiches and teriyakiburgers, but if you speak nicely to the maitre d' in the dining room, you can order up a meal from the regular menu—miso-shiru (soy bean soup), sashimi (fresh tuna or sea bass from Fisherman's Wharf, thinly sliced, and raw) and tempura (butterfly shrimps and vegetables deep fried in a special tempura batter).

And if you really want to pamper yourselves, pick up the telephone and order room-service massage.

NAME: Miyako Hotel
INNKEEPER: Charles McCaffree (operated by Western International Hotels)

ADDRESS: Post & Laguna, San Francisco, Calif. 94119

TELEPHONE: 415-922-3200

DIRECTIONS: Ask for the Japanese Trade Center, or look for its peaked Peace Pagoda; a 5-minute cab ride from Nob Hill, about 10 minutes from Fisherman's Wharf.

RATES: EP—$28 to $38 for rooms, $75 for suites.

MEALS: Breakfast (to 10 a.m.), lunch, dinner (to 10 p.m.), coffee shop downstairs in the Trade Center; jacket and tie in the evening; room service.

SEASONS: Year round.

ALTA MIRA
Sausalito, California

Translated, Alta Mira means the High View. You'll find it halfway up the precipitous hill behind Sausalito—a town that likes to think of itself as very Mediterranean. Up here on the terrace, beneath the sun umbrellas with their floral print, surrounded by vivacious people enjoying life, you could almost be on the Mediterranean. But Sausalito's high view is probably more dramatic—across the bay to Alcatraz, the Bay Bridge and the skyline of San Francisco.

This hotel is popular with visiting advertising and television types, which says a lot for it because staying there means they have to drive twenty minutes to and from their appointments across the Golden Gate Bridge. The Alta Mira is a combination Spanish villa and Swiss chalet, a group of cottages in a hilly garden. Fourteen of its thirty-five rooms are in the main lodge. No two rooms are alike. Rooms #11 and #8 are probably your best bets; #7 has a good view but you have to share a bathroom; #22 is a cottage all to itself, with two bedrooms, if you want to splurge in the interests of privacy; #26 has a fireplace and porch, and #16 is a suite with fire, kitchen and a view of Alcatraz. No air conditioning (you don't need it), no television.

The most popular feature of the inn, though, is the terrace restaurant with its sun umbrellas. It has an adjectival menu—"sumptuous," "colossal," "sensational"—but you can enjoy a fine dinner of abalone steak, veal parmigiana, butterfly prawns, and so on. The prices are almost as steep as the hill up to the inn—$5.50 for breast of capon, $7.50 for the abalone steak. But then, someone has to pay for the adjectives—and the *alta mira.*

NAME: Alta Mira Continental Hotel
INNKEEPER: Bill Wachter
ADDRESS: P.O. Box 706, Sausalito, Calif. 94965
TELEPHONE: 415-332-1350
DIRECTIONS: Coming from the Golden Gate Bridge, turn left at the first traffic signal, and keep going up the hill until you see the signs.
RATES: EP—from $20 (for something called Residential Exposure rooms) to $35 (the category of most of the rooms mentioned above).
MEALS: Breakfast, lunch, dinner (to midnight); informal; room service to 10 p.m.
SEASONS: Open, and busy, all year.

SAUSALITO INN
Sausalito, California

Feeling heroic? Spend a night in General Grant's bed—a hulking construction with a victoriously carved headboard so tall it would go right through the roof of a motel.

Grant's bed is the *pièce de résistance* in a rather unusual inn. You enter the Sausalito through a modest doorway and up a narrow stairway to a tiny lobby with bold blue wallpaper and potted plants. The inn has only fifteen rooms, all different, but each one a valentine of Victoriana. The prizes are the Marquess of Queensberry (with Grant's bed, a corner fireplace, velvet sofas and chairs, campaign chests and bric-a-brac) and the Queen Victoria (a corner room with bay windows, golden drapes and potted plants). Both the Marquess and the Queen have private bathrooms; some of the others have washbasins only, and you have to walk down the hallway to the toilet. But why not? The charm of Sausalito is said to be its "Europeanness." Everything is bright and fresh, because the inn came under new management in late 1972 (the owner is Mr. Hiller, who owns the clothing store downstairs).

There's a separate restaurant downstairs, but the inn serves a complimentary help-yourself Continental breakfast (if you want it in your room, one of you has to toddle off down the hall to get it). The inn is right smack in the middle of Sausalito, between the main street and the waterfront. That's where the action is. It's also where the noise is in summer: don't say you weren't warned.

NAME: Sausalito Inn
INNKEEPER: Barbara Stone
ADDRESS: 12 El Portal, Sausalito, Calif. 94965
TELEPHONE: 415-332-0577
DIRECTIONS: On the waterfront in the heart of town, above Hiller's clothing store.
RATES: EP—$17.50 without bath, $22.50 with bath.
MEALS: Complimentary breakfast only (to noon).
SEASONS: Open all year.

SUTTER CREEK INN
Sutter Creek, California

Swinging couples you've heard of, but swinging *beds?* This pendulous experience is something you can look forward to in "The

Hideaway" or "The Patio." The beds are suspended (securely, unless you have in mind something very peculiar) from the ceiling by sturdy old chains from ghost mines, which is only natural since this is the heart of the Mother Lode Country.

The Inn itself is a 115-year-old house, the former home of a California Senator, and became an inn only a few years ago when Jane Way happened to be passing by and fell in love with it. It wasn't for sale, so she waited until it was (or maybe she willed it—she's that kind of lady). Having acquired the house, and with no more experience of running an inn than any other housewife who has reared a family, she then set about transforming it into one of the most delightful country inns on either side of the Great Divide.

And ingeniously, too. She scoured the antique shops and auctions for cranberry scoops that became toilet paper holders, old washtubs for shower stalls, a sled for a magazine rack, a portable bidet for a coffee table. The rooms are now stuffed with canopy beds, handpainted chairs, rockers and other antiques and curios.

There are now sixteen rooms, in the main cottage and in a cluster of smaller cottages in the garden. Take your pick. Some suggestions: The Hideaway, The Patio, The Cellar (which has a fireplace, patio and pencil post bed), the Lower Washhouse, The Canopy Room (canopied twin beds, but slightly cramped), and The Library (a comfy room, but unfortunately on the ground floor between the kitchen and the parlor; if you don't want to embarrass the other guests, or be disturbed, you can while away the minutes until they've all gone to bed by reading something from the shelves—say, *Design for Steam Boilers and Pressure Vessels, New Patterns in Sex Teaching* or *What the Bible Is All About*).

Sherry on the house, brandy in the coffee

Jane Way has also filled her inn with friendly little touches, like strategically located decanters of sherry; when you feel like a snort you simply help yourself. And if you're astir before breakfast, you can help yourself to coffee with a dash of brandy "to get you ready for an afternoon nap." Breakfast is taken family style in the brass-and-copper colonial kitchen. Daughter Lindsey rustles up sumptuous meals of eggs and bacon or hotcakes, with fresh-made rolls and breads and jams; then the poor girl has to do the washing up, plunging her hands into nasty detergent when they'd rather be playing Scott Joplin on the parlor piano. In summer, breakfast is served in the arbor surrounded by lilacs and roses. (To get to the arbor guests go through The Library, so don't choose this room unless you're an early riser—or very, *very* cool.) After breakfast, you're on your own. There's nothing to do here—no pool, no television—but just enjoy yourself. You can lounge around the garden in the shade of the flowering quince, willows and daphne. You can play chess or parcheesi in the pale-green parlor. Or settle into one of the deeply-upholstered sofas by the fire and read *Punch*.

Abandoned mine shafts, antique stores

Otherwise, take a stroll down the arcaded main street of Sutter Creek, and check out the antique stores. Or go for a drive through the foothills of the Sierras and discover the relics of Mother Lode and all her little nuggets—abandoned mine shafts, the tumbledown shacks of Forty-niners, cemeteries where simple headstones mark the graves of young men who died old deaths. You can even try your hand panning for gold (the best time is spring, when the snows melt).

NAME: Sutter Creek Inn
INNKEEPER: Jane Way
ADDRESS: 75 Main Street, Sutter Creek, Calif. 95685
TELEPHONE: 209-267-5606
DIRECTIONS: About 50 miles southeast of Sacramento, 3 miles north of Jackson on historic California 49 (which links the old mining towns).
RATES: EP—from $16.50 to $30, including breakfast, all year.

MEALS: Breakfast only (family style at 9 a.m.); no lunch or dinner, but Jane Way will give you a list of some interesting country restaurants in the neighborhood, or just step across the street for some hearty Mexican food.

SEASONS: Busiest in summer, but you can relax here any time of the year.

NOTE: No children, no pets, no cigars.

HOTEL LEGER
Mokelumne Hill, California

It looks exactly like an authentic hotel of the Wild West, with a two-storied pillar-and-rail veranda for pushing bandits over, and when it began life as a tent beer hall in 1851, the Leger probably had its share of authentic fisticuffs and gunfights. (In its heyday, "Moke Hill" managed to squeeze seventeen murders into one hell-bent weekend.)

The place is never that boisterous these days, even with all the saloon's amplifying equipment going full tilt. The saloon/restaurant is the most interesting part of the hotel, a medley of potted plants, striped wallpapers and Franklin stoves—Gold Rush days with a dash of Greenwich Village. You won't find motel-modern conveniences upstairs, but the guest rooms have all been refurbished in more or less the manner of the days when Forty-niners came to town to whoop it up—or be wiped out. If the panning was good they splurged on one of the parlor suites (now $20); if they blew their nuggets on a poker game they had to settle for a room with semi-private bath (now an inexpensive $12 double). There's a small pool in a grove of orange trees at the rear of the hotel.

NAME: Hotel Leger
INNKEEPERS: Tim and Alice Cannon

ADDRESS: Box 50, Mokelumne Hill, Calif. 95245
TELEPHONE: 209-286-1312
DIRECTIONS: Seven miles south of Jackson, where old California
49 meets California 26.
RATES: $12 and $13 for rooms with semi-private bath, $16 and
$17 for doubles with private bath, $20 for parlor suites with
private bath.
MEALS: Breakfast, lunch, dinner (to 9:30 p.m.); no room serv-
ice; very informal.
SEASONS: Open all year *but closed on Tuesdays.*

THE MINE HOUSE
Amador City, California

The Old Keystone Consolidated Mining Company put up this
building a hundred years ago to house its head office. Now the
office is one of the oddest little hotels in California.

Its eight rooms have preserved as many as possible of the
original fixtures. The Retort Room, for example, has a shower
stall which was once the vault where they stored the bullion
(over the years, more than $23½ million worth of the stuff);
the Keystone Room still has a dumbwaiter that used to carry
the bullion to the vault; and the Vault Room still has the big
safe that stored the bullion before it was shipped by Wells Fargo
to San Francisco. The orthodox bedroom fixtures are more or
less in the style of the period. Not the plushest hotel in the
area, but pleasant, clean and comfortable. It has a small pool,
but no coffee shop or restaurant; when you wake up in the
morning and feel like breakfast, simply press a button and the
Daubenspecks will bring over your complimentary tray of orange
juice and coffee.

NAME: The Mine House
INNKEEPERS: Marguerite and Peter Daubenspeck

ADDRESS: P.O. Box 226, Amador City, Calif. 95601
TELEPHONE: 209-267-5900
DIRECTIONS: Six miles north of Jackson on California 49.
RATES: $15 to $22.50.
MEALS: Breakfast only (complimentary, in rooms).
SEASONS: Year round; 2-day minimum stay on weekends from March through September.

NORTHERN CALIFORNIA AND ALL THE WAY TO OREGON

. . . for love is heaven, and heaven is love . . .
BYRON

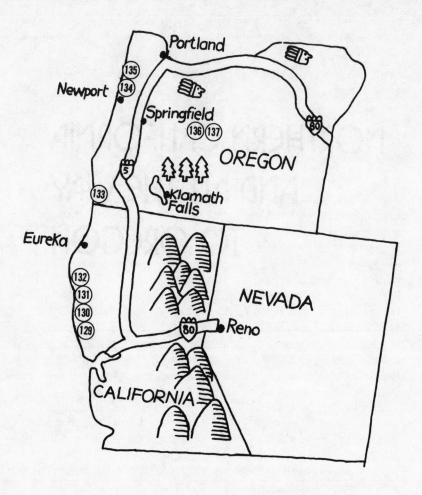

129. Timber Cove Inn

130. Sea Ranch Lodge

131. Heritage House

132. Little River Inn

133. Ireland's Rustic Lodges

134. The Inn at Otter Crest

135. Salishan Lodge

136. The Inn of the 7th Mountain

137. Sunriver Lodge

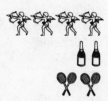

TIMBER COVE INN
near Jenner, California

The shower stalls here (or at least some of them) have floor-to-ceiling windows looking out to the ocean, and you can stand and scrub each others' backs while you watch the gulls and the surf, or, if it's February, the big gray whales migrating south.

Timber Cove is about as close as you'll ever come to the perfect blending of setting and inn. On one side, the inn overlooks Timber Cove itself; on the other, the ocean. But this is timber country, and the inn looks almost as if Paul Bunyan's son had built a matchstick house on top of a cliff. The timbers still look like *trees,* and the inn seems to grow naturally out of a rocky garden. Even the swimming pool swirls naturally among the rocks and beneath the gallery around the lobby, with a Bunny Buffano statue rising Aphrodite-like from the water.

The lobby is a cavernous hall of glass, with timber pillars, a walk-in fireplace at one end and an art gallery running around two walls. The bar separates the lobby from the dining room. It's a great place to be on a blustery afternoon, with the cassette player spinning through Richard Strauss's "Ein Heldenleben" ("We always play Richard Strauss, he seems just right for this setting somehow").

Franklin stoves and hibachis

The forty-seven guest rooms maintain the rustic atmosphere—timber walls, timber ceilings, tree-trunk pillars, dresser tops and bedside tables of timber. Even the bases of the bedside lamps are rough-hewn timber, and the decorations are hunks of drift-

299

wood, prints of Ansel Adams photographs (many of them of
the neighborhood) and serigraphs by Dorothy Bowman. About
half the rooms have Franklin stoves, and the newest rooms (the
"Fifties" group) have fireplaces that double as hibachis (you
can buy the pre-prepared steak in the kitchen). No telephone
or television.

"A place to be in love"

The man we can thank for this perfect blend of inn and setting
is a former head of the Peace Corps in Central America and
a designer in San Francisco—Dick Clements. He even did some
of the construction work himself, getting his redwood from the
mill round the corner, and the rocks from the garden. He wanted
Timber Cove to be "a place of peace and beauty . . . a place
to be in love."

Indian paintbrush, nosy raccoons

The peace and beauty include a garden that sprouts poppies,
narcissus, daffodils and wild rhododendron. And Indian paint-
brush. And wild iris.

Wildlife includes sea otters, deer and a family of raccoons
that often come up and peer through the lounge windows at
night. Occasionally a wild boar turns up on the menu. But the
two most formidable-looking animals are harmless—the resident St. Bernards, Neil and Rotunda.

The cove itself is a secluded place for strolling and beachcombing (but not swimming, unless you're an Eskimo); there
are a couple of tennis courts about a mile up the road, and
riding at Sea Ranch fourteen miles north.

After a windswept walk or an afternoon of beachcombing,
most people head for the bar. Here's a better idea: take a
shower. Watch the sun go down as you scrub backs.

NAME: Timber Cove Inn

INNKEEPER: Michael Jordan

ADDRESS: North Coast Highway, Jenner, Calif. 95450

TELEPHONE: 707-847-3231

DIRECTIONS: On the Sonoma Coast, 3 miles north of Fort Ross (where the Russians built a fort way back in trapping days), which means 90 miles or 2½ hours by car from San Francisco; the inn suggests a leisurely and scenic route following U.S. 101 to the Washington Street cut-off at Petaluma, across to Bodega Bay, then up the coast on California 1; or a longer route—101 to Santa Rosa, then follow the Russian River to the sea.

RATES: EP—from $25 to $40.

MEALS: Breakfast (to 10:30 a m.), lunch, dinner (to 9 p.m.); informal.

SEASONS: Open, and popular, all year; try to come in midweek; otherwise make a reservation early for weekends at any time of the year. June, July, August and September are the busiest months, but this is a place to be in love when the wind is a gale and the sea's a cauldron.

SEA RANCH LODGE
Sea Ranch, California

Here's another spectacular clifftop location on the Sonoma Coast, but completely different from its neighbor fourteen miles down the coast at Timber Cove. Sea Ranch looks like a transplanted Expo exhibit—contemporary California architecture with modern sans serif lettering, bold colors and a dramatic "Aries" logo announcing its presence.

Sea Ranch is part of Rancho de Herman, one of the last great Mexican land grants—a windswept tract covering 17,580 acres.

It's now a real estate project, developed by a company called Oceanic Properties Inc., but the site is still uncrowded so you don't have the feeling of staying in a subdivision.

The ranch's contemporary redwood design encloses custom-made furniture in natural woods, canvas roman blinds, chunky fabrics, wall cabinets, timber coffee tables and headboards, tiled bathrooms, central air conditioning with individual thermostats, picture windows facing the ocean and the clifftops. No TV or telephone, but some rooms have fireplaces.

Like Timber Cove, it's a place for enjoying the zesty pleasures of nature. Walking on the beach. Walking in the wind along the clifftop. Riding sprightly horses (the inn has its own stable). Picnicking in the forests. Hiking in the hills. Or you can simply relax in the solarium lounge and listen to a gale.

NAME: Sea Ranch Lodge
INNKEEPER: Bill Hill
ADDRESS: P.O. Box 44, The Sea Ranch, Calif. 95497
TELEPHONE: 707-785-2371
DIRECTIONS: Follow California 1 all the way—105 miles or 2½ hours from the San Francisco Bay Area; or follow U.S. 101 to Geyserville, then go west on California 128 to the coast; the lodge is 29 miles north of Jenner.
RATES: EP—$20 to $25 year round.
MEALS: Breakfast (to 11 a.m.), lunch, dinner (to 9 p.m.); informal; no room service.
SEASONS: Open year round, busiest in summer.

HERITAGE HOUSE
Little River, California

Take a walk around the cove. Sing love songs into the wind. Put your arms around each others' necks to keep the wind out. Listen to the ocean raging at the land.

A hundred years ago this site was a cove for shipping redwood ties, and for smuggling in liquor and Chinamen. The original farmhouse, dating from 1877, is now the inn's reception lobby, dining room and kitchen—a yellow clapboard building, with carriage lamps and a red door with bronze doorknobs, a refugee from New England; in fact, the whole setting looks like a picture of Maine that's been reversed, with the sun setting where it should be rising.

The Dennens spotted the old house in 1949, and decided to turn it into an inn (which is only fair, since it was built originally by Dennen's grandfather). Since then, they've added some more cottages to their hillside, and what they have now is not so much an inn as a village. The "village green" is a duck pond surrounded by elders; the gardens burgeon with azaleas, daffodils, nasturtiums or wild blackberries; red lichen highlights the cliffs, and the Albion buoy gongs away steadily offshore.

Apple house and water tower

Some of the inn's forty-six rooms are in new villas, but most of them are in buildings imported from other farms and sites along the coast—some of them with ingenious twists. An old apple storage house has become the inn's lounge, a clubby room with walk-in fireplace, card tables and a bar. There are a few guest rooms upstairs—the most popular one being "Salem," mainly because of its seventeenth-century solid cherry fourposter bed (and an "invalid's chair," which is a euphemism for something you can discover for yourself). The most unusual room in the

inn, maybe on the entire coast, is the Water Tower—a duplex that once really was a water tower. The bedroom is in the "tank" and a spiral staircase swirls down to a lounge with tall windows looking across the duck pond to the ocean. The only problem with the Water Tower is that other guests are so intrigued, and envious, they want to take a peek inside, and you may find yourself spending the day giving guided tours. The "Firehouse" room has lamps made from old fire hydrants; and the headboard in the "Schoolhouse" is the original sign for Greenwood School 1898, and the bedside tables are old classroom desks. No pool, no TV, no room phones—just good innkeeping.

Old-fashioned hospitality, new Maserati

The presiding genius behind this inn-village, Don Dennen, learned his trade at the Clift Hotel in San Francisco. He has since built up a loyal staff; most of them have been with him for years, and seem to share his ideal—"Old-fashioned hospitality," he explains, as he slides behind the wheel of his sleek

Maserati. His special brand of old-fashioned hospitality includes nice little touches like having the waitress let the housekeeper know when you sit down to breakfast so that the maid can dash off to your room and fix the bed. "Just having the bed tidied up makes the place look so much neater when you get back to your room." It may not sound like much, but it makes all the difference between an average inn and a place where people care.

Fresh rhubarb, granola and hotcakes

And when you see the gargantuan breakfast table, you might get the impression that it was created to give the maids plenty of time. Here you don't so much break your fast as shatter it. The meal begins with a buffet table groaning under a selection of juices; a choice of six fresh fruits (including rhubarb and figs); granola, porridge; followed by a choice of eggs, hotcakes, ham and bacon. You don't even have to wait for your coffee and toast: the coffee is on your table almost as soon as you sit down, and many tables have their own toasters so you can make your own toast to your own taste, from a choice of three types of bread.

All of which prepares you for a day in the open air—that walk around the cove, or a picnic in the forest where you can stand and kiss beneath a giant redwood tree. Or ride The Skunk, an old logging train that follows Pudding Creek and Noyo River for three hours and forty miles through the redwood forests.

NAME: Heritage House
INNKEEPER: Mr. and Mrs. L. A. Dennen
ADDRESS: P.O. Little River, Calif. 95456
TELEPHONE: 714-937-5885
DIRECTIONS: On California 1, 17 miles south of Fort Bragg; from U.S. 101 take the exit marked Rte. 253 (Boonville), just south of Ukiah, then turn right when you get to the coast.

RATES: MAP—$32 to $55, all year round (except for the Water Tower, which is $65).

MEALS: Breakfast (to 10 a.m.), dinner (to 8 p.m.), no lunch; no room service; informal, but jackets and ties are usually worn at dinnertime.

SEASONS: Open all year, except during December and January; no groups; for weekends, reserve 6-8 weeks in advance; for Thanksgiving 3 *years* in advance.

LITTLE RIVER INN
Little River, California

This inn, like the main lodge at Heritage House just down the Mendocino Coast, is a hundred-year-old Maine-style mansion. Silas Coombs built it when he settled in these parts and made a fortune in lumber and shipbuilding. Now his great-granddaughter and her husband run the old home as an inn, but its Victorian lobby still looks like the entrance to a prosperous home.

The most interesting rooms are the attics of the inn itself, brightly recreated in early Californian style, with shower stalls added. Unfortunately, there are only half a dozen of these rooms, and the remaining forty-four rooms are in a motel-like wing and cottages behind the eucalyptus trees—clean, comfy rooms, but nothing special.

There's a wood-paneled bar and dining room, where you can have dinner for $4.50 to $7.50—mostly steaks and seafoods, and home-made breads, soups and desserts. It's a gathering place for people from miles around, and "for the benefit of early morning risers and golfers" the bar keeps the same hours as the dining room—which means you can have your first snort of the day from seven-thirty a.m. The inn sits well back from the highway, and there's a view through the telephone wires all the way to the ocean. Take a stroll over there and follow a pathway down to the beach. Or play the inn's own nine-hole golf course on the hill at the back door. Or just sit and watch the fishing fleets go by, as they have done every day since Silas Coombs built his house and planted his eucalyptus trees.

NAME: Little River Inn
INNKEEPERS: Ole and Cora Hervilla, Mark and Susan Kimberly
ADDRESS: Little River, Calif. 95456
TELEPHONE: 707-937-5942
DIRECTIONS: Same as for Heritage House, which is 3 miles to the south.
RATES: EP—$14 (in the inn), $16 to $22 (in the motel wing).
MEALS: Breakfast, lunch, dinner (to 8 p.m.); informal; background music; no room service.
SEASONS: Open all year, except for 3 weeks in December; busiest in summer.

IRELAND'S RUSTIC LODGES
Gold Beach, Oregon

After a day of beachcombing or jogging or sightseeing, you settle back in your rustic cottage, feet up in front of the fire, and at six-thirty there's a knock on your door: the Swiss lady is bringing you your dinner. Three courses—steak or fish or chicken, right in your lodge, for $4 or $5. That's the nice thing about Ireland's—it's so homey.

Otherwise it wouldn't be in these pages, because the location breaks one of the guide's yardsticks—Ireland's Rustic Lodges are right on motel row, between Highway 101 and the beach. But they *are* screened by trees and they *are* rustic, so we'll overlook the location. The eight lodges have knotty pine walls, pine rockers, pine furniture—and unrustic wall-to-wall carpets, tiled baths or showers, and color TV. They all have log fires and an evening's supply of chopped logs on the porch. And that's it. There's a garden with some benches and tables beneath the pine trees, and a pathway winding between the lodges to the beach and the driftwood. Life is simple here. Settle back in front of the fire and enjoy it.

NAME: Ireland's Rustic Lodges
INNKEEPER: Corabelle Ireland
ADDRESS: P.O. Box 774, Gold Beach, Ore. 97444
TELEPHONE: 503-247-7718
DIRECTIONS: On U.S. 101, a few miles north of the California state line.
RATES: EP—$14.
MEALS: Breakfast (to 8:45 a.m., in the lobby/lounge) and dinner (6:30 p.m. in your room); no lunch; informal.
SEASONS: Open all year, except November 15 to February 15; busiest in summer.

THE INN AT OTTER CREST
Otter Rock, Oregon

The inspiration for the inn is one of those teetering pastel villages that decorate hillsides along Italy's Amalfi Drive. Here it's been translated into the setting of an Oregon pine forest, with weathered cedar replacing the stucco, and a restless ocean replacing the placid sea.

The inn's two-story lodges are stacked higgledy-piggledy with covered walkways and stairways, with the undergrowth and tumbled timbers lying around undisturbed for a natural look. A self-operated lift takes you from the top of the inn down the hill to the top of the cliff, where you can admire a dramatic sea-scape: Gull Rock straight ahead, Otter Rock on the left, and Cape Foulweather—the high cliff on the right—which was given its unflattering name by Captain James Cook, who anchored offshore in 1778 when he came searching for a harbor and found instead high winds, high seas and high cliffs.

There are 320 rooms in all, 150 of them with fireplaces; the decor is modern, fairly subdued, and the occasional dreary painting is overwhelmed by the cedar interiors and picture windows. Ask for one of the rooms with a loft—bedroom and bathroom upstairs, kitchen and lounge downstairs.

Razor clams and king salmon

Where the cliff juts out into the sea there's a restaurant vaguely (very vaguely) modeled on the dining room of an ocean liner. It's a red-and-lilac room called The Flying Dutchman, and its flying Dane chef produces a wide-ranging cuisine—butter-fried razor clams, paupiettes of sole Rotterdam, butter-sautéed yearling oysters and king salmon with oyster dressing (prices around $5).

A few steps from the restaurant there are a heated pool, a therapy pool, a sauna (which are open all year) and a glass-enclosed sun terrace; another few steps brings you to a pathway leading down to the beach and a state-owned marine garden with enough curious-looking species to make it worth your while to flip on a snorkeling mask. The inn also has two year-round tennis courts (free), and a rec room with billiards and ping-pong.

There's not much nightlife in these parts. You can dance in the cocktail lounge or drive a few miles to Newport for dinner at Mo's, a modest harborside seafood place that became famous when it hosted Paul Newman and Bobby Kennedy.

Best of all, you can go back to your room, throw a few Prest-o-logs on the fire, open the balcony door, snuggle up on the rug and listen to the ocean snap and snarl at the base of Cape Foulweather.

NAME: The Inn at Otter Crest
INNKEEPER: Hollis Hammond
ADDRESS: Otter Rock, Ore. 97369
TELEPHONE: 503-765-2111
DIRECTIONS: Just off U.S. 101, about 7 minutes north of Newport, 5 minutes south of Depoe Bay.
RATES: EP—$22 to $26 for rooms, $30 to $42 for one-bedroom suites.
MEALS: Breakfast, lunch and dinner; no room service; informal.
SEASONS: Open all year, busiest in summer; groups the remainder of the year.

SALISHAN LODGE
Gleneden Beach, Oregon

How many hotels do you know that print their own botanical guides? And tide tables? Or where every room has a leaflet extolling the habits of seagulls because the manager's favorite pastime is photographing gulls (and had been for many years before Jonathan Livingston flew on to the bestseller lists)?

Salishan is that kind of special place.

It was built by a wealthy Oregon manufacturer, John D. Gray, who used to vacation on this part of the coast and decided to build a hotel here. Something that would be a credit to Oregon, something that might also make some money. He picked a serene setting—a hill that looks over a lagoon and a promontory of beach to the ocean (but, unfortunately, across the highway); there he built what one architect has called "one of the most beautiful hotels in the world," and filled it with works of art, landscaped the grounds, tagged the plants, and hired one of the best managers in the country.

Ceramic walls, teak reliefs, 200-pound red oak doors

John Gray and his team created a lovely lair for lovers. Ceramic walls decorate garden courtyards. A dozen sculptured teak panels gleam on the walls of the dining room. Driftwood "sculptures" guard the driveway, and the red oak doors that welcome you weigh 200 pounds each. Even the therapy pool has a Japanese-style garden with Oregon grape, huckleberry and vine maple. All very seductive. Enough to make you forgive any shortcomings. But you won't have to—Alex Murphy runs a tight ship, and even a faulty nozzle in the therapy pool doesn't escape his eagle eye.

Salishan's 125 guest rooms are in fifteen villas, linked by covered walkways and bridges, and constructed of Douglas fir, hemlock and cedar. The woodsy character is retained in the close-to-luxurious interiors. All rooms have picture windows and every window faces a treescape. But the trees have tough competition from the interiors: open fireplaces (with a well-stocked supply of, alas, Prest-o-logs, not real timber), oversize beds, club armchairs, hand-woven light fixtures, floor-insert electric heaters, soundproofing, TV, radio, individual heat controls.

Seven-page menu

The Salishan's dining room is on three levels, with lots of windows so that everyone can get a good view of Siletz Bay and the distant Pacific once they've feasted their eyes on the teak sculptures. A handsome dining room is one thing, but how about the food? What's the food like in Oregon? The lodge's seven-page menu begins with, say, fresh Tillamook Bay oysters on the half shell ($2.75), Beluga caviar ($3.50), quenelles Maison ($2.25, and excellent); continues through a choice of nine salads to Dungeness crab legs Pompadour ($7.75), fresh Chinook salmon filet ($6.75) and grenadines de boeuf aux morilles with cognac ($8.25). In Oregon? In Oregon.

And not even in San Francisco will you find as comprehensive a wine list as the one at Salishan—from an extravagant Chateau Lafite Rothschild ($85) or Romanee Conti ($75), step by step down the oenological hierarchy to a private reserve Beaulieu Vineyard Cabernet Sauvignon 1967 ($9) and Soave Bolla ($4.50). Surprise: for a dryish white wine to go with the Chinook Salmon, try an Oregon wine—the Bjelland. From Oregon? From Oregon—and not bad at all.

How do you fill your Oregon days between grapefruit juice and Chateau Lafite?

You can whack a ball around the 6,437 yards of the lodge's seventy-two–par course, or thunk another kind of ball around a couple of tennis courts. You can swim in the lodge's new indoor pool (it has a solarium roof and hydrostatically-controlled humidity to avoid that cloying damp smell you usually find in indoor pools); work out in the exercise rooms (separately—they're not coed), or together you can plunge into the 102-degree hydro-therapy pool (a big one, with a dozen nozzles) and contemplate the huckleberry and vine maple.

Kinnikinnick, salmonberry and three miles of driftwood

You can follow the old logging road up into the hills and enjoy almost virgin Oregon. Don't forget to take along your botanical guide—here a kinnikinnick, there a salmonberry, everywhere a juniper.

Best of all, wander over to the beach. It's just across the highway on the peninsula. There you'll find three miles of virtually private beach curving toward the sunset—and decorated with one of the world's most dramatic collections of driftwood. Not the occasional branches and stubs you usually see, but forestfuls of timbers, weathered and worn into grotesque and gruesome shapes. Come at sunset. It's spooky. All those grotesqueries, the wind sighing in the reeds, gulls wheeling overhead, and when you look toward the setting sun you may be startled by the head of a curious sea lion a few yards out at sea. Stare back. Throw it kisses.

NAME: Salishan Lodge

INNKEEPER: Alex Murphy

ADDRESS: Gleneden Beach, Ore. 97388

TELEPHONE: 503-764-2371

DIRECTIONS: On U.S. 101, 20 miles north of Newport, 90 miles south of Portland; by private or charter plane to the 3,000-foot runway half a mile south of the lodge.

RATES: EP—$25 to $32 from March 1 through April 30; $28 to $34 during May, June and October; $32 and $36 from July 1 through September 30; $24 and $29 from November through February.

MEALS: Breakfast (all morning), lunch, dinner (to 11 p.m.); coffee shop; informal *or* jacket-and-tie dining; room service.

SEASONS: Open all year; busiest in summer; small groups and conventions in spring, fall and winter (but unboisterous groups—like seminars of environmentalists, that sort of thing).

THE INN OF THE 7TH MOUNTAIN
Bend, Oregon

The name is romantic enough, that's for sure. Ditto the setting —among the tall pines, red-barked manzanitas and blue sage of Oregon's High Country, surrounded by forest trails, rivers and waterfalls and a private lake stocked with trout, with Mount Bachelor popping its almost perfect cone above the pines. 7th Mountain should be 7th Heaven—but it falls short (say, 5th Heaven), probably because it's primarily a condominium development (it's run by the people who operate the Inn at Otter Crest), which means that the emphasis is on real estate rather than traditional innkeeping. But give it a try.

In winter it's a ski resort (9,000-foot Mount Bachelor has the longest season in the country, November through June, and the U.S. Olympic team chose it as training camp). For the rest of the year, the inn's a mountain playground with tennis (three courts, free), tennis clinics, ice skating, basketball courts, an outdoor chess set with handcarved three-foot-high pieces, raft trips down the rapids, sailing and rowing on the lake, swimming in two heated pools and a therapeutic pool, two saunas, riding on forest trails, and golf on any of four courses in the neighborhood.

Mountain views, bedroom lofts

The guest rooms are in rows of cedar-sided villas around the perimeter, so that *all* the picture windows look out onto views of the lake, the forest and the mountains. The rooms are smartly designed in cozy cedar, stone and bold furnishings, with fireplaces and contemporary furniture throughout, color TV, tiled bathrooms and thermostatically-controlled temperatures. The rooms are divided by air walls, and even the steps are dampened to deaden sound. Some of the bedrooms are small. Your best bets are the Loft Houses, each of which has a gallery with twin beds and bathroom upstairs, and a lounge, small kitchen, fire-place and sun-deck downstairs; or the Ponderosa Suites which have beds that fold up into the wall, bench-type dining tables, kitchen, roman blinds and color TV.

If you want to mingle, wander over to the Red Toe Restaurant and find yourself a spot in the conversation pit before the big fire.

NAME: The Inn of the 7th Mountain
INNKEEPER: Peter Rogers
ADDRESS: P.O. Box 1207, Bend, Ore. 97701
TELEPHONE: 503-382-8711
DIRECTIONS: Seven miles south of Bend; stay on U.S. 97 through Bend until you come to a sign for Century Drive, a scenic route, where you'll find the inn.
RATES: EP—$18 without kitchen, $25 with kitchen, year round.
MEALS: Breakfast, lunch and dinner; informal; no room service.
SEASONS: Open all year; busy on weekends in winter with skiers, and during the summer; watch for groups and conventions in spring and fall.

SUNRIVER LODGE
Sunriver, Oregon

This may be the only hotel in the country with an ecologist-in-residence. And almost certainly it's the only one with an Ecologium—a mini natural-history museum where ecologist Jay Bowerman interprets the surrounding wildlife and nature.

And there's plenty of both. Sunriver's 5,000 acres, a lake basin formed some 2,000 years ago by a lava flow, is surrounded on three sides by a national forest with 156 lakes. This is the country of black bear, elk and pronghorn antelope, of bald eagles and china pheasants, where German brown and rainbow trout out-

sparkle the crystal water of mountain streams. It's a place to fill
your lungs with clean air and enjoy the wide open spaces: fifteen
miles of cycle tracks (and more bikes than cars), three dozen
horses chomping on the bit in the stables, waiting to trot you
around the meadows and forests (this is one place where twosomes can go cantering off on their own), a championship golf
course. The eight tennis courts are floodlit so that your outdoor
fun doesn't stop when the sun sets over the Cascades. You can
go canoeing on the river, bird watching in the meadow or rock
hunting among the lava beds. You never have to wear a jacket
or tie. Which doesn't mean you're going to rough it: in a setting
like this, most people would settle for a log shack, but up at
Sunriver you enjoy wall-to-wall comfort. *You're* spoiled, not the
countryside.

Sunriver is a planned community—but it looks as much like
the average real estate blotch as a Rolls-Royce looks like a bull-
dozer. No more than one family per acre; *no* buildings on the
banks of the river; all utilities underground, and so on. The man
behind the project is the same John Gray who gave you Salishan
Lodge, which means that the surroundings are respected and
little details of design are in impeccable taste (note the direction
signs, or the "sculptured" angled, inclined sun terraces around
the swimming pool).

The main lodge is an unusual timber-and-lava-stone building, a creation of the Pacific in its blend of Oregon and oriental; and the twenty-three guest lodges dotted around the fairways have pitched roofs, sun-decks, fireplaces, color TV and, in some cases, kitchens. Over in the lodge you'll find sauna baths, a rumpus room to keep the teenagers out of your hair, a coffee shop and a handsome restaurant where you can enjoy veal Cordon Bleu or chicken a la Kiev with a view of the 600-acre meadow, a Japanese bridge and the Fuji-like cone of Mount Bachelor. It's an unpolluted setting—and Jay Bowerman's there to help keep it that way.

NAME: Sunriver Lodge
INNKEEPER: Bill Wismer
ADDRESS: Sunriver, Ore. 97701
TELEPHONE: 503-593-1221
DIRECTIONS: Fifteen miles south of Bend and 2 miles west of U.S. 97; by scheduled air service to Redmond (33 miles north of Sunriver), or by private or charter flight to Sunriver's own 4,500-foot airstrip.
RATES: $18 a room, $30 a suite in winter (November 1 through March 18); $24 and $38 in summer.
MEALS: Breakfast (to noon), lunch and dinner (to 9 p.m.); room service to noon only; informal.
SEASONS: Open all year, busiest in summer; small seminar-type groups throughout the year.

P.S.

Maybe your favorite hideaway was overlooked in this guide, and maybe you're sighing with relief. On the other hand, if you'd like to share your good fortune with others who share your interest in nice places, let me know. Maybe it can be included in subsequent editions. Also, if any of the places in this guide don't live up to their reviews, again, let me know. There's no point in having people wasting their time going to places which have deteriorated.

Please address your letters:
Ian Keown
c/o Macmillan Publishing Co., Inc.
866 Third Avenue
New York, N.Y. 10022

Alabama, 184, 185
Alisal, the, 267, 268
Alta, Utah, 202, 203
Alta Lodge, 202, 203
Alta Mira, 288, 289
Amador City, California, 294, 295
American Plan (AP), xvii
Amherst, Massachusetts, 78, 79
Annapolis, Maryland, 114, 115
AP (American Plan), xvii
Arizona, 218–43
Arizona Biltmore Hotel, 236–39
Arizona Inn, 218–21
Auberge Des Quatre Saisons, 100, 101

Bedford, Virginia, 134, 135
Bel-Air Hotel, 261–64
Bend, Oregon, 314, 315
Beverly Hills, California, 257–61
Beverly Hills Hotel, 257–61
Big Meadows Lodge, 127, 128
Bishop's Lodge, the, 207–9
Blantyre Castle, 67–69
Boar's Head Inn, 135, 136
Boca Raton, Florida, 165–67
Boca Raton Hotel and Club, 165–67
Bourne, Massachusetts, 12, 13

Breakers, The, 161–64
Bromley House, 38–40

C Lazy U Ranch, 192–94
California, 247–307
Carefree, Arizona, 239, 240
Carefree Inn, 239, 240
Carmel Highlands, California, 274–76
Carmel Valley, California, 285, 286
Carmel-by-the-Sea, 277–82
Carolina Hotel, the, 146, 147
Casa Blanca Inn, 233, 234
Century Inn, 106, 107
Charleston, South Carolina, 147–50
Charlottesville, Virginia, 135, 136
Chester, Vermont, 43, 44
Chester Inn, 43–44
Chocorua, New Hampshire, 57–59
Clauson's Inn & Golf Resort, 13, 14
Cloister, The, 153–56
Colorado, 189–95
Connecticut, 8–10, 86–92
Cumberland Island, Georgia, 158–61
Cypress West Inn, 278, 279

Del Monte Lodge, 271–74
Durango, Colorado, 191–92

Earl of Stirling Bar, the, 5, 6
El Prado, New Mexico, 217, 218
EP (European Plan), xvii
Essex, Connecticut, 8–11
European Plan (EP), xvii

Far View Lodge, 189–90
Farrell Lodge, 60–62
Florida, 161–69
Flying Cloud Inn, the, 71–74
Four Columns Inn, the, 40–43

General Wolfe Inn, the, 52–54
Georgia, 153–61
Gleneden Beach, Oregon, 311, 313
Gold Beach, Oregon, 307, 308
Golden Lamb, the, 173, 174
Grafton, Vermont, 34–38
Granby, Colorado, 192–94
Grand Hotel, 184–85
Gray Gables Ocean House, 12, 13
Greenbrier, The, 137–39
Greyfield, 158–61
Griswold Inn, 8–11
Gurney's Inn, 3, 4

Hacienda de San Roberto, 217, 218
Hacienda del Sol, 221–23
Hancock, New Hampshire, 49–51
Harrison Inn, 91, 92
Harrodsburg, Kentucky, 175–78
Harwichport, Massachusetts, 14–17

Hawk Mountain, 47–49
Heritage House, 303–6
Hermosa Inn, 235, 236
Highlands Inn, 274–76
Hillsdale, New York, 93, 94
Hilton Head Inn, 151–53
Hilton Head Island, South Carolina, 151–53
Hinton, West Virginia, 140, 141
Holly Inn, 145, 146
Homestead, The, 129–32
Hot Springs, Virginia, 129–33
Hotel Edelweiss, 216
Hotel Leger, 293, 294
Hotel Maison de Ville, 180–81

Inn at Otter Crest, the, 308–10
Inn at Pleasant Hill, the, 175–78
Inn at Rancho Bernardo, 247–49
Inn at Rancho Santa Fe, 254–57
Inn at Sawmill Farm, 31–34
Inn at Steele Hill, 56–57
Inn of the 7th Mountain, 314, 315
Ireland's Rustic Lodges, 307, 308
Irvington, Virginia, 116–19

Jared Coffin House, 19, 20
Jenner, California, 299–301
John Gardiner's Tennis Ranch (Arizona), 230, 231
John Gardiner's Tennis Ranch (California), 283, 284
John Hancock Inn, the, 49–51

Kennebunkport, Maine, 25–27
Kentucky, 175–78
Key West, Florida, 167–69

Kilravock Inn, 89–91
King & Prince Hotel, 157, 158

La Jolla, California, 251–54
La Valencia Hotel, 251–54
Laconia, New Hampshire, 56–57
Lake of the Ozarks, Missouri, 178–80
Lake Ozark, Missouri, 178–80
Lebanon, Ohio, 173–74
Lenox, Massachusetts, 57–69
Litchfield, Connecticut, 89–91
Litchfield Park, Arizona, 241–43
Little River, California, 303–7
Little River Inn, 306, 307
Lodge at Snowbird, the, 199–212
Lodge of the Four Seasons, 178–80
Long Island, New York, 7, 8
Longfellow's Wayside Inn, 83–86
Lord Jeffery Inn, 78, 79
Los Angeles, California, 261–64
Louisiana, 180–84
Lumberville, Pennsylvania, 101–3

Maine, 25–27
MAP (Modified American Plan), xvii
Maryland, 111–15
Maryland Inn, 114–15
Massachusetts, 12–20, 65–86
Mayflower Inn, the, 86–88
Mesa Verde National Park, Colorado, 189, 190
Middletown, Virginia, 123–25
Mills Hyatt House, 147–50
Mine House, the, 294, 295

Missouri, 178–80
Miyako Hotel, 286–88
Modified American Plan (MAP), xvii
Mohonk Lake, New York, 97–99
Mohonk Mountain House, 97–99
Mokelumne Hill, California, 293, 294
Montauk, New York, 3, 4
Montecito, California, 264–67
Mt. Jackson, Virginia, 128, 129
Myerstown, Pennsylvania, 103–6

Nantucket, Massachusetts, 17–21
Narrow Passage Inn, 125, 126
New England, 8–11
New Hampshire, 22–24, 49–62
New Marlboro, Massachusetts, 71–74
New Mexico, 207–18
New Orleans, Louisiana, 180–84
New York (State), 3–8, 93–101
Newfane, Vermont, 40–43
Normandy Inn, 281–82
North Carolina, 145–47
North Falmouth, Massachusetts, 13, 14

Ohio, 173, 174
Old Deerfield, Massachusetts, 75–77
Old Deerfield Inn, 75–77
Old Tavern at Grafton, the, 34–38
Oregon, 307–17
Orpheus Ascending, 69–71
Otter Rock, Oregon, 308–10

Oxford, Maryland, 111–13

Palm Beach, Florida, 161–64
Paradise Valley, Arizona, 235, 236
Peaks of Otter Lodge, 134, 135
Pebble Beach, California, 271–74
Pecos, New Mexico, 213, 214
Pennsylvania, 101–7
Peru, Vermont, 38–40
Phoenix, Arizona, 236–39
Pier House, 167–69
Pine Inn, 277, 278
Pinehurst, North Carolina, 145–47
Pipestem Resort, 140, 141
Pittsfield, Vermont, 47–49
Point Clear, Alabama, 184–85
Portsmouth, New Hampshire, 22–24
Provo, Utah, 195–98
Publick House, the, 79–82

Quail Lodge, 285, 286

Rancho Bernardo, 247–49
Rancho Encantado, 210–13
Rancho La Costa, California, 249–51
Rancho La Costa Resort Hotel & Spa, 249–51
Rancho Santa Fe, 254–57
Red Lion Inn, 65–67
Robert Morris Inn, 111–13

Saddle and Surrey Ranch, 229, 230
Sagebrush Inn, 214, 215
Saint Bernard Hotel and Chalets, 216

Saint Louis Hotel, the, 182–84
St. Simons Island, Georgia, 157, 158
Salishan Lodge, 311–13
San Diego, California, 247–49
San Francisco, California, 286–88
Sandpiper Inn, 280, 281
Santa Barbara, California, 264–67
Santa Barbara Biltmore Hotel, 264–67
Santa Fe, New Mexico, 207–14
Sausalito, California, 288–90
Sausalito Inn, 289, 290
Scenery Hill, Pennsylvania, 106, 107
Scottsdale, Arizona, 230–34
Sea Island, Georgia, 153–56
Sea Ranch, California, 301, 302
Sea Ranch Lodge, 301, 302
Seacrest Inn, 25, 26
1740 House, 101–3
Shakertown, Kentucky, 175–78
Shawmut Inn, 26, 27
Sheffield, Massachusetts, 74, 75
Shelter Island, New York, 5, 6
Shelter Island House, 5, 6
Shenandoah National Park, Virginia, 126–28
Ships Inn, 20, 21
Ship's Knees Inn, 16, 17
Sisterville, West Virginia, 174, 175
Sky Chalet, 128, 129
Skyland Lodge, 126, 127
Snowbird, Utah, 199–202
Solvang, California, 267, 268
South Carolina, 147–53
South Sudbury, Massachusetts, 83–86

Southbury, Connecticut, 91, 92
Stafford's-in-the-Field, 57–59
Stagecoach Hill Inn, 74, 75
Steamboat Springs, Colorado,
  · 194, 195
Stockbridge, Massachusetts,
    65–67, 69–71
Stony Brook, New York, 7, 8
Strater Hotel, 191, 192
Sturbridge, Massachusetts, 79–
    82
Sundance, 195–98
Sunriver, Oregon, 315–17
Sunriver Lodge, 315–17
Sutter Creek, California, 290–
    93
Sutter Creek Inn, 290–93
Swiss Hutte, 93, 94

Tanque Verde Ranch, 223–27
Taos, New Mexico, 214, 215
Taos Ski Valley, New Mexico,
    216
Tecumseh Inn, 60–62
Three Village Inn, 7, 8
Thunderbird Lodge and Chalets,
    216
Tides Golf Lodge, the, 118,
    119
Tides Inn, the, 116, 117
Timber Cove Inn, 299–301
Timbers, the, 194, 195
Tom Young's Tres Lagunas
    Guest Ranch, 213, 214

Tucson, Arizona, 218–30
Tulpehocken Manor Farm,
    103–6

Utah, 195–203

Valley View Inn, 132, 133
Vermont, 31–49
Virginia, 116–36

Washington, Connecticut, 86–88
Waterville Valley, New Hamp-
    shire, 60–62
Wayside Inn, 123, 125
Wells Inn, 174, 175
Wentworth-by-the-Sea, 22–24
West Dorset, Vermont, 31–34
West Virginia, 137–40, 174, 175
Westwood Village, California,
    261–64
White Elephant, the, 17–19
White Sulphur Springs, West
    Virginia, 137–39
Wigwam Resort, the, 241–43
Wild Horse Racquet and Ski
    Club, 227, 228
Wolfeboro, New Hampshire,
    52–55
Wolfeboro Inn, 54–55
Woodstock, Vermont, 44–46
Woodstock, Virginia, 125, 126
Woodstock Inn, 44–46
Wychmere Harbor Club, 14–16